SOUL-WINNING SERMONS

SOUL-WINNING SERMONS

Volume I

R. A. TORREY

FLEMING H. REVELL COMPANY

Westwood, New Jersey
London E.C.4—29 Ludgate Hill
Glasgow C.2—229 Bothwell Street

Library of Congress Catalog Card Number: 56-8503

Printed in the United States of America

INTRODUCTION

Reuben Archer Torrey was born on January 28, 1856, at Hoboken, New Jersey. The Torrey family lost its wealth in the financial crash of 1857. Later, however, Torrey's father became a successful manufacturer and wealthier than ever.

"Archie" Torrey went off to Yale University in 1871. Blessed of God with keen powers of intellect, he was able to do his college work with comparative ease. He turned to a life of worldliness: dancing, card playing, gaming, and horse racing. Endowed with great mental powers, supported by a wealthy father, having a "good time" in the world, what more could a young man want? But things never bring lasting satisfaction. It was so with Torrey. Confessing disappointment, despair, and utter wretchedness, he was on the verge of suicide. Only then did he turn to the Lord. And the Lord, who is "merciful and gracious, slow to anger, and abundant in lovingkindness and truth" received him. Later he discovered that it was in answer to his mother's prayers that he turned to the Lord.

That this young man had given himself with abandon to his worldly living is attested by the words of his first convert: a young lady who had been in the same crowd before his conversion. Won at last to the Saviour, she said to Torrey: "I thought if Jesus Christ could save you after what I knew you used to be, He could save anybody."

And Reuben Archer Torrey was saved; he had met God. Life was different and it was going to be more different. After graduation from college and seminary, the young theologue took postgraduate work at two schools in Germany: Leipzig and Erlangen. There he picked up the popular unbelieving higher criticism of the day. But the root of the matter was in him. He had a battle, but victory finally was his. He said simply: ". . . the time came when I was convinced by proofs that were overwhelming that the Lord Jesus was a Teacher sent from God, who spoke the very words of God, and today I 'believe in the Lord Jesus' from the crown of my head to the soles of my feet, and if every scholar on earth should say one thing and the Lord Jesus Christ should say another, I would believe the Lord Jesus Christ against the whole bunch.

". . . The Lord Jesus has stood the test of nineteen centuries, and German scholarship or any other scholarship, never stood the test of nineteen consecutive years; and so I, as a reasonable man, prefer to believe in the Lord Jesus and be saved, than to believe in the latest scholarship and be damned! I would be a fool, if I didn't."

Looking back on the record of his life, it seems inevitable that he would do exactly what he did. His own battles prepared him to be used of God to help people of like passions. His early contacts with Moody were undoubtedly ordered of the Lord. Torrey had assisted in the inquiry room during Moody's campaign in New Haven. Then, on no less than his honeymoon, Torrey assisted in the inquiry room during Moody's campaign in Cleveland! But such service was not incidental. Ministries in Garrettsville, Ohio, and in Minneapolis, Minnesota, saw the young minister as a winner of souls.

What was more to be expected than that Mr. Moody would bring him to what later was called Moody Bible Institute as its first superintendent? Torrey was thirty-four years old at the time. It was a master stroke. As J. Wilbur Chapman said: "The Rev. R. A. Torrey . . . is, without question, the most capable man that Mr. Moody could have found for this very important position." It is no exaggeration to say that R. A. Torrey, under God, is more responsible for the delineation of the purpose and putting into effect the fundamental principles of the Bible Institute than any other man. The groundwork was so well laid that it continues as the norm for Bible institutes to this day. Additions have been made, strides forward have been taken by these schools now scattered all across the nation, but Torrey was used to give the movement its own particular genius.

And what was more to be expected than, after having taught students for over a decade, he would follow in the steps of Moody and become God's evangelist to the world?

First superintendent of Moody Bible Institute of Chicago, first dean of the Bible Institute of Los Angeles, beloved pastor of Moody Memorial Church, world-famous evangelist, stalwart defender of the faith, faithful husband and father, winner of souls: these distinctions are but a few of those granted to this giant in the faith.

Soul-Winning Sermons epitomizes Dr. Torrey. Here is the heart-warming gospel, the inexorable logic, the awe-inspiring truth of judgment to come, the absolute devotion to the Lord Jesus Christ and the Word of God, the telling recitation of illustrations, the passionate love for the souls of men that all spell the name Reuben Archer Torrey.

William Culbertson
President, Moody Bible Institute

CONTENTS

I

GOD IS

"He Is."—Heb. 11:6.

MY subject tonight is, God Is. Two short words, tremendous significance: God is. If the thought that there is in those two words gets into your mind and heart and stays there, those two words will determine all your thinking; they will determine your science, your philosophy, they will determine your conduct, your character, your life here on earth, and they will determine your eternity. God Is.

We are told in Psalm 14:1, " The fool hath said in his heart, There is no God." Please notice just where he says it, *" in his heart."* That is to say, the fool denies the existence of God not because he has any reason for believing that there is no God, but because he does not wish to believe in the existence of God. Now, any man who denies a fact simply because he does not wish to believe it is a fool. And it is a fact that there is a God.

I. Nature Proves the Existence of God

Everywhere in nature we find order, beauty, symmetry, law, design, adaptation of means to end, conclusively proving the existence of an intelligent and beneficent Creator of the material universe. You may look at nature in the vast, or you may look at nature in the minute. You may take your telescope and turn it up toward those wonderful and stupendous worlds of light that we call stars, about which the astronomers are telling us such amazing things in our day, or you may take your microscope and turn it down upon the minutest form of animalculæ discernible by the most powerful of microscopes, and it is everywhere the same, order, beauty, symmetry, law, design, adaptation of means to end, conclusively proving, as I say, the existence of an intelligent and beneficent Creator of the material universe.

11

Suppose I should take out my watch and ask you, " Do you think that that watch had an intelligent maker?" You would reply, " Of course, that watch had an intelligent maker." Then suppose I should ask you a second question, " Why do you believe that watch had an intelligent maker?   Did you see the watch made?"   " No."   " Did you ever see a watch made?" " No."   " How, then, do you know that the watch had an intelligent maker?"   You would reply at once, " Everything about the watch shows the marks of intelligent design.   The dial of the watch, the figures upon the dial in orderly procession, one, two, three, four, five, six, seven, eight, nine, ten, eleven, twelve; the three hands of the watch, the second hand revolving once a minute, the minute hand revolving once an hour, and the hour hand revolving once in twelve hours; the case of the watch, the hinge in the back of the case, the winding apparatus, everything about the watch proves that it had an intelligent maker."   Then suppose I should say, " No, you are mistaken, the watch did not have an intelligent maker.   The atoms that constitute the watch danced around through endless aeons until at last by a ' fortuitous concurrence of atoms ' they danced together into their present form, and so the watch came to be." What would you say?   I'll tell you what you would say.   You would go out of this place tonight saying, " That man may think he is very wise; he may have taken various university degrees in this country, and studied at various universities in Germany, but he talks quite like a fool."   And you would be altogether right.

But what is that watch, as a mere piece of mechanism, to say nothing of the chemical reactions, to your eye?   But when any-one stands on a public platform and tells you that your eye, and all the other countless million eyes of men and beasts, and all the other innumerable forms of utility and beauty that go to make up this wonderful thing that we call the universe, came into being without an intelligent Creator; tells you that the atoms that constitute the universe danced around through end-less aeons and at last by a " fortuitous concurrence of atoms " danced together into their present form, you call that man a philosopher.   But if he talked to you that way about the com-mon ordinary affairs of everyday life, you would not call him a philosopher, but you would spell the first syllable of that word with two " o's " instead of an " i " and call him a " foolosopher;" or, in plain language, you would call him a fool. Nature proves to a demonstration the existence of God.

But someone will say, " Hold on, Dr. Torrey, you forget the modern evolutionary hypothesis, and how it has taken all the force out of the argument from design in nature." No, I do not forget the evolutionary hypothesis which, by the way, is not at all modern. Even Charles Darwin was born quite a little more than a hundred years ago, and he wrote his first sketch of his evolutionary hypothesis in 1844, eighty years ago, twelve years before I was born, and he published the *Origin of Species by Natural Selection* in 1859, sixty-five years ago—when I was only three years old. But the evolutionary hypothesis did not begin with him, nor did it even begin with Lamarck; nor, going back for many centuries, did it begin with Lucretius. It treks away back to at least six centuries before Christ. But I do not forget it whether ancient or modern. I have given some considerable thought to it for the last fifty-one years, when I first ran up against it.

Now let us suppose that the evolutionary hypothesis were true. I do not say that it is true, I do not believe that it is true in any sweeping all-inclusive way. I once was greatly disposed to believe it, as most students are at a certain stage in their intellectual career, but I gave it up. I gave it up not for religious reasons; I do not know any conclusive religious reasons against it: I gave it up for purely scientific reasons. I gave it up because it was absolutely unproven, and all really scientifically discovered and proven facts were against it instead of for it. A great many uninformed people, and some people who ought to know better, talk about " the missing link." The missing link? All the links are missing, there is not one single link. That is to say, there is not one single instance of scientifically observed and recorded transmutation of species; development of varieties there are, but always with a tendency to revert to type, but not one single instance of scientifically observed and recorded transmutation of species. If you doubt that statement I refer you to any well-informed teacher of science. Put to him the question, " Is there one single instance of scientifically observed and recorded transmutation of species?" and if he is really well informed he will

tell you, " No, of course there is not, for if there were a case
of transmutation of species it would take so long to take place
that it could not be scientifically observed and recorded."
There are other facts that are proven and known to be true,
but which the obsessed evolutionists try to ignore or obscure,
that are against rather than for an all-inclusive theory of
evolution.

But never mind that. Let us suppose for the sake of the
argument that the evolutionary hypothesis were true; let us
suppose that the entire universe as we see it today, with all
its countless forms of beauty and utility, came into being by
a process of development from some unorganized primordial
protoplasm. If that were true it would be in a way a more
striking proof of the existence and wisdom and power of God,
than if the universe were created outright as we see it today,
for the question would at once arise with every really intelligent man, " Who put into the primordial protoplasm the power
of developing into the world as we see it today?" Which
would be more wonderful, for a man to make a watch outright as you see that watch today, or for a man to make a
second hand with an inherent capacity for developing into a
watch? And just so it would be a more marvelous display
in some ways of the wisdom and power of God if He had
created some primordial protoplasm with an inherent capacity
of developing into this marvelous universe as you and I know
it today, than for Him to have created the material universe
outright as we see it today. Nature proves the existence of
God.

II. HUMAN HISTORY PROVES THE EXISTENCE OF GOD

In the second place: *The history of the human race proves
the existence of God*. When we look at history in a small
way, the history of a single nation for a few years, history
oftentimes looks to us like an endless jar and jangle of conflicting passions and ambitions of men, might always right and
the weakest going to the wall. But when we look at history
in a large way, not the history of a single nation but of all
nations, and not for a few years but looking throughout the
centuries, we soon discover back of the conflicting passions
and ambitions of men a restraining, constraining, all-control-

ling moral force overruling the follies and sins of men, and instead of might always being right and the weakest going to the wall, in the final outcome right is always might and the wickedest goes to the wall. We soon discover, as Samuel Taylor Coleridge put it many long years ago, that " Throughout all history one increasing purpose runs;" or, as Matthew Arnold put it at a later day, " There is a power, not ourselves, that makes for righteousness." We soon discover, if we are open-eyed and candid, that it is just as true in history as it is recorded in the Word of God in Psalm 76:10, that God makes the wrath of men to praise Him, and the remainder of wrath doth He restrain. Nothing is clearer to a really intelligent and profound student of history than that men do not shape the destinies of nations but that God shapes them, that God controls all the forces of human history; that in the final outcome everything in human history conspires to punish sin and reward virtue; and that it is just as true in the history of the nations as in the history of individuals, that whatever nations sow that shall they also reap. If we ever had any doubts of this before, we certainly need to no longer doubt it after our last and appalling war. There is no force, nor power, nor reason sufficient to account for the final outcome of that war, but God, a righteous God. Time and time again the God who hates iniquity and loves righteousness took a hand in that war and brought the calculations of men to naught; and " He that sitteth in the heavens laughed, and Jehovah had them in derision." (Ps. 2:4.) And today the condition of affairs in Germany and in other lands conclusively proves that God is, and that God reigns. History proves the existence of God.

III. THE STORY OF JESUS OF NAZARETH PROVES THE EXISTENCE OF GOD

In the third place, *There is one particular history that proves in a special way the existence of God, and that is the history of Jesus of Nazareth as recorded in the Four Gospels.* It is one of the simplest and most universally believed principles of modern science that every effect must have an adequate cause, and the only cause that is at all adequate to account for the sinless character of Jesus of Nazareth, His matchless teaching, His works of supernatural power, and His resurrection from the dead, is God standing back of that history. Of course I know perfectly well that a very strenuous effort is being made in our day to eliminate the supernatural element from the four gospels and to so reconstruct the story of Jesus of Nazareth from the material that we have in the four gospels, as to leave out the miracles and have His character and conduct and teaching left. This attempt is called by a certain superficial people, who boast of a scholarship which they do not possess, " The *modern* view of the Bible," but there is nothing at all modern about it. Only one who is totally uninformed as to the history of Biblical criticism and interpretation, or else who deliberately falsifies, will call it " The modern view." The ablest attempt that was ever made to reconstruct the story of Jesus of Nazareth so as to leave out the miracles and have only the character and conduct left, was made by David Strauss. David Strauss was a remarkable man; he was a man of very wide and very profound scholarship; he was a man of almost matchless powers of critical analysis; he was a man of untiring industry. And he brought to bear all the powers of his singularly gifted mind on the Four Gospel accounts of the birth, life, death and resurrection of our Lord, with the purpose of doing away with the miracles and so reconstructing the story as to have the character and conduct and teaching left; but the miracles all gone. If anybody could have succeeded in that attempt David Strauss was the man. At last he gave the results of his labour to the world in his celebrated, epoch-making " Leben Jesu," published in the year 1833, ninety-one years ago, twenty-three years before I was born, and I am not very young; published when my father, who if he were living today would be one hundred and two years old, was only eleven years old; and yet these " scholarly critics " call this the modern view. As I have said, if any man could have succeeded in such an attempt, David Strauss was the man, and for a time it seemed as though David Strauss had succeeded. His " Leben Jesu " swept all the universities of Germany, France, England, Scotland, to a less extent those of America, as the modern destructive criticism has never swept them. David Strauss' " Leben Jesu " seemed to many so conclusive and unanswerable that anyone who did not accept David Strauss' construction of the

life of Jesus was thought to be not quite up to date. But
when David Strauss' "Leben Jesu" was itself subjected to
rigid critical analysis it fell all to pieces, and there is not a
single scholar on earth today who accepts David Strauss' construction of the life of Jesus. Some do accept his conclusions
as to the miracles because they start out with the determination to believe his conclusions, but they do not accept David
Strauss' explanation of his conclusions in his construction of
the life of Jesus whereby he seeks to justify his conclusions.

Where David Strauss failed, Ernest Renan tried his hand.
Ernest Renan was not by any means so great a man or scholar
as David Strauss, nevertheless he was a man who towered
far above the average thinker of his time. He was a man of
some considerable Semitic scholarship, a man of subtle imagination, a man who was a master of an almost matchless literary style. He was universally regarded, I think, as the greatest literary master of his day in France. He gave the result
of his labour to the world in his celebrated " Vie de Jesus,"
or " The Life of Jesus," and it seemed to some for a while that
Ernest Renan had succeeded where David Strauss had failed,
and that the miracles must go. But when Ernest Renan's
" Life of Jesus " was itself subjected to rigid critical analysis
it also fell all to pieces, and there is not a single scholar on
earth today who accepts Ernest Renan's construction of the
life of Jesus.

Every other attempt of a similar character, and they have
been countless, has come to the same end, and today at least
this much is proven (I believe that much more than this is
proven, but this is enough for my present purpose), that the
story of Jesus of Nazareth as recorded in the Four Gospels
is at least substantially accurate history. I believe that much
more than that is proven, but that is enough for our present
purpose. If Jesus of Nazareth lived as the Four Gospels say
He lived; wrought as the Four Gospels say He wrought;
taught as the Four Gospels say He taught; died as the Four
Gospels say He died; and was raised again as the Four Gospels say He rose again, then beyond a peradventure back of
that history with its sinless life, its miracles of creative power,
its matchless teaching, its atoning death, and the triumphant
resurrection of His crucified body from the dead, stands God.

IV. THE EXPERIENCE OF THE INDIVIDUAL BELIEVER PROVES THE EXISTENCE OF GOD

In the fourth place, *The personal experience of each individual believer proves the existence of God.* My firm and unshakable belief that there is a God does not rest today upon the argument from design in nature; it once did. It does not rest upon the argument from the hand of God in human history; it once did. That is the argument that originally brought me back from blank and utter agnosticism into faith in the existence of a personal and righteous and beneficent God. My firm and unshakable belief in the existence of God does not even depend upon the argument from the story of Jesus of Nazareth as recorded in the Four Gospels; it once did. But today I know God in personal experience. I know God more truly and more intimately than I know any human being. God is the one fact of which I am absolutely sure. God is to me the one great reality that gives reality to all other realities. I know that there is a God as surely as I know that I exist. There was a certain man, Rev. William S. Jacoby, with whom for years I was more intimately associated than with any other man. I knew him better than I knew any other man; we were together daily and we opened our hearts freely to one another. But I know God far more intimately and surely than I knew William S. Jacoby. Now it is quite conceivable that some man might have undertaken to prove to me by some subtle system of idealistic philosophy that William S. Jacoby had no objective existence, that he was simply a form of my own subjective thought, and when this philosopher got through his argument I might not have been able to put my finger upon the weak spot in his argument, and yet after all I would still have known that William S. Jacoby is. Just so, someone might undertake to prove to me by some subtle and elusive system of philosophy that God had no objective existence, that God was simply a form of my own subjective thinking, and when the man got through I might not be able to put my finger upon the weak spot in his argument, nevertheless after all I would still know that God is.

Suppose you were to go up to an opening in a wall and order beefsteak and potatoes, and beefsteak and potatoes were passed out; and the next day you ordered lamb chops and

pumpkin pie, and lamb chops and pumpkin pie were passed
out; and the next day you ordered turkey and cranberry sauce,
and turkey and cranberry sauce were passed out, and that went
on day after day and you got what you asked each time. Even
though you saw no person back of that opening, would you
not know that there was some intelligent person there listening
to your requests? Well, that is my exact experience with God.
Day after day, week after week, month after month, year after
year, I have walked up to that aperture in heaven which men
call " prayer," and I have asked God for many things of many
kinds, and God has answered my prayer and given me the
very things that I asked, oftentimes when no human being
knew I needed it, and sometimes when it could not by any
possibility have come except by the direct action of God. I
have asked God for fifty dollars, and fifty dollars came; for
a hundred dollars, and a hundred dollars came; for five thousand dollars, and five thousand dollars came; for a hundred
thousand dollars, and got it.

I shall never forget a day during the World's Fair in Chicago. Mr. Moody was carrying on, as you know, a great
campaign involving the expenditure of many thousands of dollars. A little group of us, forming the inner circle of advisers,
met every day for dinner in Mr. Moody's rooms in the Bible
Institute in Chicago. One day as we gathered together, before we sat down to eat, Mr. Moody said, " We needed seven
thousand dollars today for our work. I have already received
one thousand dollars, but before we eat I propose that we ask
God for the other six thousand dollars." We all knelt in
prayer. Mr. Moody, with that childlike trust that characterized his relation to God, led us into the very presence of
our Father and asked for the six thousand dollars which was
needed at once for the work. We arose from our knees and
sat down at the table. We were a long time at the table discussing various phases of the work. Before we arose from
the table there came a knock at the door, and I said, " Come
in," and one of my students at the Institute entered with a
telegram in his hand. He took it to Mr. Moody and Mr.
Moody opened it and read it and said, " Here, take it to Mr.
Torrey," and then he said to me, " Read it to the others."
And I read, " Mr. Moody—your friends in Northfield had a

feeling you needed money for your work in Chicago. We have just taken up a collection and there is six thousand dollars in the basket, and more to follow." It was signed by H. M. Moore of Boston. Some months after I met Mr. Moore and told him our end of the story. He said, " Let me tell you our end of the story." Then he continued, " As we drew near to the close of our morning session at Northfield, Dr. A. J. Gordon (who was presiding in the absence of Mr. Moody) called me to the platform and said, ' Mr. Moore, I have a feeling that Mr. Moody needs some money for his work in Chicago. What do you say to our taking up a collection?' " Mr. Moore approved. A collection was taken and God put it into the hearts of three thousand people in Northfield, nearly one thousand miles away, to put into the basket the exact sum we had asked for in Chicago. I think it would have been difficult at that time to have convinced any one of us that there was no God, or that God does not answer prayer.

Many years ago I determined to put the theory that there was a God, and that the God of the Bible was the true God, and that He answered prayer on the conditions laid down in the Bible, to the test of rigid, practical, personal experiment. I say the theory that there was a God, for at that time it was to me a theory, a theory that I firmly believed, but nevertheless a theory. I determined that I would risk all that men hold dear upon that theory, and upon that theory I did risk my health, my life, my reputation, the life, health and welfare of my wife and four children whom I had at that time. On that theory I risked everything that men hold dear, and if there had been no God, or if the God of the Bible were not the true God, or if He did not answer prayer upon the conditions laid down in the Bible, years ago I would have lost all that men hold dear. *But I risked and I won,* and today I know that there is a God, and I know that the God of the Bible is the true God. There was a time in my life when I literally lived by prayer. In a single day I cut off every source of income that I had had before for myself, my family, and my work. I gave up my salary, I gave up all collections and all subscriptions for the work. I determined that I would ask no one for one single penny for the support of myself and wife and children, for the payment of hall rent, for the

support of missionaries, or for any part of the work. I do
not think that God asks all men to do that, nor do I think
that He asks one man to do it all the time, but I was clear
that God told me to do it then. I had had a strong society
back of me, and a generous society, but I felt sure that God
had asked me to take that step at that time, and so I asked
the society to hand the work over to me. They handed the
work over to me and very properly cut off all support in a
day. From that time on every penny that was obtained for
myself and my family, and all the work in all its phases was
obtained by prayer. And the money came day after day,
week after week, month after month, sometimes in small
amounts, sometimes in large amounts, sometimes in ways most
ordinary and sometimes in ways apparently most extraordi-
nary—but it came. Never one penny of debt was incurred
for one single hour; I had taken the ground that I owe no man
anything either for myself, the family, or the work, for running in debt is not trusting God, it is disobeying God, for He
says, " Owe no man anything." As I say, the money came,
and when I got through I knew that there was a God, and I
knew that the God of the Bible was the true God. I and my
family literally lived from hand to mouth, from God's hand to
our mouth, but we never went hungry.

It is clear from these various arguments that I have presented to you, it is sure beyond a question, that there is a God.
The best proven fact in the universe is the existence of God—
that God is. Now we have seen that a man who denies a fact
simply because he does not wish to believe it, is a fool, but
the man who denies the supreme fact because he does not
wish to believe it is the supreme fool. And not only is it a
fact that there is a God, but that is the supreme fact. The
profoundest and loftiest philosophy that was ever written is
found in the first four words of the Bible, " In the beginning
God." In the beginning of all true history, God; in the beginning of all correct science, God; in the beginning of all
real philosophy, God; in the beginning of all right conduct,
God: " *in the beginning, God.*" The existence of God is the
supreme fact, the fact of facts, and therefore anyone who
denies it simply because he does not wish to believe it is a
supreme fool, the fool of fools. So it is written in God's own

Word, " *The* fool (that is, the supreme fool, the fool of fools, the prince of fools, the colossal, archetypal fool) has said in his heart, There is no God." Yes, beyond a peradventure, beyond the possibility of any honest doubt or question, God is.

V. GOD IS INFINITELY GREAT

The second thing that the Bible teaches about God is, *that God is a being of infinite greatness and majesty.* We would all do well to ponder the words which we find in Ps. 147:5:

> " Great is our Lord, and mighty in power:
> His understanding is infinite."

The whole Bible, from the tremendous words of Genesis 1:1: " In the beginning God created the heavens and the earth," to the last verse of Revelation, gives voice in countless ways to the thought of the infinite greatness and majesty of God.   Indeed, one of the chief points of difference between Bible thought and much that is called " Modern Thought " and " New Thought " is, that in the Bible we have a very great God and a very small man except as " God's gentleness makes him great " (Ps. 18:35); whereas in much that is called " modern thought " and " New Thought " we have a very small God and a very great man.   One of the most popular of modern novelists said, " God owes it to man to explain to man the mystery of evil."   Ah, me!   Ah, me!   *God owes it to man?*   A popular preacher in this city announced one Sunday morning as his subject, " God's duty to man."   *God's* duty to *man?*   Ah, me!   Ah, me!

And who is man?   Who are you?   Who am I?   I will tell you exactly who you are, and exactly who I am.   You are one of about one billion five hundred millions like you inhabiting this globe today.   Not very big, are you?   One out of one billion five hundred million!   And what is this globe?   A very small part of the known universe.   This globe is so small a part of the known universe that compared with one of the heavenly bodies, and that by no means the largest, the sun, that if the sun were hollow and a hole were bored into it you could pour into it one million two hundred thousand earths like our own, and there would still be room enough left for them to rattle around.   You one out of the one billion five

hundred millions that inhabit this globe, and this whole globe
so small a part of the universe that one million two hundred
thousand of them could be poured into the sun. Not very
big, are you? And what is the sun? What is the whole solar
system? I was told some years ago upon Mt. Wilson, when
inspecting the great telescope there, the most powerful telescope at the time in the world, I was told by the one who has
charge of that telescope that until that telescope was installed
there had been two hundred million stars observed, but in the
last few years since using this telescope one hundred million
more had been observed in our known universe. Three years
ago when I was on my way to Vancouver to take the steamer
for China, I stepped off the train at one of the cities in Oregon.
As I was walking up and down the pavement a gentleman came
up to me and said, " Are you not Dr. Torrey?" " Yes."
" Well, I was professor of astronomy at ———— College when
you were there. I have just been spending a few months up
on Mt. Wilson making some observations with the telescope
there." I said to him, " Will you tell me how many stars have
been actually observed with that telescope?" He replied,
" Of course it is more or less a matter of conjecture. There
are probably five hundred million stars, but it would be perfectly safe to say three hundred and fifty million." So then
you are one out of one billion five hundred million persons
inhabiting this globe that we call the earth; the earth so small
a part of the known universe that one million two hundred
thousand earths like ours could be poured into the sun and
there still be room enough left for them to rattle around; and
our sun one out of three hundred fifty million known suns that
go to make up our known universe, and our known universe
may be, for all we know, one out of an infinite number of uni-
verses—and God made all of them. And yet you undertake
to say what you think God ought to do?

Do you wish your exact size stated with mathematical precision? Divide one by one billion five hundred million; divide that by one million two hundred thousand; divide that by
three hundred fifty million, and divide that by infinity—and
that's you. But now do you wish to know God? Multiply
one by one billion five hundred million; multiply that by one
million two hundred thousand; multiply that by three hundred

and fifty million, and multiply that by infinity—and that's God. And yet you undertake to say what you think God ought to do? Thou fool! If ever a man seems like the double concentrated quintessence of consummate, inane, imbecile and hopeless asininity, it is when *he* undertakes to say what he thinks God ought to do.

VI.   God is Infinitely Holy

The next thing that the Bible teaches about God is, that *God is infinitely holy*. Oh, how the entire Bible from beginning to end swells, pulsates and throbs with the stupendous thought of the infinite holiness of God. That is its constantly repeated message. What mean those stern judgments upon sin recorded in the Old Testament—the destruction of the entire old world by a flood; the destruction of Sodom and Gomorrah; the blotting out of the Canaanite nations, men, women and children; God's stern and awful judgments upon Israel which we see continued before our own eyes today? What does it all mean? It means that God is holy and that He hates sin with infinite hatred.

What means that constant flow of blood beginning in the Garden of Eden when sin first entered, and ever widening and deepening book after book, the shedding of the blood of thousands and tens of thousands of turtle doves, innocent lambs, bullocks, sheep and goats; that awful river of blood—what does it mean? It means that God is holy and man is a sinner, and that "Without shedding of blood there is no remission."

What means that supreme tragedy of all human history, when the only sinless man this world ever knew is nailed to the cross, and mocking mobs pass by and hurl at Him their jests and jibes as He hangs there in dying agony, and even the face of God is veiled from Him until with breaking heart He cries, "My God, my God, why hast Thou forsaken me?" What does it mean? It means that God is holy and that man is a sinner, and that without the offering of a sufficient substitute sacrifice there is no forgiveness of sin possible for any man.

Perhaps the supreme expression of the holiness of God

found in the whole Bible is in I John 1:5: "*God is light,* and in Him is *no darkness at all.*"

In the sixth chapter of Isaiah which we read for our Scripture lesson tonight, Isaiah gives us a leaf from his own autobiography. Isaiah was perhaps the holiest man of his day, and yet he tells us that in the year that King Uzziah died he saw the Lord sitting upon the throne, high and lifted up, and His train filled the Temple. Above Him stood the seraphim (seraphim is a Hebrew word meaning "burning ones," burning in their own intense holiness): each one had six wings; with two he covered his face, with two he covered his feet, and with two he did fly (burning in their own intense holiness and yet covering their face and feet in the presence of the infinitely Holy One). And one cried unto another (kept crying) and said, "Holy, holy, holy, is Jehovah of Hosts: the whole earth is full of His glory." And when Isaiah saw and heard, holy man though he was, he covered his face and cried, "Woe is me! for I am undone; because I am a man of unclean lips, and I dwell in the midst of a people of unclean lips: for mine eyes have seen the King, Jehovah of Hosts." And if there should burst upon this audience this moment just one glimpse of God as He is in His infinite holiness, this whole audience would fall on its face to the floor and cry, "God, be merciful to me a sinner."

VII. WE MUST ALL MEET THIS GREAT AND HOLY GOD

There are many other things which the Bible tells us about this wonderful Being whom we call God which we have not time to take up tonight, but there is one great fact about God that this Bible tells us which I must mention before I close, and that is that you and I must meet God. These are the startling words God Himself speaks in Amos 4:12: "Prepare to meet thy God." We must all meet God. We must each one of us as individuals meet God face to face. There are no exceptions; the rich man must meet God, and the poor man must meet God; the king upon his throne must meet God, the labourer in the ditch must meet God; the great university professor, the man of science, the brilliant orator, must meet God, and the illiterate man that digs in the trench must meet God. We must all meet this being of infinite greatness and majesty;

we must meet this infinitely Holy One in whose presence the very seraphim veil their faces and feet and do perpetually cry, "Holy, holy, holy, is Jehovah of Hosts." So the question of questions, the question of greatest importance, that confronts you and me tonight is this, "Am I ready to meet God?" How soon we must meet Him none of us can tell. Within a year, according to the average death rate of men, at least a hundred persons in this audience tonight will have met God. In five years far more than five times as many; in ten years far more, in twenty years almost everyone of us that is here tonight, and in forty years practically every one of us. Are you ready to meet God?

Any one of us may meet God within twenty-four hours. When I was holding meetings in Sherman, Texas, I ran over early one Sunday morning to the city of Dennison and held an early morning meeting for men only in the theatre. I spoke upon the same subject upon which I am speaking tonight. As I drew to a close I said, "Someone here this morning may meet God within twenty-four hours." The following week a minister came down from Dennison to Sherman and recalled to me my words, and then he said, "There was a young man in your audience that morning perfectly well and strong. He was a laundryman and very early the next morning, as he was driving along in his laundry wagon, he came in contact with a live wire that had fallen and was instantly killed. And," he continued, "within the week since you were in Dennison twelve of our citizens have passed into eternity." Oh, how soon we must meet God! Are you ready to meet God?

What constitutes readiness to meet God? There is but one ground upon which any sinner, and we are all sinners, can meet a holy God with exultant joy, and not with overwhelming fear and dismay and despair, and that ground is the shed blood of Jesus Christ. On the ground of that shed blood of Christ the vilest sinner that ever lived on earth, but who has turned from sin and accepted Jesus Christ as his personal Saviour, can walk into the very presence of this infinitely Holy God and look up into His face without fear, in loving confidence, and call Him "Father." But outside of the shed blood of Jesus Christ the best man or woman who ever walked this earth cannot stand in God's presence for one moment. So the question, "Am I ready to meet God?" resolves itself into this, "Am I under the atoning blood of Jesus Christ?"

How does one get under the atoning blood? The answer to this immeasurably important question is plainly given in God's Word. There is but one way in which any man can get under the atoning blood of Jesus Christ, and that is by accepting Jesus Christ as his personal Saviour, surrendering to Him as His Lord and Master, openly confessing Him as such before the world, and a life of daily conformity to His revealed will by which he proves the reality of his faith. Listen to the way God puts it in His own Word, John 3:36: "He that believeth on the Son hath everlasting life: and he that believeth not the Son shall not see life; but the wrath of God abideth on him." Listen to Romans 10:9, 10: "If thou shalt confess with thy mouth the Lord Jesus, and shalt believe in thine heart that God hath raised Him from the dead, thou shalt be saved. For with the heart man believeth unto righteousness: and with the mouth confession is made unto salvation." Matt. 10:32, 33: "Whosoever therefore shall confess me before men, him will I confess also before my Father which is in heaven. But whosoever shall deny me before men, him will I also deny before my Father which is in heaven."

I repeat the question, "Are you under the shed blood?" I put it to each one of you here tonight, even though you may be a church member, even though you may be nominally a very active church worker, "Are you under the blood?" Are you sure that you are under the blood? If not, will you get under the blood right now?

To sum it all up: God Is; God is infinitely great; God is infinitely holy. You and I must meet God. There is only one way to meet Him with exultant joy and not with craven, cowering, agonizing fear, and that is to be under the blood. There is only one way to get under the blood, by accepting Jesus Christ as your personal Saviour, surrendering to Him as your Lord and Master, confessing Him as such before the world, and living a life of daily conformity to His will, thereby proving the genuineness of your faith. Are you under the blood? Will you get under the blood right now?

II

THREE REASONS WHY I BELIEVE THE BIBLE
TO BE THE WORD OF GOD

MY subject tonight is, "Three Reasons Why I Believe the Bible to Be the Word of God." The most fundamental and the most important question in religious thought is, "Is the Bible the Word of God?" If the Bible be the Word of God, a revelation from God Himself regarding Himself, His nature, His character, His purposes, His will, His plans, His methods, His work, and concerning man, his nature, his fall, his ruin, the way of his salvation, his duty and his destiny, then we have a sure starting point from which we can proceed to the conquest of the entire domain of religious and ethical truth. But if the Bible is not the Word of God, if it is merely the product of man's own thinking, speculating, and guessing regarding the great subjects with which it has to do, not at all trustworthy, then we are all at sea, not knowing whither we are drifting, but we may be sure that we are not drifting toward any safe port.

Let me say here, at the very outset, that I did not always believe the Bible to be the Word of God. I doubted whether the Bible was the Word of God. I doubted whether Jesus Christ was the Son of God. I sometimes doubted whether there was a personal God. I was not an infidel—I was a skeptic. I was not an atheist—I was an agnostic. I did not deny—I questioned. But I made up my mind that I would find out. If the Bible was the Word of God, I would find that out and act accordingly; but if the Bible was not the Word of God I would find that out and act accordingly. If Jesus Christ was the Son of God, I would find that out and act accordingly; but if Jesus Christ was not the Son of God I would find that out and act accordingly. If there were a God, I would find that out and act accordingly; but if there were no God I would find that out and act accordingly. I found out. I found out to an absolute certainty that there is a God. I found out for a certainty that Jesus Christ is the Son of God. I found out to an absolute certainty that the Bible is the Word of God.

I will give you tonight, and on the two following nights, some of the reasons why I believe the Bible to be the Word of God. I will not give you all of my reasons—it would take months to give them. I am not even going to give you my best reasons; for my best reasons are of such an intensely personal character that each one must work them out for himself, but before I get through I will tell you how you may work them out for yourself. However, I will give you on these three nights reasons so conclusive and decisive that they will make any doubt that the Bible is the Word of God absolutely impossible on the part of any candid seeker after the truth; that is, to any one who desires to know the truth and is willing to obey it when he discovers it. They will not convince one who is determined not to know the truth, or who is unwilling to obey it. Such a one must be left to his own deliberate choice of error and sin, but he has no one to blame for it but himself.

The reasons, however, that I shall give have satisfied thousands of thinking men and women around the world, men and women of every class of society from the brilliant professional man, prominent university teachers and students, down to men of the artisan class and of the labouring class.

I. I Believe the Bible to be the Word of God Because of the Testimony of Jesus Christ to That Fact

In the first place, I believe the Bible to be the Word of God because of the clear and definite testimony of Jesus Christ to that fact. We live in a day in which many people say, " I accept what Jesus Christ teaches, but I do not know about the rest of the Bible. As for what Jesus Christ says, that goes with me, but as to what Paul said, or John said, or Peter said, or Moses said or is said to have said, or David said or is said to have said, or Isaiah said or is said to have said, or the rest of them said, I do not know about that; but what Jesus Christ says I accept." Now at the first glance that looks like an eminently rational position, but, in point of fact, it is utterly irrational and impossible. It is irrational and impossible for this reason: if we accept the teaching of Jesus Christ, we must of course accept everything upon which He sets the stamp of His endorsement. To say that you accept the authority of Jesus Christ and then to throw overboard that upon which He sets the stamp of His endorsement, is to be utterly irrational. And Jesus Christ sets the stamp of His endorsement upon the entire Bible, upon the entire Old Testament and entire New Testament; and, therefore, if we accept the authority of Jesus Christ we are logically compelled to accept the entire Old Testament and the entire New Testament as the Word of God.

As to our Lord's endorsement of the Old Testament, you will find it, for example, in Mark 7:13. Here our Lord, in reasoning with the religious leaders of His day, said, " you do make *The Word of God* of none effect through your tradition." He had just been drawing a sharp contrast between their traditions and the teachings of the law of Moses, not merely of the Decalogue but of other parts of the Pentateuch as well, and having drawn this contrast He says these words, " Making *the Word of God* of none effect through your traditions;" thus in so many words calling the law of Moses " the Word of God."

When I was holding meetings in England, a prominent dignitary and scholar in the Church of England, in a private correspondence with me, took me to task for calling the Bible "the Word of God," and said, " The Bible nowhere claims to be the Word of God." In reply, among other passages, I called his attention to the one just quoted and showed him how the Lord Jesus Himself in so many words called the law of Moses " the Word of God."

Now turn to Matthew 5:18, where you will read these words of the Lord Jesus, " Verily I say unto you, Till heaven and earth pass, *one jot or one tittle shall in no wise pass from the law,* till all be fulfilled." Now a " jot," as every Hebrew scholar knows, is the Hebrew character " Yodh," the smallest character in the Hebrew alphabet, less than half the size of any other character in the Hebrew alphabet; and a " tittle " is only a part of a letter, the horn that the Hebrews put on some of their consonants, less than the cross that we put on a "t." So our Lord Jesus here sets the stamp of His endorsement upon the law of Moses, as originally given, as being absolutely inerrant down to its smallest letter or smallest part of a letter. That is " verbal inspiration " with a vengeance, and it is from our Lord Jesus Christ Himself.

Of course, this only covers the first five books of the Old Testament, but if you can accept them you will not have much trouble with the rest of the Old Testament, for this is the very part of the Bible where the hottest controversy is being fought today, and always has been fought, between the rationalists and the believers in the Bible as the inerrant Word of God. It is in this part of the Bible that we read the story of creation, the story of the Fall, the story of the Flood, the story of Sodom and Gomorrah, the turning of Lot's wife into a pillar of salt, the destruction of the Canaanite nations, and pretty much all the other things on which the objectors to a Bible verbally inspired most violently pour out their condemnation and their scorn. And is it not a remarkable fact that our Lord Jesus Christ, looking down through the coming centuries and anticipating the controversies of today, should have put the stamp of His endorsement in the most unmistakable way upon that very portion of the Bible where the hottest conflict would be waged eighteen centuries later?

Now turn to John 10:35. Here the Lord Jesus says, " The scripture cannot be broken." He had just quoted Psalm 82:6 as ending all controversy in the matter in dispute between Himself and His opponents, and having done it He utters the words quoted above, " The Scripture cannot be broken," thus setting the stamp of His endorsement upon the absolute irrefragability or inerrancy of the Old Testament Scriptures. Turn now to Luke 24:27, " And beginning from Moses and all the prophets, He expounded unto them *in all the scriptures* the things concerning Himself." And now read the 44th verse of the same chapter, " *All things must be fulfilled,* which were *written in the law* of Moses, and *in the Prophets, and in the Psalms,* concerning Me." The Hebrew in our Lord's time divided his Bible, our present Old Testament, into three divisions: " The Law," that is the part we call the Pentateuch; " The Prophets," including not only most of the books that we call prophetical, but many of the historical books as well, the material for which was derived from the prophets; and

" The Psalms," or " Hagiographa " or sacred writings, including all the remaining books of our present Old Testament.
So our Lord in these verses takes up each one of the three
recognized divisions of the Jewish Bible of His day, our
present Old Testament scriptures, and sets the stamp of His
endorsement upon each and every one of them.   Therefore,
if we accept the authority of Jesus Christ we are logically
compelled to accept the entire Old Testament as the Word
of God.

Furthermore, as regards the Divine origin and authority of
the Old Testament, our Lord Jesus says in Luke 16:31, " *If
they hear not Moses and the prophets,* neither will they be
persuaded, though one rose from the dead."   In these words
He endorses in a most emphatic way the infallible truth of
the Old Testament.   He says again in John 5:47, " If ye
believe not His (Moses') writings, how shall ye believe my
words?"   In these words He set the stamp of His authority
upon the teaching of Moses as being as truly from God as
His own, and declares that the same spirit that led men to
reject the teachings of Moses would lead them to reject His
own teachings.   So, then, if we accept the authority of Jesus
Christ we are compelled to accept the entire Old Testament
as the Word of God.

*But how about the New Testament?   Did our Lord Jesus
set His stamp of approval upon that also?* He did.   But
someone will say, " How could He, was the New Testament
written when He was here on earth?"   No, not a single book
of it.   How then could He set the stamp of His endorsement
upon books that were not as yet written?   The answer is simple, by way of anticipation.   Turn to John 14:26 and you
will hear Jesus saying, " But the Comforter, which is *the Holy
Spirit,* whom the Father will send in My name, He shall *teach
you all things,* and *bring all things to your remembrance,*
whatsoever *I have said unto you."*   In these words our Lord
Jesus set the stamp of His endorsement not only upon the
teaching of the Apostles as being Divinely inspired, but also
upon their recollection of what He said as being also Divinely
inspired.   The question is often asked me, " How do we know
that in the four gospels we have an accurate record of what
Jesus Christ said?   Did the Apostles take notes of what our

Lord Jesus said at the time, and if not, may they not have forgotten and misreported Him?" To this question I would say, " There is reason to suppose that the Apostles did take notes at the time of what the Lord Jesus said; that Matthew, the author of the first gospel, and Peter, from whom Mark derived his material for the second gospel, and that James, the brother of John, from whom there is reason to believe Luke derived much of his material for the third gospel, took down what Jesus said in Aramaic, and that John took down what the Lord Jesus said in Greek, for we must remember that when our Lord Jesus was here on earth the people among whom He lived were a bilingual people, speaking sometimes Greek, sometimes Aramaic. But all this does not matter for our present purpose; for our Lord Jesus Christ Himself distinctly tells us that in the Apostolic records of what He said we would not have the Apostles' recollection of His words but the Holy Spirit's recollection, that *the Holy Spirit would bring to their remembrance all that He had said unto them;* and, while it was possible that the Apostles might forget and misreport, the Holy Ghost could never forget nor misreport.

Now turn to John 16:12, 13. There you will read these words, " I have yet many things to say unto you, but ye cannot bear them now. Howbeit, when He, the Spirit of truth, is come, He will guide you into all the truth." In these words our Lord Jesus declares that the Apostles' teachings were not only all to be Divinely inspired, but that furthermore they would contain more truth than He Himself taught, that indeed they would contain " *all the truth.*" So if we accept the authority of Jesus Christ, we are logically compelled to accept the New Testament as being Divinely inspired, as containing more truth than Jesus Christ Himself taught, as indeed containing " *all the truth.*"

There was a fad cry that arose some years ago in England, and was taken up in this country, " Back to Christ." By this men meant, " Do not tell us what Paul said, do not tell us what John said, do not tell us what Peter said, back to Christ Himself, back to the original source of authority." Very well, " Back to Christ "; I rather like the cry myself, but when you get back to Jesus Christ you hear Him saying, " On to the Apostles; I have many things to say that I could tell you, but

you are not ready to hear them yet; but when the Holy Spirit
is come, He will guide you into all the truth." So, then, if
we accept the authority of Jesus Christ, we are compelled to
accept the authority of the entire New Testament, as being
divinely inspired, as containing more truth than He Himself
taught, as indeed containing " all the truth."

Here, then, is the point at which we arrive; if we accept the
authority of Jesus Christ, we must accept the entire Old
Testament and the entire New Testament as the Word of God.
It is either Christ and a whole Bible—or else, no Bible and
no Christ. There are many in these days who say that they
" Believe in Christ, but not in the Christ of the New Testament." But there is no Christ but the Christ of the New
Testament. Any other Christ than the Christ of the New
Testament is a pure figment of the individual imagination,
just as much an idol made with men's brains as an idol men
make with their hands.

So then if we accept the authority of Jesus Christ, we are
logically compelled to accept the entire Old Testament and the
entire New Testament as the Word of God. But, if we
honestly face the facts in the case, we are compelled to accept
the authority of Jesus Christ, for Jesus Christ is accredited
to us by five unmistakably Divine testimonies.

First of all, Jesus Christ is accredited to us by the testimony
of the Divine life that He lived, for He lived as never man
lived. If any man will take the four gospels for Himself and
lay them side by side and read them through carefully and
honestly, even once, he will discover two things: The first
thing that he will discover is, that the story here related is
the story of a life that was actually lived here upon earth,
and not a mere romance. To suppose that any one man
imagined such a character as that of Jesus of Nazareth when
such a life was never lived here upon earth, is to suppose a
greater miracle than any one recorded in any of the four gospels. But to suppose that not only one man did it, but that
four different men did it and that each one of the four not
only succeeded in making his story consistent with itself, but
consistent also with the other three, is to suppose the absolutely preposterous and impossible. There is no possibility
of honestly questioning that the story recorded in the four

gospels is the story of a life that was actually lived here upon earth. The second thing that he will discover, will be that the life here recorded stands absolutely apart from any other life ever lived upon earth. Napoleon Bonaparte, late in life, was discussing Jesus of Nazareth with some of his friends, and he is reported to have said, " I know men (and if he did not know men, who ever did?), and Jesus of Nazareth was no man." By this, of course, he meant that Jesus Christ was not merely a man; for man He was.

In the second place, Jesus Christ is accredited to us by the Divine words that He spoke. If anyone will take the four gospels and just read with candour and open mind the words spoken by our Lord Jesus Christ, he will soon discover that there is a quality in these words that distinguishes them from all other words ever spoken on earth. He will be compelled to say what the officers said who were sent to arrest Jesus but came back without Him, " Never man spake like this man."

In the third place, Jesus Christ is accredited to us by the Divine works that He wrought, not only healing the sick, which many others have done, but cleansing the leper by a mere word, opening the eyes of the blind by a mere word, raising the dead by a mere deed, stilling the tempest and the sea by a mere word, turning water into wine, and feeding five thousand people with five small loaves and two small fish, which was a creative act. These works of Divine power are clear credentials of a God-sent Teacher. We cannot study them carefully and not come to the same conclusion that the great Jewish teacher of the day, Nicodemus, came to, when he said, to quote his words in the exact order of the Greek, " We know that *from God* Thou art come a Teacher, for no man can do these signs which Thou doest, except God be with Him." (John 3:2.)

Of course, I do not forget that very strenuous efforts are being made in our day (in point of fact they have been made for many, many years, though some of our university professors are telling us it is the " *modern* view " of the Bible) to eliminate the supernatural element from the story of the life of Jesus Christ, that is to reconstruct the life of Jesus of Nazareth as we find it in the four gospels in such a way as to leave out the miraculous and to leave the character and teaching of

Jesus Christ intact. But all attempts of this character have resulted in total failure, and all future attempts will result in the same failure. The most able effort of this kind that was ever made, was that made by David Strauss in his " Leben Jesu." David Strauss was a remarkable man, he was a man of very broad and very profound scholarship, a man of almost matchless powers of critical analysis, a man of untiring industry, and he brought all the powers of his singularly gifted mind to bear upon the four gospel records of the life of Jesus for the purpose of reconstructing it in such a way as to leave out the miraculous and have the character and conduct of Jesus left. If any man could succeed in that attempt David Strauss was the man. He gave the results of his labours to the world in his celebrated, epoch-making " Leben Jesu," published in 1833. Please note the date. We are constantly informed by theological professors of the modernistic school, and by various university professors of the same school, and other leaders, that this view of the Bible is " the *modern* view," but this ablest attempt of the kind ever made was published ninety years ago, published twenty-three years before I was born and when my father was only eleven years old. Where have these scholarly gentlemen who insist upon this being the " *modern* view " been living for the last hundred years?

It seemed for a time to many as if David Strauss had succeeded in his attempt and that the miraculous must go. David Strauss' " Leben Jesu " swept all the universities of Germany, and France, and England, and Scotland, and Ireland, and to a less extent those of America, as the modern destructive criticism has never swept them, swept them until it was thought that anyone who did not accept David Strauss' construction of the life of Jesus was not up-to-date, that he was not scholarly but the slave of tradition, an " obscurantist." But when David Strauss' " Leben Jesu " was itself submitted to rigid, critical, analysis, it fell all to pieces, and there is not one, single, scholar on earth today who accepts David Strauss' construction of the life of Jesus.

Where David Strauss failed, Ernest Renan tried his hand. He was not by any means so able a man as David Strauss, but he was a man who towered far above the average man in ability and genius. He was a man of some considerable Semitic scholarship. He was a man of subtle imagination, of a rare literary skill, of singular adroitness and finesse, the acknowledged literary master of all France in his day. His " Life of Jesus " was read with interest and admiration in many lands. The work was done with a rare and fascinating skill. And some fancied that Ernest Renan had succeeded in his attempt where David Strauss had failed. But when Renan's " Life of Jesus " was subjected to a rigid critical analysis, it also fell all to pieces, and there is not a single scholar on earth today who accepts Ernest Renan's construction of the life of Jesus. Every other attempt of a similar kind, and they have been almost countless, has met with a similar fate, for they attempt the impossible; and today at least this much is proven—I believe far more than this is proven, but this is enough for our present purpose—that the story of Jesus of Nazareth as recorded in the four gospels is at least substantially accurate history. If that be true, and it unquestionably is, if it be true that our Lord Jesus lived as recorded in the four gospels and wrought the works that are attributed to Him in the four gospels, *then beyond a peradventure Jesus Christ bore unmistakable credentials from God Himself that He was a Teacher sent from God.*

In the fourth place, Jesus Christ is also accredited to us by His Divine influence upon all subsequent history. Jesus Christ was, beyond an honest peradventure, one of three things: He was either the Son of God in a unique sense, a Divine person, God incarnate in human form, or else He was one of the most daring impostors that ever lived, or else one of the most hopeless lunatics. That Jesus Christ claimed to be the Son of God in a unique sense does not admit of a moment's question. He says in Mark 12:6, that while all the prophets of the old dispensation, even the greatest, were " servants," He Himself was the " Son " and the " one " and only " *Son* " of God (see R. V. and Greek). He did not hesitate to say in John 10:30, " I and My Father are one." He went so far as to say in John 14:9, " He that hath seen Me, hath seen the Father," and He even went so far as to say in John 5:22, 23, that all men should honour Him, " The Son even as they honour the Father." That He claimed in these passages to be a Divine person is beyond question. He was then either the Divine person that He claimed to be, or else the most daring impostor the world has ever known, or else the most hopeless lunatic. The modern Unitarian position, that Jesus Christ was not a Divine person except in the sense that we are all divine, but that He was a good man, perhaps the best man that ever lived, is the very acme of irrationality and absurdity. Whatever Jesus Christ was, He was not " a good man," that is to say, if He was not more than man He was not good. Some years ago when I was speaking to business and professional men on these subjects in the city of Atlanta, Georgia, one of the most brilliant lawyers in the city sent me a message in these words, " Tell Dr. Torrey for me that he has proven at least one thing, that Jesus of Nazareth was not a good man." A few days later he came out and took his stand and openly confessed Jesus Christ as his Divine Saviour. To come back to our main point, Jesus Christ was, as we have said, either a Divine person, God incarnate, or else He was the most daring and blasphemous impostor that ever lived; or else one of the most hopeless lunatics. Now let me ask you two questions: Was the influence of Jesus of Nazareth upon subsequent history the influence of an impostor? No one whose own heart is not cankered with fraud and imposture, would dream for one moment of asserting it. Was the influence of Jesus of Nazareth upon subsequent history the influence of a lunatic? Nobody but a lunatic would dream of asserting it. Here then is the inescapable conclusion—not an impostor, not a lunatic, then beyond an honest peradventure the Son of God.

In the fifth place, Jesus Christ is accredited to us by His resurrection from the dead. We have not time now to go into the argument for the resurrection of Jesus Christ from the dead. I have done it time and time again, and it can be easily shown that the historic evidence for the resurrection of Jesus Christ is so absolutely and overwhelmingly convincing, that doubting the resurrection of Jesus Christ from the dead is impossible on the part of any man competent to weigh evidence and who will sit down before the evidence of His resurrection and carefully examine it with the single-hearted desire to know and obey the truth. But this clearly proven resurrection of Jesus Christ from the dead is the Lord God Almighty's stamp of endorsement upon Jesus Christ's claims.

Jesus Christ, as we have seen, claimed to be a Divine person. He was put to death for making that claim. When I was a minister in the city of Chicago, one of the leading liberal preachers of that city made the assertion one Sunday morning in his sermon that " Jesus of Nazareth was crucified by the Orthodox people of the day." I called him down the following Sunday by calling his attention to the fact that Jesus of Nazareth was crucified by the Unitarians of the day on the specific charge that He claimed to be the Son of God. This liberal preacher was honest enough to admit that I was right, and afterwards quit the ministry and went into newspaper work. I repeat, Jesus Christ was put to death for making the claim to be the Son of God, but, before they put Him to death for making that claim, He said in substance, " You will put me to death for claiming to be the Son of God, but after you have put Me to death God will set the stamp of His endorsement upon the claim by raising Me from the dead." Put Him to death they did; take Him down from the cross and lay Him in Joseph's sepulcher, they did; roll a stone to the door of the sepulcher and seal it with a Roman seal, which to break was death, they did; but when the appointed, exactly predicted hour came, the breath of God swept through that sleeping clay and Jesus Christ was raised triumphant over death, and God spoke more clearly to all coming ages than if He should speak with audible voice from the open heavens above us today, " This man is what He claims to be, He is My beloved Son, hear ye Him."

We must then, if we are honest, accept the authority of Jesus Christ, and consequently we must accept the entire Old Testament and the entire New Testament which He endorsed as being the Word of God, as being in reality such. Therefore, I believe the Bible to be the Word of God because of the testimony of Jesus Christ to that effect. I would be a fool if I did not.

A school of criticism has arisen in your day and mine that assumes to set its authority up above the authority of Jesus Christ. This school of criticism demands that we give up the authority and infallibility of Jesus Christ and of the Apostles, and accept their authority and their infallibility in their stead. That is a stupendous claim to make, but I for one, am perfectly willing to listen to the claim. But before I accede to the claim I demand that this School of Criticism present its credentials. We cannot yield to the claim of authority and infallibility of anyone until he presents his credentials, and they must be very clear and convincing credentials. Jesus Christ presents His credentials. First of all, He presents the credential of the Divine life that He lived. What has this school of criticism to present over against that? They love to tell us about the beauty of the lives of some of these destructive critics, and we have not the slightest desire to deny the claim, but over against the fairest life that was ever lived by any destructive critic, or modernist, we lay the life of Jesus of Nazareth. Which suffers by the comparison? If there is any force in the argument, and there is great force in it, " If a man's life is in the right, his doctrine cannot be in the wrong," it bears immeasurably more for the authority of Jesus Christ than it does for the authority of any critic who ever lived on earth.

Jesus Christ presents His second credential, the Divine words that He spoke. What has this school of criticism to present over against that? Nothing at all adequate; for while the words of Jesus of Nazareth have stood the test of eighteen centuries and more, and shine out with greater luster and glory today than ever before, what school of criticism has ever stood the test of eighteen years? If one has to choose between the teaching of Christ and that of any school of criticism that ever existed upon earth, it will not take him long to decide which to accept, if he is a man of any intelligence and candour.

Jesus Christ presents His third credential, the Divine works that He wrought, the unmistakable seal of God upon His claims. What has this school of criticism to present over against that? Absolutely nothing. The only miracles they offer us are miracles of literary ingenuity, by which they attempt to make the preposterous appear like the plausible.

In the fourth place, Jesus Christ presents the credential of His Divine influence upon all subsequent history. What has this school of criticism to offer over against that? Less than nothing; for while the influence of Jesus of Nazareth has been all together wholesome, uplifting, and saving, beyond a question the influence of this school of criticism has been all together pernicious and destructive. It is robbing thousands and tens of thousands of our young men and women in our high schools and universities, and theological seminaries, of their faith; it is robbing the Church of candidates for the ministry; it is robbing those who have entered the ministry and gone to the foreign field of all power in their work. Man after man came to me as I went around the world, even as long ago as 1902, and confessed that the destructive criticism and new theology had left him without a message. It is robbing our treasuries of contributions for the work at home and abroad, and is paralyzing missionary effort and evangelistic effort in every field where it has gone. This I know by personal observation, and not by hearsay.

Jesus Christ presents His fifth credential, His resurrection from the dead. What has this school of criticism to present over against that? Nothing whatever! Therefore I, for one, positively refuse to bow to the claim to authority and infallibility of any Pope, protestant popes as well as Roman Catholic Pope, or any preacher, or any priest, or any theological professor, or any school of criticism, when that claim of authority and infallibility is absolutely unproven; but most gladly do I bow to the completely demonstrated claim of authority and infallibility of Jesus Christ; and, therefore, I accept the entire Old Testament, and the entire New Testament, which He endorsed as being the Word of God, as being in reality such. There is nothing else left for me to do, as a man who gladly bows to the inexorable logic of facts.

II. I BELIEVE THE BIBLE TO BE THE WORD OF GOD
BECAUSE OF ITS FULFILLED PROPHECIES

My second reason for believing the Bible to be the Word of God is because of its fulfilled prophecies. The subject of fulfilled prophecy is a large one, and to go into it in any fullness would take many hours; but I think I can sufficiently outline it in a few minutes for you to see its unanswerable force.

There are two kinds of prophecy in the Bible: first, the explicit verbal prophecies, and, second, the prophecies of the types and symbols.

Let us take up first the explicit verbal prophecies. These are of three kinds; first, prophecies regarding the coming Messiah; second, prophecies regarding the Jewish people; third, prophecies regarding the Gentile nations. We will limit ourselves this evening to the prophecies concerning the coming Messiah, and take only five of them by way of illustration.

First of all, Isaiah 53, the entire chapter. A very determined effort is being made in our day to discredit the Messianic application of Isaiah 53. This is done by both the rationalists and by the unbelieving Jews. It is very natural that both of these classes should deny the Messianic application of this chapter, for if Isaiah 53 is Messianic, then beyond a peradventure there is a predictive element in prophecy, and one of the fundamental principles of the rationalists is, that "there is no predictive element in prophecy." Also, if Isaiah 53 is Messianic, then beyond a peradventure Jesus of Nazareth was the Messiah, and of course unbelieving Jews are not willing to admit that, so we are told that Isaiah 53 is not Messianic. But two things prove to a certainty that Isaiah 53 is Messianic: first, because the Jews themselves taught it was Messianic until Jesus of Nazareth came and fulfilled it, and then, as they did not wish to admit that He was the Messiah, they began to deny the Messianic application of this prophecy. The second thing that proves it is Messianic is, that, if it does not refer to the Messiah, the question at once arises, to whom does it refer? The best answer that those who deny that it refers to the Messiah can give, and the answer they constantly do give, is that the sufferer of Isaiah is suffering Israel. But anyone who will read the chapter through even once carefully, especially if he reads the Revised Version, will see that this explanation is impossible: for this reason, that we are distinctly told that the sufferer in Isaiah 53 was suffering for the sins of others than himself. This we are told again and again; for example, we are told "He was wounded for our transgressions, He was bruised for our iniquities: the chastisement of our peace was upon Him; and with His stripes we are healed." We are told furthermore that the

others than Himself for whose sins He was suffering, were
Israel. Now put these two facts together—the sufferer suffering for the sins of others than Himself, and the others than
Himself for whose sins He was suffering, Israel, then certainly
the sufferer cannot have been Israel.

Some years ago a Jew wrote to one of the most learned and
best known rabbis in America asking him if Isaiah 53 referred
to Jesus of Nazareth. To this the brilliant Rabbi replied,
" It seems to, but don't." The answer was astray in only
one or two words, " It seems to *and does.*"

The other passages to which I call your attention are,
Micah 5:2; Daniel 9:25-27; Jeremiah 23:5, 6; Psalm 16:8-11.
In these five passages we have predictions of a coming King
of Israel. We are told the exact place of His birth, and the
exact time of His manifestations to His people; we are told
of the precise family of which He was to be born, and the condition of that family at the time of His birth, a condition entirely different from that existing at the time the prophecy
was written, and contrary to all the probabilities in the case;
we are told of the manner of His reception by His people, a
reception entirely different from that which would naturally
be expected; we are told of His death, the exact manner of
His death by crucifixion, and other details regarding His
death; we are told of His burial and the details in connection
with His burial, and of His resurrection and His victory subsequent to His resurrection. Every one of these predictions
was fulfilled centuries later with the most minute precision
in Jesus of Nazareth. Now I submit that any book that
has the power of looking centuries into the future, and predicting with minuteness and precision and accuracy of time,
person, place, and circumstance, events to occur centuries
later, must have for its author the only person in the universe
who knows the end from the beginning—that is God. Of
course, it is quite possible for a far-seeing man, by studying
causes now operant, to predict *in a general way* the condition
of affairs a few years in the future. Gladstone did that in
England; James G. Blaine did it in America. But that is
not at all our present problem. It is not a few years but
many centuries, for you can bring these prophecies down to
the latest date the most daring destructive critic ever thought

of assigning to them, and still they were centuries before the birth of Jesus of Nazareth; and they are not predictions of a general kind, but predictions characterized by minuteness, precision and accuracy of time, person, place and circumstance; and they are not of things the causes for which were operant and observable, but of things for which there were no causes then operant and observable, and these predictions were fulfilled to the very letter. I submit again, that any book that has this power of looking centuries into the future, and predicting with minuteness, precision and accuracy of time, person, place, and circumstance, events to occur centuries later, must have for its author the only being in the universe that knows the end from the beginning, that is, God.

There is a noteworthy and significant fact regarding the prophecies of the Bible, and that is, that oftentimes there are two seemingly contradictory lines of prophecy, and it seems as though if the one line of prophecy were fulfilled, the other could not by any possibility be fulfilled, and yet these two seemingly contradictory lines of prophecy will converge and be fulfilled in one person. For example, in the Old Testament we have two apparently contradictory lines of prophecy regarding the Messiah: one line predicts a suffering Messiah, " despised and rejected of men," " a man of sorrows and acquainted with grief ", One who should lay down His life as an atoning sacrifice for sin on the cross, one whose earthly mission should end in death and ignominy. The other line of prophecy predicts with equal clearness and definiteness a Messiah who should be an all-conquering Messiah, a King who should rule the nations with a rod of iron. How could these two lines of prophecy both be true? This was the problem that confronted the ancient Jew; and the best answer he could give was, that there were to be two Messiahs, one a suffering Messiah of the tribe of Joseph, and the other an all-conquering Messiah of the tribe of Judah; but in the actual fulfillment in Jesus of Nazareth, we find both lines of prophecy converging and fulfilled in the one person: the first line of prophecy, that of a suffering Messiah who should die an atoning sacrifice for sin, being already fulfilled in His first coming which culminated in His crucifixion on the cross of

Calvary; the second line of prophecy to be fulfilled in His
second coming as an all-conquering King to rule in Jerusalem
over all the nations of the earth.

But if the explicit verbal prophecies are conclusive, the
prophecies of types and symbols are even more conclusive.
If you ask the ordinary, superficial, student of the Bible how
much of the Old Testament is prophetical, he will answer
something like this, " Isaiah is prophetical, and Jeremiah is
prophetical, and Ezekiel and Daniel, and the minor prophets,
are prophetical;" he may add that " there are also prophetical
passages here and there in the Psalms and in the Pentateuch."
But if you ask a thoroughgoing student of the Bible how
much of the Old Testament is prophetical, he will reply that
the entire Old Testament is prophetical, that its historical in-
cidents are prophetical, that its personages are prophetical,
that its institutions, ceremonies, offerings, sacrifices, and
feasts, are all prophetical. If you doubt his statement, and
you have a perfect right to doubt it until you investigate it,
but you have no right to remain a doubter unless you take the
trouble to investigate it, if you will take time, he will sit down
and take you through the whole Old Testament, from the first
chapter of Genesis to the last chapter of Malachi, and will
show you everywhere unmistakable foreshadowings of things
to come. He will show you in Abraham, Isaac, Joseph,
David and Solomon, and also in every sacrifice and offering,
in the Tabernacle and every part of the Tabernacle, its outer
court with its brazen altar of sacrifice, its Holy Place with its
seven branched candlesticks and table with the loaves of shew-
bread upon it, in the golden altar of incense before the curtain
separating the Holy Place from the Most Holy Place, in the
curtain itself, in the Ark of the Covenant beyond the curtain,
with its perfectly kept law overshadowed by the blood-
sprinkled Mercy Seat, in its coverings, and even in its boards
and its tenons and sockets, and the various covers of skins,
indeed in every minutest part of the Tabernacle, in every
sacrifice and offering, in its laws regarding cleansings, and in
its feasts, and all its ceremonies, the most unmistakable foreshadowings and types of Jesus Christ; His twofold nature,
Divine and human; His sinless character, His atoning death,
His resurrection and return, and all the outstanding facts of

Church and Jewish history. Now at first this will seem to
you merely accidental, a happy coincidence, but as you go
on chapter after chapter, and book after book, the theory of
" happy coincidence " is ruled out by the law of mathematical
probabilities and you are forced to see that it is intended;
you will find every fundamental truth that was to be fully
revealed in the New Testament prefigured in the types and
symbols of the Old Testament. Now I submit that any book
that has the power of putting into a legislation intended in
the first place to meet the immediate needs of the people then
living, the clearest foreshadowings of happenings and truths
not to be fully revealed for at least fifteen hundred years,
must have for its author the only being in the universe who
knows the end from the beginning—that is God. A wisdom
is here discernible of such a profound and infinite character
as can only be the wisdom of God. The modern critical
theories regarding the composite character of Exodus, Levit-
icus, Numbers, and Deuteronomy go all to pieces when con-
sidered in the light of the meaning of the types of the Old
Testament. I have never once been able to find one single
destructive critic that knew anything to speak of regarding
the types. I have challenged the destructive critics in the
university towns and elsewhere of Germany, England, Scotland, Ireland, and America, to name one single destructive
critic that knew anything of a thorough character about the
types, and they have never been able to name one. One cannot study them thoroughly without being profoundly convinced that the real author of the Old Testament, back of the
human authors, is God.

III. I Believe the Bible to be the Word of God Because of the Unity of the Book

*My third reason for believing the Bible to be the Word
of God is because of* THE UNITY *of the Book.* This is an
old argument but it is not only a good one but an unanswerable
one. The Bible is composed, as I presume most of you know,
of sixty-six separate portions, or books. These sixty-six
books were written in three different languages, Hebrew,
Greek and Aramaic. The period of their composition ex-
tends over at least fifteen hundred years. They were writ-

ten in countries hundreds of miles apart. They were written by at least forty different human authors. They were written by men upon every plane of political and social life, from the king upon his throne down to the herdman, the shepherd, the fisherman, and the petty politician. They display every known form of literary structure. We not only have in the Bible both prose and poetry, but we have every known form of prose and every known form of poetry. We have in the Bible epic poetry, lyric poetry, didactic poetry, erotic poetry, elegy and rhapsody. We have also every form of prose. We have in the Bible historic prose, didactic prose, epistolary prose, argument, theological treatise, proverb, parable, apothem, allegory, satire, and oration. In a book so marvelously composite, made up of such divergent parts, composed at such remote periods of time, and under such divergent circumstances, by so many different persons, what would we naturally expect? Variance and discrepancy, absolute contradiction and discord, utter lack of unity. In point of fact, what do we find? We find, as every thorough Bible student knows, the most marvelous unity known anywhere in literature. Every part of the Bible fits every other part of the Bible, one ever-increasing, ever growing, ever deepening thought pervades the whole. It is sometimes said, and men think they are particularly wise when they say it, that " the Bible is not a book, it is a library." That is partly true and largely false and foolish. It is true that the Bible is a library, in fact it is a whole literature, but at the same time it is the most intensely and unvaryingly one of any book known in literature. In the last thirty years I have written something over thirty different books, but I venture to say that in the thirty books written by one author in the short period of thirty years, there is not the unity that there is in these sixty-six books written by forty different human authors in a period covering at least fifteen hundred years. Now here is a fact, an astonishing fact—how are we going to account for it? It demands accounting for. If we were simply theologians or philosophers of the evolutionary type, who do not bother with facts but simply weave their theories out of their inner consciousness, we would not have to notice or account for this fact; but being hard-headed, common sense, everyday men and women, we must account for facts, and here is a fact that demands accounting for. How shall we account for it? There is one very simple way of accounting for it, and only one way for accounting for it at all. What that very simple and only way is, I will indicate in a few moments.

Before taking up the very simple and only way of accounting for this marvelous unity of the Bible, let me call your attention to the character of this unity, for that also is most significant. Two things about the character of the unity of the Bible demand attention. First of all, it is not a superficial unity, but a profound unity. It is not a unity that lies on the surface, it is a unity that only comes out of careful and protracted study. On the surface we often find apparent discrepancies and discord, but as we study and go far below the surface, the apparent discrepancies and discord disappear and the deep underlying unity appears. The more deeply we study, the more complete do we find the unity to be.

The second characteristic of this unity is, that it is an organic unity—that is to say, it is not the unity of a dead thing, like a stone, or even of a building, but of a living thing, like a plant or a tree, where you have first the seed, then the young plant, then the mature plant, then the bud, then the opening blossom, then the ripened fruit. In the early books of the Bible we have the germinant thought; as we go on we have the plant, then further on the bud, then the blossom, and then the ripened fruit. Revelation is, as every thorough student of the Book knows, simply the ripened fruit of Genesis.

Now how are we to account for this unity? It is, as I said, a fact demanding accounting for by level-headed men and women who are concerned not so much with theories as with realities, not with fine-spun speculations of cloistered theologians and utterly prejudiced so-called scientists, dreaming apart from the substantial realities of life, and not concerned with facts but with the theory they are bound to support at any cost. Now there is one very easy and very simple way of accounting for it, and there is only one rational way of accounting for it at all. This only rational way of accounting for it is, that back of the forty or more human authors was the One all-governing, all-controlling, all-superintending, all-shaping mind of God.

Suppose it were proposed to build in our capital city, Washington, D. C., a temple that should display the stone productions of every State in the Union. Some of the stones were to come from the marble quarries of Marlboro, N. H.; some from the gray granite quarries of Quincy, Mass.; some from the brownstone quarries of Middletown, Conn.; some from the white marble quarries at Rutland, Vt.; some from the gray sandstone quarries at Berea, Ohio; some from the porphyry quarries below Knoxville, Tenn.; some from the redstone quarries near Hancock, Mich.; some from the brownstone quarries at Kasota, Minn.; some from the redstone quarries near Flagstaff, Ariz.; some from the gypsum quarries of the Far West; some from the gray and blue granite quarries of Oglesby and Elberton of Georgia; some from every State in the Union. These stones were to be of all conceivable sizes and shapes—some large, some small, some medium, some were to be cubical, some spherical, some cylindrical, some conical, some trapezoidal, and some rectangular parallelopipedons. Each stone was to be cut into its final shape in the quarry from which it was taken. Not a mallet or chisel was to be touched to a stone after it reached its destination. Now the stones have all arrived and the builders at Washington go to work. As they build, they find that every stone fits exactly into every other stone, and into its appointed place. They find that there is not one stone too many, nor one stone too few; until at last when the builders' work is done there is not a stone small or great left over, and not the smallest niche or crany where a stone is lacking, and there rises before you a temple with its side walls, its buttresses, its roof, its pinnacles, and its domes, its naves, its arches, its transepts and its choirs, perfect in every outline, and perfect in every detail, and not one stone too many and not one stone too few, and every stone fitting into its place, and yet every stone hewn into its final shape in the quarry from which it was taken. How would you account for it? There is one very simple way of accounting for it, and only one way of accounting for it at all: this very simple and only way of accounting for it is this, that back of the individual quarry-

men who wrought in the quarry was the master mind of the
architect, who planned the whole building from the beginning
and gave to each individual quarryman his specifications for
the work.   Now this is precisely what we find in the temple
of eternal truth which we call the Bible, the stones for which
were quarried in places remote from one another by many
hundreds of miles of space and at periods of time fifteen centuries apart, stones of all conceivable sizes and shapes, and
yet every stone fitting exactly into its place and fitting every
other stone, until when the last book is added there rises before you this matchless and marvelous temple of God's eternal
truth, perfect in every outline and perfect in every detail, not
one book too many, and not one book too few, and yet every
stone cut into its final shape in the quarry from which it was
taken.   How are you going to account for it?   There is one
very simple way of accounting for it, and only one way of
accounting for it at all, that is, that back of the human hands
that wrought, was the Master-mind of God that thought and
planned the whole building from the beginning and gave to
each individual workman his specifications for the work.   I
challenge any man to answer it—it cannot be answered.   It
is an indisputable fact that proves to a demonstration that the
Bible is the Word of God.

III

FOUR MORE REASONS WHY I BELIEVE THE
BIBLE TO BE THE WORD OF GOD

M Y subject tonight is, *"Four More Reasons Why I
Believe the Bible to be the Word of God."* I gave
you last night three reasons why I believe the
Bible to be the Word of God:

First, *because of the testimony of Jesus Christ to that
effect.* We saw that Jesus Christ set the stamp of His endorsement upon the entire Old Testament and entire New
Testament, and that if we accepted the authority of Jesus
Christ we were logically compelled to accept the entire Old
Testament and entire New Testament as the Word of God.
That it was either Christ and the whole Bible, or else it was
no Bible and no Christ. We next saw that, if we faced the
facts in the case, we were compelled to accept the authority
of Jesus Christ; for He was accredited to us by five unmistakably Divine testimonies. First, the testimony of the
divine life that He lived, for He lived as never man lived.
Second, the testimony of the divine words He spoke, for He
spoke as never man spoke. Third, the testimony of the divine works that He wrought, for He wrought as never man
wrought. Fourth, the testimony of His divine influence upon
all subsequent history. And fifth, the testimony of His
resurrection from the dead, the best proven fact of history
and the Lord God Almighty's stamp of endorsement upon
Jesus Christ's claims. Therefore we were compelled to accept the authority of Jesus Christ, and consequently were
compelled to accept the entire Old Testament and entire New
Testament, which He endorsed as being the Word of God, as
being in reality such.

The second reason that I gave you for believing the Bible
to be the Word of God was, *because of its fulfilled prophecies.*
We saw by various explicit prophecies to which I referred
you that the Bible had the power of looking centuries into
the future and predicting with minuteness and precision and

accuracy of time, person, place and circumstance, events to occur centuries later, and we saw that these predictions had been fulfilled to the very letter in Jesus of Nazareth. And we saw that any book that had this power of looking centuries into the future and predicting with minuteness and precision and accuracy of time, person, place, and circumstance, events to occur centuries later, must have for its author the only being in the universe who knows the end from the beginning, that is God.

The third reason that I gave you for believing the Bible to be the Word of God was, *because of the unity of the Book.* We saw that the Bible was composed of sixty-six separate portions, or books, thirty-nine in the Old Testament and twenty-seven in the New Testament. We saw that these sixty-six books were written by at least forty different human authors, the period of their composition extending over at least fifteen hundred years, that they were written in three different languages, Hebrew, Greek, and Aramaic; that they were written by men upon every plane of social and political life from the king upon his throne down to the shepherd, the herdman, the fisherman, and the petty politician. We saw that they displayed every known form of literary structure, that we had in the Bible not only poetry and prose, but every known form of prose and every known form of poetry. And yet we saw that this wonderfully composite Book was the most intensely one of any book in literature. And we saw that the only rational way of accounting for this indisputable fact was, that back of the forty or more human authors was the one all-shaping, all-governing, all-controlling mind of God. At that point I stopped last Sunday night.

I. I Believe the Bible to be the Word of God Because of the Immeasurable Superiority of Its Teachings to Those of Any Other Book or All Other Books.

My fourth reason for believing the Bible to be the Word of God is, *Because of the Immeasurable Superiority of Its Teachings to Those of Any Other Book or of All Other Books Put Together*. It was quite the fashion when I was studying in the University to compare the teachings of the Bible with those of the ethnic philosophers and sages, with the teachings, for example, of Socrates, Plato, Aristotle, Isocrates, Marcus Aurelius Antoninus, Seneca, Buddha, Zoroaster, Confucius, Mencius, and Mohammed, and it is getting to be the fashion again. Fashions in thought are recurrent just as are fashions in women's dresses. Anyone who institutes such a comparison and puts the Bible in the same category with these ethnic philosophers and sages must be either ignorant of the teachings of the Bible, or else ignorant of the teachings of the ethnic philosophers and sages, or, what is more frequently the case, densely ignorant of both. There are three points of radical difference between the teachings of the Bible and those of any other and all other books.

First, *The teachings of these ethnic philosophers and sages contain truth, it is true, sometimes precious truth; but it is truth mixed with error; whereas the Bible contains nothing but truth.* There are gems of thought in these ethnic philosophers and sages, but as Joseph Cook pointed out nearly half a century ago, they are " Jewels picked out of the mud."

" Did not Socrates teach in a way worthy of our attention how a philosopher ought to die?" we are oftentimes asked. He did, but those who put Socrates in the same category with the Bible forget to tell us that Socrates also taught a woman of the town how to conduct her business, and that was not quite so pretty.

" Did not Marcus Aurelius Antoninus teach in a way that is worthy of our thought today the excellencies of clemency and moderation?" these men ask. He did, but they forget to tell us that this same Marcus Aurelius Antoninus also taught that it was right to put men and women to death for no other crime than that of being Christians, and being himself Emperor of Rome, and having the power to do it, he practiced what he preached, one of the most awful persecutions, that in which the holy Polycarp died, being under the especial patronage of this same Marcus Aurelius Antoninus.

" Did not Seneca teach in a thoughtful and suggestive way the excellencies of poverty?" these men ask us. He did, but they forget to tell us that at the very time Seneca was writing so beautifully about the excellencies of poverty he himself was one of the most notorious spendthrifts in Rome, the

single item of onyx tables in his Roman mansion costing a
fabulous fortune; and furthermore, Seneca was the tutor of
the most infamous Emperor in Roman history, Nero, under
whom Nero was trained for his awful work.

"Did not Confucius teach the duty of children to parents
in a way that is worthy of our attention today?" these men
ask. He did, but they forget to tell us that Confucius also
taught that it was right to tell lies, and unblushingly tells us
in a fragment of his own life which he has left us how he
himself told lies on occasion. And there is nothing in which
his most devoted disciples, the modern Chinese, have proven
themselves such adept pupils of their great master as in this
single matter of lying; for the Chinese are the one nation of
the earth that have reduced lying to a fine art. The typical
Confucianist Chinaman will tell anything to "save his face."

*The second point of radical difference between the teach-
ings of the Bible and all other books is, that the Bible contains All the Truth, while those other books contain only
fragments of the truth.* There is not one single known truth
on moral or spiritual subjects that cannot be found for substance between the covers of the Bible. Oftentimes in speaking to audiences largely composed of secularists and infidels
I have challenged anyone to produce one single truth on moral
or spiritual subjects which I could not find for substance
somewhere between the covers of the Bible. Of course it is
quite possible that somebody should be able to do that, for
I do not pretend to know everything that is in the Bible. I
have been studying it closely for only forty-seven years and
do not pretend to know all that there is in it, but no one has
ever been able to do it yet, and if you think you can, you
might try your hand on it at the close of this address. The
Bible is a very old Book, the last part of it was written over
eighteen hundred years ago, and yet in all the thinking that
men have done in the many long centuries since they have
not been able to strike out one single truth, on moral or spiritual subjects, that cannot be found in substance between the
covers of this old, old Book. Is not that a remarkable fact?
Is it not a very suggestive fact? Does it not point unmistakably to God as the author of the Book? Let me put it
this way: If all the other books in the world were destroyed,

and the Bible left, we would not lose one single known truth on moral or spiritual subjects.

The third point of radical difference between the Bible and all other books is, that the Bible Contains More Truth than All Other Books put Together. You can go to the literature of all ages and of all nations, the literature of ancient Greece, ancient Rome, ancient Persia, ancient China, ancient India, and to all modern literature as well, and cull out of it all that is good, set aside all that is bad or comparatively worthless, and put the results of your labour together into one book, and even then you will not have a book that will take the place of this one book. In other words, man in all his thinking through all the centuries of human history has not been able to produce as much truth as is found in this one Book. As I have already said, if you should destroy every other book in the world and have the Bible left, you would not lose any known truth on moral or spiritual subjects: on the other hand, if you should destroy the Bible and have all other books left, the loss would be irreparable. It is as clear as day then that the Bible stands absolutely in a class by itself, and that while other books are men's books, this Book is God's Book. No really intelligent and candid mind can come to any other conclusion in the light of these indisputable facts. I appeal to you, isn't that so?

II. I Believe the Bible to be the Word of God Because of the History of the Book, Its Omnipotence Against All of Men's Attacks.

My fifth reason for believing the Bible to be the Word of God is, Because of the History of the Book, Its Omnipotence Against All of Men's Attacks. It is as plain as day that what man has produced, man can destroy. Why then, if man produced the Bible, have eighteen centuries of assault upon the Bible been unable to destroy the Bible? Scarcely was the Bible given to the world when men discovered three things about the Bible. They discovered that the Bible condemned sin. They discovered that the Bible demanded renunciation of self. They discovered that the Bible laid human pride in the dust. Men were not willing to give up sin, they were not willing to renounce self, and above all they were not willing to have their pride laid in the dust; therefore, they hated the book that made these demands. Men's hatred of the Bible was most intense, most persistent, most practical, most active, most energetic and most relentless. They determined to destroy the Book they hated. Fronto, the most accomplished rhetorician of his day, the man whom the great Emperor Antoninus Pius chose to be the tutor of his still greater son, Marcus Aurelius Antoninus, brought all the powers of his matchless rhetoric to bear against the Bible, with the intention of discrediting and destroying the Bible, but he failed. Then Celsus tried it with the brilliancy of his genius, and he failed. Then Porphyry, beyond a question the leading neo-Platonic philosopher of his day, tried it, with all the depth of his philosophy; but he failed. Lucian tried it, with the keenness of his satire, but he failed. Then Diocletian came upon the scene of action and brought to bear against the Bible other weapons. He summoned all the military and political forces of the mightiest empire the world ever saw, Rome at the zenith of its glory, to discredit and destroy the Bible, but he failed. He issued edicts that every Bible in the Roman Empire should be destroyed and that failed. Then he issued sterner edicts, that everyone who had a Bible in his possession should be put to death, and that failed. And for eighteen long centuries the assaults upon the Bible have gone on. Every engine of destruction that human reasoning, human science, human philosophy, human wit, human satire, human cunning, human force, and human brutality, could bring to bear against a book has been brought to bear against this Book. With what result? That the Bible has a stronger hold upon the confidence and affections of the wisest and best men and women in the world than it ever had before. There have been times when all the great men of earth were against the Bible and only an obscure and despised remnant for it, and yet the Bible still stands. If the Bible had been man's book it would have gone down and been forgotten centuries ago, but because there was in this Book " the hiding " of not only God's wisdom, but also " of God's power," it has wonderfully fulfilled in other than their original significance those stupendous words of the Lord Jesus Christ, " Heaven and

earth shall pass away, but *my words* shall not pass away."
(Matt. 24:35.)

Of course there have been times when, in the midst of the
smoke of battle and din of conflict, it has seemed to some
weak-hearted men and women as if the Bible must have gone
down; but in every instance, when the smoke has rolled up
from the field of battle, this citadel of God's eternal, impreg-
nable and imperishable truth has been seen to rear its lofty
head toward heaven without one single stone dislodged from
lowest foundation to highest parapet, and each new attack
upon the Bible has simply served to prove anew the absolute
and divine impregnability of this indestructible rock of God's
eternal Word.

I, for one, am glad every time a new attack is made upon
the Bible. That may sound like a strange thing for a minister of the Word to say; but what I mean is this, I tremble,
of course, for certain weak-hearted and weak-headed men and
women who are willing to swallow anything which they are
told with sufficient confidence is " the assured result of the
latest scholarship "—but for the Bible I have no fears. A
book that has successfully withstood eighteen centuries of
assault by the devil's heaviest artillery is not going down before the air-guns (oftentimes hot air at that) of " modern
Biblical criticism." This demonstrated indestructibility of
the Bible is proof positive of its Divine Origin.

III. I Believe the Bible to be the Word of God Be-
        cause of the Influence of the Book, Its Power
        to Lift Men Up to God.

*My sixth reason for Believing the Bible to be the Word of
God is, Because of the Influence of the Book, Its Power to
Lift Men Up to God.* It cannot be denied that there is a
power in the Bible to gladden, and beautify, and ennoble
human lives, a power to lift men up to God, that no other
book possesses. Now it is one of the most fundamental principles of modern science that, no stream can rise higher than
its source; and I submit that, *a book that has a power to lift
men up to God that no other book possesses, must have come
down from God in a way that no other book has.* In literally
millions of cases this Book has demonstrated its power to

reach down to men and women in the deepest depths of iniquity and degradation, and ruin, and lift them up, up, up,
until they were fit for a place beside the Christ upon the
throne.   There comes before me as I speak the face and form
of a man whom I knew intimately and greatly loved.   He
was one of the most brilliant orators that I ever heard upon
the public platform.   He had a law practice of twenty-five
thousand dollars a year.   But he had been brutalized, and
stupefied, and demonized by strong drink and had gone down
until his law practice was all gone, his law office shut up, his
law books pawned, and even his watch pawned, for drink.
When he had gotten down so low, I met him on the street
and I said to him, " John, you ought to accept the Lord Jesus
Christ as your Saviour."   He replied, " I don't believe in your
Christ, and I don't believe in your Bible.   I am an agnostic."
I said, " John, it doesn't make a particle of difference what
you believe; if you will accept the Lord Jesus Christ He will
save you; if you reject Him, you are a ruined man."   He
turned from me and went down the street with a hollow, mocking laugh.   He sank even lower, he got to the very bottom.
He was a wanderer on the streets of New York, sleeping in
a wretched garret.   One day he stood on the curbstone and
saw a procession of brewers and their wives pass by.   As he
saw the evidences of their prosperity, he became very angry
and he said to himself, " Those diamonds that shine upon
those shirt fronts are my diamonds, those costly robes that
adorn the persons of their wives are my wife's robes that went
for drink."   In bitterness of soul he went to the wretched garret where he was staying, and flung himself upon his knees,
and threw to the winds his agnosticism and accepted the Bible,
and the Christ of the Bible; and by the power of this Book
he was transformed into one of the noblest, truest, gentlest,
and humblest men I ever knew, a man so honoured from the
Atlantic to the Pacific that in one of our presidential cam-
paigns he ran for President of the United States on the Prohibition ticket.   Now I submit that a book that has this
power to reach down, down, down into the deepest depths of
sin and take hold of men and women utterly lost, and lift
them up, up, up, until they are fit for a place beside the Christ
on the throne, a book that has a power to lift men up to God

that no other book possesses, must have come down from God in a way no other book has, and I challenge anyone to give a really reasonable answer to the argument. It can't be done.

But there is a power in this Book not merely to lift up individuals, but to lift up communities and nations. Ten years ago what, by almost universal acknowledgment, were the three greatest nations of the earth? England, America, and Germany. To what did these three greatest nations of the earth owe all that was best in their social life, in their commercial life, in their political life, in their moral life, in the individual lives of their citizens? Beyond a peradventure they owed it to the Bible. But one of these nations gave up its faith in the Bible. For the Bible of Luther they substituted the philosophy of Nietzsche, and the evolutionary science of Haeckel, and the destructive criticism of Gräfe and Wellhausen and Kuenen. For the God of the Bible, they substituted, to use the language of some of their own leaders, " the good old German God of War," and today that nation lies prostrate, wrecked and ruined, in the dust. And yet, in face of these well-known facts, many of our leading educators in America today, in our Universities, Colleges, and even in our High Schools and Grammar Schools, and even in our Theological Seminaries, are trying to get us to substitute for the whole Bible, the Word of God, the emasculated Bible of the German criticism that wrecked Germany, and a philosophy of essentially the same character as Germany adopted, and a crass evolutionism of the same Haeckelian type as Germany adopted, and a sociology akin to theirs. Will the American people consent to do it? Not unless we are hopelessly blind to the teachings of history or have gone stark mad. The most dangerous enemy that there is today to the state, to true democracy, to social order, and to wholesome morals, is the man who seeks to undermine in the slightest degree our faith in the whole Bible as the inerrant Word of God. Never forget that.

IV. I BELIEVE THE BIBLE TO BE THE WORD OF GOD BECAUSE
    OF THE CHARACTER OF THOSE WHO ACCEPT IT AS THE
    WORD OF GOD.

In the seventh place, I Believe the Bible to be the Word of God Because of the Character of Those Who Accept It as

*the Word of God, and Because of the Character of Those Who
Reject It as Not Being the Word of God.*   Two things speak
for the Bible and its divine origin.   First, the character of
those who accept it as being the Word of God, and second,
the character of those who reject it as not being the Word of
God.   Sometimes when I meet a man or woman who says
with a quiet confidence, " I believe the Bible to be the Word
of God," and when I look at the purity, and probity, and in-
tegrity, and uprightness, and self-sacrifice, of their life, how
near they are living to God, I feel like saying, " I am glad to
hear you say that you believe the Bible to be the Word of
God.   The fact that a man who lives so near God as you do,
and knows God so well, thinks the Bible to be the Word of
God, is a confirmation of my own faith that it really is."
But when I meet another man of an entirely different type
who says to me with a jaunty toss of his head, " I do not believe the Bible to be the Word of God," and then I look at
the selfishness, and sordidness, and oftentimes the utter sensu-
ality of his life, how far he is living from God, I feel like saying, " Well, sir, I am glad to hear you say that you do not
believe the Bible to be the Word of God.   The fact that a
man who lives so far from God as you do, and knows so little
about God, doubts that the Bible is the Word of God, is a
confirmation of my own faith that it really is the Word of
God."   Now do not misunderstand me.   I do not mean to
say that every man who professes to believe in the Bible is
better than every man who professes not to believe in the
Bible, not for one moment.   But what I do mean to say is
this, show me a man who is living a life of entire surrender
to God, of whole-hearted devotion to the welfare of his fellow-
men, a life of humility and of prayer, and I will show you
every time a man who has an unshaken and unshakable faith
that the Bible is the Word of God.   But on the other hand,
show me a man who denies that the Bible is the Word of God,
or who persistently questions it, and I will show you every
time a man who is living either (mind I do not say all, I am
constantly misquoted at this point.   Men find it very difficult to answer what I really say, therefore put into my mouth
words I never dreamed of saying which are much easier to
answer)—I say I will show you a man who is leading *either*

a life of greed for gold, or a life of lust, or a life of self-will, or a life of spiritual pride, and I challenge you to tell me one single exception. As I have thrown out that challenge around the world, a number of times people have tried to name an exception, but when you have thought of the men that they named as exceptions, as leading a life of absolute surrender to God, a life of whole-hearted devotion to the welfare of their fellow-men, a life of humility, and a life of prayer, it was simply ludicrous. In other words, all of those men and women who live nearest God, and know God best, have absolute confidence in the Bible as the Word of God. Those who have the most doubts about it are those who live farthest from God and know God least. Which are you going to believe? Suppose there were found in the city of Boston a manuscript that purported to be by Oliver Wendell Holmes, but there was a great deal of discussion and question as to whether it were really by Oliver Wendell Holmes or not. Finally it was submitted to a committee of critics to decide, and it was found, that when the committee brought in their report, that all those members of the committee who had lived nearest Oliver Wendell Holmes, and knew Oliver Wendell Holmes best, and were most in sympathy with his thought, said with absolute unanimity, " the manuscript is by Oliver Wendell Holmes "; but that those who had the most doubts about it were those who had lived farthest from Oliver Wendell Holmes, known him least, and were least in sympathy with his thought, which would you believe? That is a very simple problem in literary criticism, far simpler than the problem of resolving a single verse in the Book of Judges, which was confessedly written thousands of years ago, into seven different parts and assigning these minute fragments to the seven different authors who are supposed to have written them, as is attempted in that monumental joke book of the nineteenth century, the so-called " Polychrome Bible." Now this is the exact case with the Bible: all those men and women who live nearest God, and know God best, have an unshaken and unshakable confidence in the Bible as the Word of God: those who have the most doubts about it are those who live farthest from God, and know God least. Which are you going to believe? If you are a reasonable and a candid man, you can give but one answer to that question.

There is another fact of a similar character, a fact that many of us know to be a fact by our own experience or observation; namely, that a man who at one period of his life is a sinner and an infidel, by merely giving up his sin loses his infidelity without a single argument. You and I have seen that illustrated time and time again. Did you ever know a single instance of the opposite character, of a man who was a sinner and a believer in the Bible, who by giving up his sin, lost his faith in the Bible?

Here is still another fact. Men who at one period of their life are living a life of whole-hearted devotion to God and to the welfare of their fellow-men, and have an unshaken faith in the Bible as the Word of God, but who begin, as life advances, to drift away from God into a broader and a more selfish mode of living, perhaps they have become rich and are not able to stand the strain of prosperity, and as they drift away from God they have ever increasing doubts that the Bible is the inerrant Word of God. So true is that, that whenever men and women tell me that they are beginning to be skeptical I feel like asking them, " What have you been doing?"

Some years ago I was walking down a street in a college town. A little ways ahead of me I saw one of the students whom I had known before he came to the college, in fact he was being put through college by a personal friend of mine. I quickened my steps and caught up with him and said, " Charlie, how are you getting on?" With a light toss of his head Charlie replied, " Well, Mr. Torrey, I am getting somewhat skeptical." Then I asked, " Charlie, what have you been doing?" Charlie dropped his head, for Charlie had been sinning.

Some years ago I was lecturing at a school in Massachusetts and gave the students opportunity to come to me personally and ask me questions after the lectures were over. One day a bright young student came to me and said, " I would like to talk with you." I replied, " I will be glad to talk with you. What is your trouble?" " Oh," he said, " I am getting somewhat skeptical." I said, " What makes you skep-

WHY I BELIEVE THE BIBLE

tical?" " Oh," he replied, " I have been studying philosophy."
I looked at him, and looked over him and looked through him,
and read his history, and I said to him, " Tell me, are you
not practicing a certain sin," and I mentioned the sin definitely. He dropped his head and said, " Yes, I am." I said,
" If you will give up the practicing of that sin, I think you
can go on studying philosophy with perfect safety." He said,
" I guess I can." I said, " Will you give it up?" And he
replied, " I will." I was back at that school the next year,
and at the close of one of my lectures that same young man
came to me again. I suppose he thought I had forgotten him,
but I have a better memory than I have a forgettery, and my
former conversation all came before me. He said, " I would
like to talk with you." " Very well," I said, " what would
you like to talk about?" " I am getting somewhat skeptical."
I said, " Why are you getting skeptical?" He said, " I have
been studying philosophy." Then I said, " Don't you remember that you and I had a conversation together when I
was here a year ago?" " Yes." " Don't you remember that
at that time you confessed to me you were practicing a certain sin?" " Yes," he replied. " Do you remember that you
promised me you would give that sin up?" " Yes." " Have
you given it up?" " No." " Well," I said, " if you will give
up that sin, I think you can continue the study of philosophy
with perfect safety." He replied, " I guess I can."

I have had a very large experience with skeptical men of
all ages and of all classes, I have had a great many close con-
versations with them in which, in order to help them, I had
them open to me their hearts, and I have discovered what
others have discovered, that an overwhelming per cent of all
the skepticism and infidelity in the world today comes from
two specific sins which I could name if it were not for the
mixed character of this audience.

Let me ask you a question? Where is the stronghold of
the Bible today? The pure, the happy, the Christ-like, the
heaven-like home. Where is the stronghold of infidelity
today? The race course, the gambling hell, the booze joint,
and the brothel. Now some of you will not like that, but is
it not true? If you stop to think you will know it is true.
Suppose I should come to this city a stranger and go into some

place where they still sell strong drink in spite of our prohibition laws; suppose I should go in there with a Bible under my arm and lay the Bible on the bar, and say to the bartender, " Give me a glass of whiskey straight and make it big." Would there not be great surprise? Would he not look at the book and say, " What book is that? Is not that a Bible?" " Yes." " And what did you ask for?" " A glass of whiskey straight, and make it big." There would be great surprise. But suppose I should go into that same joint with a copy of the " Mistakes of Moses," by Ingersoll, or a copy of the " Truth Seeker," or any other infidel book or magazine, no matter of how high a type, under my arm and should lay it on the bar and order a glass of whiskey straight, and make it big. Would there be any surprise? No. It would be just what they would expect. Whiskey and the Bible do not go well together—whiskey and infidelity go constantly together, they are twin sisters, and Siamese twins at that.

I said this some years ago in a meeting for business and professional men at the noon hour in Belfast, Ireland. At the close of the meeting a bright young doctor came up to me laughing. " Oh," he said, " we had an illustration yesterday of the very thing you have just said. My mother was out at your afternoon Bible reading. As she went out she dropped into a licensed grocer's to get some brandy for a friend who was ill. Without thinking of what she was doing, as she ordered the brandy she was putting her Bible into a little bag she carried, and the grocer's clerk said, ' That is right, madam, you better put it out of sight. The two don't go well together.' "

Yes, the three reasons I gave you last night prove to a demonstration that the Bible is the Word of God, and the four reasons that I have given you tonight prove the same thing. There is no room left for honest doubt that the Bible is God's Word. " Well, what of it?" you ask. Everything of it. If the Bible is the Word of God, and it is, there is a heaven of infinite glory, and a hell of awful shame and agony, and you are going to the one or the other. Whether you go to the one or the other, according to this Book, which is the Word of God, depends entirely upon what you do with Jesus

Christ. If you accept Jesus Christ, you become a child of God and will spend eternity in heaven, for it is written in this Book in John 1:12: " But as many as received Him, to them gave He the right to become children of God, even to them that believe on His name."

But if you reject Jesus Christ, you are going to spend eternity in hell, for it is written in this Book in John 3:36: " He that believeth on the Son hath everlasting life: but he that believeth not the Son shall not see life: but the wrath of God abideth on him."   And it is written again in II Thess. 1:7-9: " The Lord Jesus shall be revealed from heaven with the angels of His power in flaming fire, rendering vengeance to them that know not God, and *to them that obey not the gospel of our Lord Jesus:* who shall suffer punishment, even eternal destruction from the face of the Lord and from the glory of His might."

Which path will you take tonight, the path which we have demonstrated leads to heaven, or the path which, as we have demonstrated, leads to eternal darkness and despair? Will you accept Jesus Christ tonight as your Saviour, surrender to Him as your Lord and Master, and confess Him as such before men, or will you reject Him tonight, or deny Him by neglecting to confess Him? How will you decide? It is a question of stupendous importance, and there is but one answer that has the faintest shadow of reasonableness, " I will accept and confess Jesus Christ tonight."

IV

THREE MORE REASONS WHY I BELIEVE THE
BIBLE TO BE THE WORD OF GOD

L AST night and the night before I gave you seven reasons why I Believe the Bible to be the Word of God.
The first reason I gave you for Believing the Bible
to be the Word of God was, because of the unequivocal and
unmistakable testimony of Jesus Christ to that effect. We
saw that Jesus Christ set the stamp of His endorsement upon
the entire Old Testament and entire New Testament as the
Word of God, and that, therefore, if we accepted the authority
of Jesus Christ we were logically compelled to accept the entire Old Testament and entire New Testament as the Word
of God, that it was either Christ and a whole Bible, or else
it was no Bible and no Christ. We next saw that if we
frankly faced the facts in the case we were compelled to accept the authority of Jesus Christ, because Jesus Christ was
accredited to us by five unmistakably Divine testimonies.
First of all, He was accredited to us by the testimony of the
divine life that He lived, for He lived as never man lived.
Second, He was accredited to us by the testimony of the divine words that He spoke, for He spoke as never man spoke.
Third, He was accredited to us by the testimony of the divine
works that He wrought, for He wrought as never man wrought.
Fourth, He was accredited to us by the testimony of His
divine influence upon all subsequent history. Fifth, He was
accredited to us by the testimony of His resurrection from
the dead, which is the best proven fact of history and is the
Lord God Almighty's stamp of endorsement upon Jesus
Christ's claims. Therefore we were compelled to accept the
authority of Jesus Christ, and consequently were compelled
to accept the entire Old Testament and entire New Testament
as the Word of God.

The second reason that I gave you for believing the Bible to be the Word of God was, because of its fulfilled prophecies. We saw that the Bible has the power of looking centuries into the future and predicting with minuteness and precision and accuracy of time, person, place, and circumstance, events to occur centuries later, and we saw that any book that had this power must have for its author the only being in the universe who knows the end from the beginning, that is God.

The third reason that I gave you for believing the Bible to be the Word of God was, because of the unity of the Book. We saw that the Bible was composed of sixty-six separate portions, or books, thirty-nine in the Old Testament and twenty-seven in the New. We saw that the sixty-six books were written by at least forty different human authors, that the period of their composition extended over at least fifteen hundred years, and that they were written in three different languages, Hebrew, Greek, and Aramaic. We saw that these sixty-six books were written by men upon every plane of social and political life, from the king upon his throne down to the shepherd, the herdman, the fisherman, and the petty politician. We saw that these sixty-six books display every known form of literary structure: that in the Bible we had not only both prose and poetry, but every known form of prose and every known form of poetry. Yet we saw that in spite of the marvelously composite character of this Book, that it was the most intensely one of any book known in literature. And we saw that the only rational way of accounting for this astonishing fact was, that back of the forty or more human authors was the one all-superintending, all-controlling, all-governing, all-moulding mind of God.

The fourth reason that I gave you for believing the Bible to be the Word of God was, because of the immeasurable superiority of its teachings to those of any other book or of all other books together. We saw that there were three points of radical difference between the Bible and all other books: first, that while other books contained truth, it was truth mixed with error, whereas the Bible contained nothing but the truth. Second, that while other books contained fragments of truth, the Bible contained all the truth, that there was not a single known truth on moral or spiritual subjects that could not be found for substance between the covers of the Bible. Third, that the Bible contains more truth than all other books put together. We saw that if all other books in the world were destroyed and the Bible left, we would not lose one known truth on moral or spiritual subjects; but that if the Bible were destroyed and all other books were left the loss would be irreparable. Therefore we saw that the Bible stood absolutely in a class by itself, that while other books were man's books, the Bible was God's book.

The fifth reason that I gave you for believing the Bible to be the Word of God was, because of the history of the Book, its omnipotence against all of man's attacks. We saw that what man had produced man could destroy, but that eighteen centuries of persistent attack upon the Bible had been unable to destroy or discredit the Bible, that it was omnipotent against all man's assaults. That therefore, beyond an honest question, man never produced it, that it was not man's book but God's Book.

The sixth reason that I gave you for believing the Bible to be the Word of God was, because of the influence of the Book, its power to lift men up to God. We saw that there was in the Bible a power to gladden and beautify and ennoble human lives that no other book possesses. We saw that as a stream could rise no higher than its source, any book that had a power to lift men up to God that no other book possessed, must have come down from God in a way that no other book has.

The seventh reason that I gave you for believing the Bible to be the Word of God was, because of the character of those who accepted it as the Word of God, and the character of those who rejected it as not being the Word of God. We saw that with absolute unanimity all those men and women who lived nearest God, and knew God best, believed the Bible to be the Word of God, and that those who had the most doubts about it were those who lived farthest from God and knew God least. That therefore we were compelled to accept the testimony of all the men and women who lived nearest God, and knew God best, that the Bible was the Word of God. At that point we stopped last night.

I. I Believe the Bible to be the Word of God Because of the Inexhaustible Depth of the Book

My eighth reason for Believing the Bible to be the Word of God is, Because of the Inexhaustible Depth of the Book. It is as plain as day that what man has produced man can exhaust. If then men produced the Bible, why is it that eighteen centuries of study have been unable to exhaust the Bible? The Bible is an old, old book. The human race has had it before it for study for more than eighteen centuries, and men have studied the Bible as they never studied any other book. Men of strongest mentality, men of the most penetrating powers of perception, men of the most thorough scholarship, men of the ablest minds the world has ever known, have devoted a lifetime to the study of this Book and not one man who ever really studied the Book ever dreamed of saying that he had gotten to the bottom of it. Indeed, the more one studies the Book and the more deeply he digs into its unfathomable depths, the more clearly does he see that there is still beneath him inexhaustible depths of truth still remaining to be explored. This is not only true of individuals, it is true of whole generations of men. For eighteen centuries generation after generation of men have dug, and dug, and dug into this inexhaustible mine of truth, each generation profiting by the discoveries of the generation that has gone before, but up to the present day all of them together have been unable to exhaust this book. There are still precious nuggets of truth awaiting each new explorer. It is as true today as it was several centuries ago when John Robinson first said it, that " new light is constantly breaking forth from the Word of God." Now how are we going to account for this indisputable fact? Certainly if this book had been produced by forty men, or by any number of men, the whole human race could have exhausted it by this time, but they have not been able to. How will you account for it? It is a fact and it demands accounting for. *There is only one rational way of accounting for this indisputable fact, and that is this, that the only reason why the whole human race with all its many hundreds of years of study have been unable to exhaust this book is because that in it are* hidden the inexhaustible treasures of the wisdom and knowledge of an infinite

God. The argument is unanswerable. No really candid man will even attempt to answer it.

For all the centuries since the Bible was completed man has been growing in wisdom and in knowledge. We have outgrown every other book of the past—we have never outgrown the Bible, we have never grown up to it. The Bible is not only always up to date, the Bible is always ahead of date. Where will you find the best explanation of what is going on today in France, in Germany, in Russia, in Italy, in England, in Turkey, in the Holy Land, and even in America? Beyond a peradventure you find it in this book. If you wish to understand conditions today on the European continent, conditions that are so perplexing and bewildering the wisest statesmen today, the place to go is to this book. A few years before our last appalling war began, a religious paper having perhaps the largest circulation of any religious paper in the world, sent to different leaders of thought in this country and in Europe a questionnaire in which they asked them what they thought would be the outcome of our modern peace movements, of the Hague Convention, of the Geneva Conference, of the Peace Palace, and all the other peace movements. Did they think there would ever be another great war? One of these questionnaires was sent to me. I answered differently from the way in which most of those who were questioned answered, I said that I was in favour of anything that made for peace even temporarily, but as for their never being another great war, I knew my Bible too well not to know that the greatest and most appalling war in human history was ahead of us and not back of us. I was laughed at for saying it, many thought I was becoming a crank, but what did the outcome of events prove? We all now know that I was right. How did I know it? I am not a prophet nor the son of a prophet, but I had studied my Bible and the Bible made it clear as to what the future held. When that war ended it was everywhere proclaimed by our sociologists, and our university professors, and by many of our theologians who consulted their own wishes instead of the Bible to know what the future contains, that this war had been a war to end war and that now very near ahead of us was universal peace, and universal brotherhood, of nations, and a universal triumph of democracy. When some of us who knew our Bibles declared that there would not be peace, that " to the end " of this dispensation there " would be war," that there would be discords and overthrow of nations on every hand, and that there would be no universal peace until the Prince of Peace Himself came, we were called " pessimists " and even harder names. But the war has been over now for more than five years, were we who believed the Bible true prophets, or were we not? Look around about you at every nation of the earth and see. Read your daily papers and see. Read the reviews and magazines and the speeches of world-statesmen and think. How did we know it? Simply because we had studied and believed our Bibles. More than two thousand four hundred years ago the Bible plainly declared in Dan. 9:26, R. V., (as well as elsewhere to the same effect) that, " Even unto the end (of this present dispensation) shall be war; desolations are determined." And the Bible was, as usual, right, and history proves it was right and up to date, and ahead of date. And the Lord Jesus Christ Himself has declared:

"And Jerusalem shall be trodden down of the Gentiles, until the time of the Gentiles be fulfilled. And there shall be signs in sun and moon and stars; and upon the earth *distress of nations, in perplexity* for the roaring of the sea and the billows; *men fainting for fear, and for expectation of the things which are coming on the world:* for the powers of the heavens shall be shaken. *And then* shall they see the Son of man coming in a cloud with power and great glory." Luke 21:24-27 R. V.

And everything in world conditions today is indicating clearly that Jesus Christ was right and the Bible right.

The fact that the Bible after nineteen hundred years and up to this present moment is not only always up to date but always ahead of date, the fact that the best interpretation of the most recent events of our own day is to be found in this old book, is proof positive of its divine origin. If this book were man's book we would have fathomed it and outgrown it centuries ago, but the fact that it has proved itself unfathomable for eighteen centuries is proof positive, yes, demonstrative proof, that in this book are hidden the infinite treasures of the wisdom and knowledge of God. A brilliant Unitarian preacher and writer some years ago preached a sermon on, " The Bible Better Than Inspired," in which he took the usual Unitarian position about the Bible but presented it with unusual ability. He afterwards printed this sermon in pamphlet form and was kind enough to send me a copy of it. In this pamphlet was one of the keenest sentences I have ever read from the standpoint of the denial of the divine origin and sufficiency of the Bible. I have never forgotten it and can quote it to you verbatim. This able Unitarian writer said: " How irreligious to accuse an infinite God with having put His whole wisdom in one so small a Book!" I submit that that is keen. Let me repeat it, " How irreligious to accuse an infinite God with having put His whole wisdom in one so small a Book!" But this brilliant writer did not see how the keen edge of his Damascus blade could be turned against himself: what a testimony it is to the divine origin of the Book that such infinite wisdom can be packed in so small a compass! Who but God could do it? The Bible is not such a large Book. I hold here a copy which I carry in my vest pocket. It contains all the sixty-six books of the Old and New Testaments, and yet in this Book that I can carry in my vest pocket there is packed so much of inexhaustible wisdom that eighteen centuries of study on the part of the world's best thinkers has been unable to exhaust it even up to the present day. It is proof, it is demonstrative proof, that this book never had any one man, nor any forty men, nor four hundred men, nor any number of men, for its authors. It must have come from Him of whom alone it can be said, *" O the depth of the riches* both of the wisdom and knowledge of God! *how unsearchable are His judgments,* and His ways past finding out." (Romans 11:33.) There is no getting around that. I challenge any man on earth to answer that argument.

II. I BELIEVE THE BIBLE TO BE THE WORD OF GOD BECAUSE OF THE FACT THAT AS I GROW IN WISDOM AND IN CHARACTER, AS I GROW IN KNOWLEDGE AND HOLINESS, AS I GROW TOWARD GOD, I GROW TOWARD THE BIBLE.

My ninth reason for *Believing the Bible to be the Word of God is Because of the fact that as I Grow in Wisdom and in*

Character, as I Grow in Knowledge and in Holiness, as I grow toward God, I Grow toward the Bible. In other words, the nearer I get to God the nearer I get to the Bible. When I first began the real study of the Bible I had the same experience with the Bible that every other thoughtful student has in the beginning of his studies. I found in the Bible many things that were not only difficult to understand but difficult to believe. I found things that seemed absolutely incredible. I found some things in the Bible that seemed to flatly contradict other things in the Bible and if the one were true how could the other possibly be true? But as I went on studying my Bible, as I went on growing in wisdom and especially growing in character, I found my difficulties disappearing, ever more and more rapidly disappearing, first by ones, then by twos, then by tens, then by scores, disappearing, disappearing, ever more and more rapidly disappearing. I found that the nearer I got to God the nearer I got to the Bible, the nearer I got to God the nearer I got to the Bible. Now what is the inevitable mathematical conclusion; two lines always converging as they draw toward a given point will meet when they reach that point. The nearer I get to God the nearer I get to the Bible; the nearer I get to God the nearer I get to the Bible; the nearer I get to God the nearer I get to the Bible: when I and God meet, I and the Bible will meet, that is to say, the Bible was written from God's standpoint. There is no escaping this conclusion. This also is proof positive that the Bible has God for its real author.

When I was lecturing in England, some of the advocates of the vague and shadowy theology so highly esteemed in some quarters, objected in the public press to my " Putting theological truth with the exactness of mathematical propositions." But why should I not? I am not to blame for having a mathematical mind, I was born with it. I took all my highest standing in the university on mathematics, and I love clearness and definiteness of statement about God and spiritual things just as I love clearness and definiteness of statement in every other line of research. I like moonshine in nature, but I delight in sunshine in the realm of thought. And it is a noteworthy fact that among the men of science the mathematicians are the most likely to be believers in the Bible. Do you know why that is? Because mathematics is the only exact science and the Bible is the only exact Book.

Suppose I had to pass through a vast and dark and dangerous forest. Many a one in attempting to go through this forest had been lost and perished. As I am about to start on my perilous journey a guide is brought to me who has taken many a party through the forest in safety and has never lost a party. Under the leadership of this thoroughly tried and entirely competent and perfectly reliable guide I start out. We get along nicely together for a while and then we come to a place where two roads diverge. My guide says the road to the left is the one to take, but my reason and common sense passing upon the phenomena observable by my senses see what appear to me to be clear indications that the guide in this case is wrong, and so I say to the guide, " You have often gone through this forest before and I never have. You have led many a party through in safety and never lost a party, and therefore I have great confidence in your judgment; but in this case I am sure you are wrong for my reason and common sense passing upon the phenomena observable by my own senses see clear indications that in this case you are wrong. Now I know that my reason and common sense are not infallible, but they are the best guide I have and I cannot throw them overboard," and down I go to the right about a mile, and then I come up against an impassable barrier of rock and have to go back and go the way the guide said. Again we get on nicely for a while, but then we come to another place where two roads diverge. This time the guide says the road to the right is the road to take, but my reason and common sense, passing upon the phenomena observable to my senses, see what appear to them like clear indications that the path to the left is the path to take. Again I have my little dialogue with the guide. I say to him, " You have often passed through this forest before and I never have. You have led many a party through in safety, and have never lost a party, and therefore I have great confidence in your judgment. But in this case my reason and common sense passing upon the phenomena observable by my senses see clear indications that you are wrong. Now I know that my reason and common sense are not infallible, but they are the best guide I have and I can not throw them overboard," and down I go on the path to the left. I go about half a mile and run into an impassable morass and have to go back and go the way the guide said. Now suppose this should happen about fifty times, and every time the guide proved right and my reason and common sense, passing upon the phenomena observable by my senses, proved wrong. Do you not think that about the fifty-first time I would have reason and common sense enough left to throw my ever-erring reason and common sense overboard and go the way the infallible guide said? Now this is my exact experience with the Bible. I have come to the fork in the road more than fifty times, and, fool that I was, I threw the Bible overboard and went the way that my reason and common sense seemed to indicate, and every time I have had to come back and go the way the infallible guide said. Do you not think that the next time I come to a place where the Bible and my ever erring common sense seem to differ, that I will have reason and common sense enough left to throw my ever erring reason and common sense overboard and go the way the infallible guide says? If I haven't I will be a fool.

The most irrational thing in all the world is what men call "rationalism." What is rationalism? Rationalism plainly defined is the attempt to subject the teachings of infinite wisdom to the criticism of finite foolishness. Could anything by any possibility be more irrational? Suppose that when my son was six years of age I had taken him out on the hill near our summer home at Northfield, out behind the barn, and had pointed him to the sun that seemed to be sinking into the west and had said to him, " Reuben, the astronomers tell us that that sun is over ninety-two million miles away (they used to say ninety-six million when I was a boy)." And then sup‧ pose my boy in the ripe wisdom of six years had looked up into my face and had said, " Father, I do not wish to be discourteous, but I am sure you are wrong this time, the sun is just behind the barn." Do you think I would have looked down into the wise eyes of my little boy in mute admiration and thanked God that I had begotten a Socrates? No, I would have said, " Reuben, run into the house and let your mother put you to bed." But my boy at six years of age knew more in comparison with the wisest scientist or philosopher on earth, than the wisest scientist or philosopher on earth today knows, in comparison with an infinitely wise God. It never seems to occur to the rationalist that an infinitely wise God may possibly know a little more than he does, and may possibly have a perfectly good reason for saying or doing a thing even when he, the rationalist, can see no reason at all. One of the greatest discoveries that I ever made in my life was when one day it dawned upon me that an infinitely wise God might possibly know more than I did, and that God might possibly be right when to me He appeared to be entirely wrong, that God might have a thousand good reasons for acting in a certain way even when I could not see one single reason.

III. I BELIEVE THE BIBLE TO BE THE WORD OF GOD BECAUSE OF THE TESTIMONY OF THE HOLY SPIRIT TO THAT FACT

My tenth reason for Believing the Bible to be the Word of God is Because of the Testimony of the Holy Spirit to that Fact. We began two nights ago with the testimony of the second person of the Trinity to the divine origin and authority of the Bible; we close with the testimony of the third person of the Trinity to the same fact. To any one who puts himself in the right attitude toward God and the truth, the Holy Spirit bears direct testimony that the voice that speaks to him from the Bible is the voice of God. Our Lord Jesus Christ says in John 8:47: "*He that is of God* (literally " out of God," that is, born of God) *heareth the words of God:* for this cause ye hear them not, *because ye are not of God.*" That is to say, that everyone born of God gets a divinely given instinct whereby he knows the voice of God from every other voice, and he knows that the voice that speaks to him from this Book is the voice of God. Again our Lord Jesus says in John 10:27, " My sheep hear my voice." That is to say, that one of Christ's sheep has a divinely given instinct by which he knows the voice of the Good Shepherd from every other voice, and he knows that the voice that speaks to him from this Book is the voice of the Good Shepherd.

You will often meet a godly old lady, of perhaps no very

wide reading or culture, but who still has a firm faith that the Bible is the Word of God. If you ask her why she believes the Bible to be the Word of God she will answer, " I know that it is the Word of God." " Yes, but why do you believe it to be the Word of God?" And again she answers, " I know it is the Word of God." " Yes, yes, but *why* do you believe it to be the Word of God?" And again she replies: " I know it is the Word of God." You smile and say to yourself, " Oh, I'll not disturb the old lady's faith " (never fear, you could not if you wished to), you say, " I will not disturb the old lady's faith, but she is beneath reason." You are mistaken, she is above reason. She is a child of God and she has a divinely given instinct by which she knows the voice of God from every other voice, and she knows that the voice that speaks to her from this Book is the voice of God. She is one of Christ's sheep and she has a divinely given instinct by which she knows the voice of the Good Shepherd from every other voice, and she knows that that voice that speaks to her from this Book is the voice of the Good Shepherd.

I can tell you how anyone of you can come to this same position where you will be able to distinguish God's voice from every other voice, and to know that the voice that speaks to you from the Bible is the voice of God. But let Jesus Christ Himself tell you. He tells us this in John 7:17 (R. V.): " If any man willeth to do His will (that is, God's will), he shall know of the teaching, whether it is of God, or whether I speak from Myself." If any man will surrender his will wholly to God, to be whatever God wishes him to be, to do whatever God wishes him to do, and to go wherever God wishes him to go, he will get a power of spiritual perception by which he can detect the truth of God, and by which he will know that this Book is God's Book. Jesus Christ does not ask any man to believe without evidence; but He does demand, as He ought to demand, that every man put himself in such an attitude toward God, and toward the truth, that he is competent to weigh evidence. And there is nothing else that so clarifies the mind to the perception of truth as the surrender of the will to God. Many people confuse credulity and faith and think that they are the same thing. So far from being the same thing they are the opposite poles from one another. Credulity and unbelief are simply positive and negative forms of the same thing. What is faith? Belief upon sufficient evidence. What is credulity? Belief without evidence. What is unbelief? The refusal to believe in the face of sufficient evidence. So we see that faith and credulity are the opposite poles to one another, but that credulity and unbelief are simply positive and negative forms of the same thing, the refusal to yield the mind to sufficient evidence.

Some years ago I was lecturing to our students in Chicago on how to deal with skeptics, infidels, and agnostics, and atheists, Unitarians, and Spiritualists, and other errorists. Our lecture room was open to everybody who wished to come, irrespective of their religious opinions, and pretty much everyone came. Oftentimes we had not only Orthodox evangelical Christians from pretty much all the different evangelical denominations, but also Roman Catholics and Greek Catholics, and Unitarians, and Christian Scientists, and Theosophists, and Spiritualists, and pretty much everything else. That morning as I looked down over my audience I saw sitting side by side Mrs. A. J. Gordon, the wife of that great man of God, the late Dr. A. J. Gordon of Boston, and one of the most out and out agnostics I had ever met—I had had some conversation with him before. In the course of my lecture I told the students how to deal with skeptics and infidels, and agnostics and atheists, and Unitarians, and guaranteed that if they would get the skeptic or whatever it might be, to take certain steps that he would be brought to see that the Bible is the Word of God, and that Jesus Christ is the Son of God. At the close of my lecture Mrs. Gordon came to me and said, " Did you see that man sitting beside me in the lecture room this morning?" " Yes." " Do you know what he said when you lectured?" " No, of course not." " He said he wished you would try it on him." I said, " I would be glad to." " Well, there he is," she said, " standing down by the book-stand in the corner." I did not have to go to him, for as soon as most of the people had left the lecture room he came to me. He said in a very courteous way: " Mr. Torrey, I do not wish to seem discourteous, but do you know that my experience contradicts everything you have told your students this morning?" I replied, " Do you mean to say that you have done every thing that I told the students that if they could get a skeptic to do I would guarantee that he would come to see that the Bible was the Word of God, and Jesus Christ was the Son of God?" He said, " I have done those very things." Then I said, " Let us be definite about this." That is where you always catch the skeptic and the agnostic, when you get down to something definite. If you let him hop around here and there at will he is like a flea, but if you put your finger on him and hold him down you've got him. So I said, " Let us be definite." We left the lecture room and went into my outer office and I called out my secretary and dictated to her the following words: " I believe that there is an absolute difference between right and wrong " (I did not say I believe there is a God, for this man was an agnostic, neither affirming or denying the existence of God, and you have to begin where a man is), " I believe that there is an absolute difference between right and wrong, and I hereby take my stand upon the right to follow it wherever it carries me. I promise to make an honest search to find if Jesus Christ is the Son of God, and if I find that He is, I promise to accept Him as my Saviour, and confess Him as such before the world."

My secretary brought out to us two slips upon which this pledge was written. I handed them to him. He read them carefully and I said: " Are you willing to sign that?" He said: " Perfectly willing," and signed them both. He handed one to me, I folded it and put it in my pocket. He folded the other and put it in his pocket. He said, " But there is nothing in it, my case is very peculiar." And his case was peculiar. He was a graduate of a British University and he had been through Unitarianism, Christian Science, Theosophy, Spiritualism, and pretty much every other ism of the day. Furthermore, he had recently gone through a lawsuit involving seven million dollars and had lost the suit. " My case," he said, " is very peculiar." I said: " Never mind that, do what you promised to do." He said: " I will." " Now," I said, " do you know there is no God?" " No," he replied, " I do not know that there is no God. Any man is a fool to say that he knows that there is no God. I am an agnostic; I neither affirm nor deny the existence of God." I said, " I

know there is a God but that will not do you any good." Then
I said: " Do you know that God does not answer prayer?"
He said, " No, I do not know that God does not answer prayer.
I do not believe that He does, but I do not know that He does
not." " Well," I said, " I know He does but that will not do
you any good, but here is a possible clue to knowledge. You
admit there may be a God, you admit that it may be that He
may answer prayer. Now you know the method of modern
science. The method of modern science is this, that when
you find a possible clue to knowledge, you follow that clue out
to find out what there may be in it. You do not have to know
that there is anything in it; you follow it out to find out what
there may be in it." " Yes," he said, " that is true." " Well,"
I said, " are you willing to adopt the method of modern science
in religious investigation? Here is a possible clue to knowledge—it may be that there is a God, it may be that He answers prayer. Will you follow out the possible clue? Will
you pray this prayer? ' Oh, God, if there be any God, show
me if Jesus Christ is Thy Son or not, and if Thou showest
me that He is Thy Son, I promise to accept Him as my
Saviour, and confess Him as such before the world.' " " Yes,"
he said, " I will do that, too; but there is nothing in it, my
case is very peculiar." " Now," I said, " just one more thing,
John says in John 20:31: ' These are written (that is, the
things in the gospel of John) that ye may believe that Jesus
is the Christ, the Son of God; and that believing ye may have
life in His name.' Now John here tells us that he presents
to us in his gospel the evidence that Jesus is the Christ, the
Son of God. Will you take the evidence and read it? I do
not ask you to believe it, I do not want you to even try to
believe it; but will you take it and read it with a candid mind,
and with a willingness to receive whatever in it may prove
true?" " Oh," he said, " I have read it time and time again,
I can quote it to you," and he began to quote passages from
the gospel of John. I said: " Hold on, I want you to read it
a new way. Begin at the first chapter and the first verse
and read continuously until you get through the Book, not
all in one day, but from day to day until you finish the Book.
Do not read too many verses at any one time. Pay careful

attention to what you read, and each time before you read offer this prayer:

" 'Oh, God, if there be any God, show me what of truth there is in the verses I am about to read, and what you show me to be true, I promise to accept and take my stand upon.' "

He said, " Yes, I will do that, too; but there is nothing in it. My case is very peculiar." " All right," I said, " do what you have promised." He replied, " Oh, I will." Then I went over the things he had promised to do and we parted. About two weeks later I was lecturing in a hall on the south side in Chicago and I saw my agnostic friend in the audience. He came up to me at the close of the lecture and said: " There was something in that." " Oh," I said, " I knew that before." He said, " Ever since I have done what I promised you I would do, it seems just as if I had been caught up by the Niagara River and was being carried along, and the first thing I know I will be a shouting Methodist." I became a Methodist for the occasion and said, " Praise the Lord!" I went East to lecture at some schools in Massachusetts. I came back to Chicago and there was a reception. This man was present at the reception and he came to me and said, " Are you busy?" " Not too busy to talk with you." We went aside into another room where we would be alone and he said to me: " I cannot understand how I ever listened to those men," and he mentioned a number of erratic teachers to whom he had listened. I remember the names of two of them, Colonel Robert Ingersoll, the brilliant agnostic, and Dr. Robert Collyer, the gifted Unitarian preacher—" I do not see how I ever listened to those men. It is all foolishness to me now." " Oh," I said, " the Bible explains that in I Cor. 2:14: ' The natural man receiveth not the things of the Spirit of God: for *they are foolishness unto him:* neither can he know them, because *they are spiritually judged.'* You have put yourself in the right attitude toward the truth and God has given you to see it." He came out into a clear faith that the Bible was the Word of God, and that Jesus Christ was the Son of God, and continued in that faith, and today he is up yonder in the glory. Do you doubt that story? Well, try it yourself and then you will have one of your own to tell.

Let me tell you before I close another incident. It was

in my first pastorate.   Living almost directly across the road
from me was an elderly man who was an agnostic, and though
he was an agnostic and I was a reasonably orthodox preacher,
we were intimate friends.   I went over to see him almost every
day, for I always felt that a minister of the gospel should associate with all classes and conditions of men.   I have no sympathy whatever with this common way of dividing human society into three classes, men, women, and preachers.   I believe
a preacher should be a man among men.   I do not regard a
preacher, as so many seem to, as a delicate article of vertu
that needs to be put under a glass cover lest he should be
defiled by contact with ordinary mortals.   I believe that all
preachers should mingle in the closest possible intimacy with
all classes and kinds of men.   I read in my Bible that my
Master, the Lord Jesus, was " a friend of publicans and sinners," and I am certainly not better than my Master.   I read
again that the Lord Jesus said in Matt. 5:13: " *Ye are the
salt of the earth,*" and I cannot see for the life of me how
the salt can preserve the meat, if you put the salt in one barrel
and the meat in another.   So I have always striven to come
into the closest contact with all kinds of men, the most ar-
rant unbelievers as well as the most devout believers.   And
so, though this man was an utter agnostic, while he never
darkened the doors of a church, and I was an Orthodox
preacher, he and I were intimate friends.   One evening I went
over to his house a little after sunset, and we were standing
on his front lawn and there was a wonderful glow following
the sunset that fell upon the earth with a strange and solemn
light, and I think he felt the effect of it.   Suddenly he turned
to me and said: " Mr. Torrey, I am sixty-six years of age,
I cannot live many more years, and I have nobody to leave
my money to (he had quite a lot of it) and I would give every
penny of it if I could believe as you do."   " Oh," I replied,
" that is easy, I can tell you how."   " I wish you would," he
said.   " Let us go into the house," I replied.   We went into
the house and I asked his wife for a sheet of paper and on
this paper I wrote substantially these words: " I believe there
is an absolute difference between right and wrong."   Mark
you, I did not say I believe there is a God, for this man was
an agnostic, neither affirming nor denying the existence of

God, and as I said before, you always have to begin where a
person is. " I believe there is an absolute difference between
right and wrong, and I hereby take my stand upon the right
to follow it wherever it may carry me.   I promise to make an
honest search to find if Jesus Christ is the Son of God, and
if I find that He is, I promise to accept Him as my Saviour,
and confess Him as such before the world."   I handed it over
to him and said: " Will you sign that?"   He read it carefully
and then said: " Why, anybody ought to be willing to sign
that.   There is nothing here but what my own conscience tells
me I ought to do."   " Certainly," I said, " Will *you* sign it?"
" Why," he replied, " anybody ought to be willing to sign
that."   " Will *you* sign it?"   " Anybody ought to be willing
to sign that."   " Will You sign it?"   " I will think about
it," he replied.   He never signed it.   He died as he had lived,
without God, without Christ, and without hope.   He told the
truth about one thing, he did not take a penny of his money
with him.   He went out into the darkness of a Christless and
hopeless and awful eternity.   But whose fault was it?   A way
was shown him out of darkness into light, a way which his
own conscience told him he ought to take, but he would not
take it..   The same way has been shown to each one of you
tonight, a way that your own conscience tells you you ought
to take, a way out of the darkness, and the wretchedness, and
the moral paralysis, and the utter dissatisfaction, and the ultimate hopeless despair of unbelief, into the light, and joy, and
power, and glory, of an intelligent faith in the Bible and in
the Christ of the Bible.   Will you take that way?   If you
do not, you will have no excuse.   It will be wanton unbelief,
the determined refusal to yield to conclusive evidence.   If
you will take the right way, the way that in your heart of
hearts you know you ought to take, ahead of you lies joy and
victory and complete satisfaction in the life that now is, and
eternal glory hereafter.   If you refuse to take that way, ahead
of you is unrest, and moral weakness, and failure, and sin, and
degradation, and restlessness, and utter despair, and the eternal blackness and midnight gloom of existence in a hopeless
eternity separated from God and Jesus Christ.

V

THE FIRST QUESTION THAT GOD EVER
ASKED OF MAN

MY subject tonight is, The First Question that God Ever Asked of Man. You will find that question in Gen. 3:9, "And Jehovah God called unto Adam and said unto him, 'Where art thou?'" Please note four things about this question, first, Who asked it? Second, Of whom He asked it? Third, The circumstances under which He asked it. Fourth, What He asked.

First, Who asked it? Our text tells us that it was "Jehovah God" Who asked the question. The eternal God asked it. God asked this question of the first man, and He has been asking questions of man ever since. God's questions are very searching and very startling. For example, you will find one of God's questions in Mark 8:36, "For what shall it profit a man, if he shall gain the whole world and lose his own soul?" You will find another of God's questions in I Pet. 4:18, "And if the righteous scarcely be saved, where shall the ungodly and the sinner appear?" You will find still another of God's questions in Heb. 2:2, 3, "For if the word spoken by angels proved stedfast, and every transgression and disobedience received a just recompense of reward; how shall we escape, if we neglect so great a salvation?" and you will find still another of God's questions in the tenth chapter of this same Book, the epistle to the Hebrews, verses 28 and 29, "He that despised Moses' law died without mercy under two or three witnesses: of how much sorer punishment suppose ye, shall he be thought worthy, who hath trodden under foot the Son of God, and hath counted the blood of the covenant wherewith he was sanctified an unholy thing, and hath done despite unto the Spirit of grace?" But the question of the text is the first question, so far as the record goes, that God ever asked of man. We shall find, before we get through tonight,

84

that it is one of the most searching, and most thought provoking, and most soul-awakening questions that God ever asked.

But of whom did God ask the question? Of Adam. Adam, the first member and the head of our race, was not a glorified ape, as H. G. Wells would have us believe in his history of the world, which he has woven from the disordered pipe dreams of his own befuddled fancy, and not constructed from the actual facts that are recorded in many ways, and easily ascertainable by any one who wishes to know them. No, Adam, the first man, was an intelligent being, possessed of all the intellectual and moral faculties that we possess, and that too of a high order; and all the discoverable facts of the primitive history of all races coincide with the view of primitive man presented in the Bible, and run directly counter to the fancies of the theory-blinded evolutionist. Actually ascertained facts count for nothing with the determined evolutionist, he lives entirely in the world of theory and the unscientific use of the imagination. Among the most illogical, credulous and really *unscientific* thinkers the world has ever seen are the rank and file of our modern so-called " scientists." They build a stupendous superstructure of dogmatic assertion upon the smallest possible foundation of scientifically ascertained fact.

But that does not much matter for our purpose tonight. Of far more practical importance is the question of the circumstances under which God asked this question of our original parent. The context clearly states the circumstances, Adam had sinned. For the first time in the history of the human race sin had entered. In the cool of the day of that first day of human sin the voice of God was heard rolling in its majesty down through the avenues of the Garden of Eden. Adam had often heard the voice of God before. Hitherto that voice had been to him the sweetest music; for in the days of his innocence Adam knew no greater joy than that of communion with his Creator and his Heavenly Father. But now all was changed, for sin had entered. And as the voice of God was heard resounding through the Garden Adam was filled with terror and tried to hide himself from God.

And now note what the question was that Jehovah God asked of Adam, " *Where art thou?* " That was the very ques-

tion that Adam most dreaded to answer. He was trying to
hide from God and now God for Adam's own good will make
him come out into the light and face Him. Every sinner
from that day to this has attempted to do just what Adam
tried to do, to hide from God. Every man and woman here
tonight at some time in your life, has attempted to hide from
God. Just as soon as sin enters our hearts and our lives we
seek earnestly to hide from God. Every impenitent sinner is
trying to hide from the presence and from the all-seeing eye
of God tonight.

The sinner's attempt to hide from God lies at the root of
all the atheism and agnosticism of today, whether it be crude
atheism and agnosticism or philosophical atheism and agnosticism. If we can only make ourselves think that there is
no God, or can even make ourselves think we cannot know
whether there is a God or not, it is a comfort to us in our
sin; and the consciousness or subconsciousness of sin in our
lives awakens a strong desire to make us doubt the existence
of God.

The sinner's attempt to hide from God lies at the root of
all the infidelity and skepticism of the day. Men will give
many reasons why they are skeptics, many reasons why they
are infidels or unbelievers of one kind or another; but in the
vast majority of cases the real reason is (though men may not
be conscious of it themselves) that men hope by the denial
that the Bible is the inerrant Word of God to hide themselves
from the discomfort of God's acknowledged and realized
presence. No book brings God so near and makes God so
real as the Bible. The God of the Bible is a very real God,
a very present God, very different from the shadowy, vague
and meaningless God of much of our modern philosophy, and
New Thought, and the New Theology, and the God of not a
little of the teaching of our universities and theological seminaries today.

The sinner's attempt to hide from God also accounts for
much of the neglect of the Bible. People will tell you they
do not read their Bibles because they have so much else to
read, and life is so crowded and busy; or they will tell you
they do not read their Bibles because they are not interested
in the Bible, and it is a dull and stupid Book to them; but

the real cause of man's neglect of the Bible is this, the Bible brings God nearer to us than any other book does, and men, as they know they are sinners, are uneasy in the conscious presence of God, so they neglect the Book that brings God near.

It is also the sinner's attempt to hide from God that accounts for much of the absence from the house of God and its services of most of the people of the present day. People will give you many reasons why they do not attend Church. They will tell you they cannot dress well enough to attend Church, or they are too busy and too tired to attend Church, or that they need one day in the week to get out in the fresh air, or they will tell you the services of God's house are dull and uninteresting; but in the great majority of cases the reason why men and women habitually absent themselves from the services of God's house is because the house of God brings God near, and makes men think of God, and makes men uncomfortable in sin, and their desire to hide from God, more or less distinct and definite, and conscious, leads them to stay away from the house of God.

The sinner's attempt to hide from God lies at the root of most of the Unitarianism and the so-called " Liberalism " of the day. If Jesus Christ was a Divine Person, actually God manifested in the flesh, that brings God very near; but, if we can only make ourselves think that Jesus Christ was a divine person only in the sense we are all divine, that makes God very unreal and shadowy, and moves God very far away; and so men, in their desire to have God as far away as possible, where He does not make them uneasy by His conscious presence, adopt Unitarian and " Liberal " views of Christ.

There are many who fancy, and are really conscientious in their fancy, that their difficulties are intellectual when in reality they are moral. A brilliant lawyer in New York City came to a friend of mine and said to him, " You surely do not believe in the resurrection of the Body of Jesus from the dead?" My friend said to him, " I certainly do, and if you will let me put the evidence of His resurrection in shape for you, and then carefully study it, you will believe in it too." The lawyer consented. My friend handed him the evidence

collated and wisely arranged. The lawyer studied it, and
came back to my friend, and my friend said to him, "What
do you think?" The lawyer replied, "I am convinced that
Jesus Christ was raised from the dead as recorded in the four
gospels." "Thank God," my friend exclaimed. "Don't be
too much in a hurry," the lawyer replied, "I am no nearer
being a Christian than I was before. I thought my difficulties were intellectual, I find that they are moral." So, at the
root, are the difficulties of most men and women with the
teachings regarding God and His Son, Jesus Christ, which are
found in the Bible, their difficulties are not intellectual, they
are moral.

But Adam did not succeed in hiding from God. God called
him out of his hiding place, and he had to meet God face to
face, and not one of us will succeed in hiding from God. God,
sooner or later, will call each one of us out from our hiding
place, whatever it may be, just as He called Adam, and each
one of us will be forced to come out of our hiding place just
as Adam was, and meet God face to face, and let His all-seeing
eyes search us through and through, and lay everything bare,
every act, every thought, every fancy, every secret act as well
as open act, every word and every secret desire.

God is putting to each one of us here tonight the same question that He put to Adam in those pristine days of human
history, "Where art thou?" Let each of us put it to ourselves ruthlessly and unsparingly, "Where art thou?" Just
where are you at? Just where do you stand morally and
spiritually? What is your exact spiritual latitude and longitude? Where do you stand as regards right and wrong?
Where do you stand as regards sin and holiness? Where do
you stand as regards God and Jesus Christ? Are you wholly
theirs or are you really against the Lord and His Christ?
Where do you stand as regards heaven and hell? For which
place are you bound? I put the question to each one of you
tonight, "Where art thou?" No! God puts it to each one
of you as an individual, "Where art thou?" Lose sight of
me, and see God standing here with His eyes of fire upon you,
looking you through and through, and saying in tones that
penetrate the innermost recesses of the soul, "Where art
thou?" Now, every truly intelligent, and, in the highest

sense, sane person here tonight will be glad to face that question. The answer may not be pleasing or gladdening, but you will wish to know. You will desire to know the actual facts, however unpleasant they may be.

In the business world at the opening of each year every careful and competent business man takes a careful inventory of his stock, casts up his debits and his credits and endeavours to find out just how much his assets exceed his liabilities. He wishes to know just where he stands. He may discover as a result of his careful investigations that he does not stand as well as he thought he did. He may find he is seriously in debt when he hoped that his capital exceeded his liabilities. But if that is true, he wishes to know it in order that he may conduct his business accordingly. Many a man has made shipwreck of his business through his unwillingness to face facts and find out just where he stands.

Many years ago I knew a very brilliant business man, a man rarely gifted along certain lines of business enterprise, but his affairs got into a tangled condition. His wisest business friends came to him and advised him to go through his books and find out just where he stood, and promised him help if he needed it. But the man was too proud to take their advice. He was too proud to admit his business was in a bad way; so he refused to look into it. He shut his teeth, clenched his fists, and set his face like a flint, and tried to plunge through. But instead of plunging through, he plunged into such utter financial ruin that, although he was, as I have said, an exceptionally brilliant business man in some directions, he made such a complete financial shipwreck that he never got on his feet again, and when he died he did not have enough money to pay his funeral expenses, and I had to pay them out of my own pocket, simply because he was not willing to humble his pride and face facts. It is just so with some of you men here tonight. You are too proud to face the fact that you are morally and spiritually bankrupt; so you are going to shut your teeth, clench your fists, set your face like a flint, and endeavour to plunge through, but in very fact you will plunge into utter and eternal ruin—you will plunge into an eternal hell.

Every really wise man wishes to know just where he stands

physically. He desires to know the exact condition of his
lungs, of his heart, of his stomach, of his nerves and of the
various vital parts of his body. So he goes to a competent
medical authority for a thorough physical examination. He
oftentimes finds he is worse off than he thought he was. He
sometimes finds that though he thought his heart was thoroughly sound it is really defective; but if that is the case, he
wishes to know it, because if he knows his heart is weak, he
will not subject himself to the strain he otherwise would.
Many and many a man lies today in a premature grave, who
might be doing good work on earth, simply because he was
not willing to find out his real condition, and subjected his
heart to a strain it would not bear, and thus brought his life
to a sudden and untimely end.

Every sailor that sails the sea wishes to know just where
his vessel is, its exact latitude and exact longitude. At the
noon hour each day a careful observation is taken upon the
sun.

I remember once in crossing the Atlantic Ocean we had
been sailing for days beneath clouds and through fogs. We
had been unable to take an observation by the sun, and had
been sailing by dead reckoning for several days. One night
I happened to be on deck, and suddenly there was a rift in
the clouds just where the North Star appeared through the
rift. Word was sent below to the commanding officer. The
captain of the vessel hurried on deck, and I remember how
he fairly lay across the compass, and how carefully he took
an observation by the North Star, that we might know exactly
where we were. But we are all sailing tonight across a perilous sea, toward an eternal port, and every truly intelligent
man and woman in this audience will desire to know just
where they are, their exact spiritual longitude and their exact
spiritual latitude.

I. How to Consider the Question

Now how should we consider this question?

1. In the first place, *We should consider the question seriously*. This is not a question to trifle with. Only a fool will
trifle with a question like this. It is a singular fact that men

and women who are intelligent and sensible about everything else, men and women who would not think of trifling with the great financial questions of the day, or the great social problems of the day, when they come to this greatest of all questions, the question of eternity, will treat it as a joke.

One night in Chicago a little bootblack was blacking my shoes and I put to this bootblack as he worked over my shoes the question, " My boy, are you saved?" and the little fellow treated it as a joke. I was not at all surprised. That is just what one would expect of a poor, illiterate, uneducated boot-black on the street; but men and women, it is not what you would expect of thinking men and thinking women, that when you come to these great eternal problems of God, eternity, salvation, heaven and hell, that they should be treated as a joke. But, alas! they are treated as a joke by some men and women of culture. I once read an address by a college president, one of the best known thinkers in America, who, in an address to the teachers of Philadelphia, treated the question of heaven and hell as a joke. Never, from that day to this have I been able to have the respect for that man that I had before; and after a brilliant career, that man and his reputation, and his influence have come to an untimely and tragic end. Any man or woman who trifles with a question like this, plays the part of a fool. I do not care what your social position may be, what your reputation for scholarship may be, how successful in business you may be, I do not hesitate to affirm tonight that, unless you have faced, or will face tonight, this great question of your spiritual condition and eternal prospect with the profoundest earnestness and seriousness, you are playing the part of a fool.

2. In the second place, *We should consider this question honestly*. There are many people in our day who are trying to deceive themselves, trying to deceive others, and trying to deceive God. Many men who in their innermost hearts know they are all wrong, are trying to persuade themselves that they are all right, and trying to persuade others that they are all right, and trying to persuade God that they are all right.

Men and women, you cannot deceive God, " God is not mocked: for whatsoever a man soweth, that shall he also reap." It will do you no good to deceive anyone else. And

it is the most consummate folly to deceive yourself. One of
our great American financial men once said, "The biggest fool
on earth is the man who fools himself." Let me add that
the most consummate fool of all is the man who fools himself
about his spiritual condition. Be honest. Be thoroughly
honest. If you are lost, own up to it. If you are on the road
to perdition, acknowledge it. If you are not a Christian, say
so. If you are an enemy of God, confess the fact. If you
are a child of the Devil, admit it. Be thoroughly honest,
honest with yourself, honest with your fellow-men, honest
with God. Face the facts.

3. In the third place, *We should consider the question
thoroughly*. There are many people who are honest enough,
and serious enough as far as they go, but they do not go to
the bottom of things. They are superficial. They give this
tremendous question a few moments' thought and then their
weak minds weary, and they say, " Oh, I guess I am all right.
I will take my chances." Listen, you cannot afford to guess
or take any chances on a question like this. In matters like
this we must not rest satisfied with probability. We must
have absolute certainty. It will not satisfy me to hope I am
saved. I must know I am saved. It will not satisfy me to
hope that I am a child of God. I must know that I am a
child of God. It will not satisfy me to hope I am bound for
heaven. I must know that I am bound for heaven. Take
this question up thoroughly and do not lay it down until you
have gone to the bottom of it, and know with an absolute certainty exactly where you stand.

4. In the fourth place, *We should consider this question
prayerfully*. God tells us in His Word, and we know in our
own experience that it is true that, " The heart is deceitful
above all things." (Jer. 17:9.) There is nothing in which
the deceitfulness of the human heart comes out so clearly
as in our estimates regarding our own moral and spiritual condition. Everyone of us by nature is exceedingly sharp-sighted
to the faults of others, and exceedingly blind to our own. But
while we are blind to our own real condition, God searches
our heart and knows it. He knows our hearts and our lives
just as they are, and is willing to show us to ourselves as He
sees us. What we need is to face this question in prayer.

You will never know where you stand until God shows you. We need to pray at least the substance of David's prayer, " Search me, O God, and know my heart: try me, and know my thoughts: and see if there be any wicked way in me," and when God pours the light of His Holy Spirit into our hearts and shows us ourselves as He sees us, then we shall know ourselves as we really are, and not till then.   The great Scotch poet, Burns, never said a wiser thing than when he wrote:

> " O wad some power the giftie gie us,
>   To see oursel's as ithers see us!
> It wad frae monie a blunder free us,
>   And foolish notion."

But there is something far better than to see ourselves as others see us, and that is, to see ourselves as God sees us. Oh! let us not leave this auditorium tonight until we see ourselves in the light of God's presence, see ourselves just as God sees us.   And we can only see ourselves as He sees us, in definite and earnest prayer to God to show us ourselves as we really are.

One morning in the city of Minneapolis I met the pastor of the church of which I had formerly been pastor.   He had a very depressed look and I said, " Brother Norris, what is the matter?"   He replied, " Brother Torrey, I have had an awful experience this morning.   You know Mrs. ————?" mentioning a member of the church of which he was now pastor and of which I had formerly been pastor.   He continued, " You know she is dying.   She sent for me this morning to come and see her.   I hurried to her home.   The moment I entered the room she cried, ' Brother Norris, I have been a professing Christian for forty years.   I am now dying and have just found out in my dying hour I have never been saved at all.' "   Oh, the horror of it, to be a professing Christian for forty years and never find out until just as your life is ending, that you have never really been a Christian at all. Better find it out even then than in eternity, when it is forever too late to set matters straight; but better far, find it out in the dawn of your professed Christian life, better find it out tonight.

I have little doubt that in this great crowd here tonight there is many a man and woman who has been a professing Christian for years, who has never been saved.

5. In the fifth place, *We should consider the question Scripturally.* God has given to us just one safe chart and compass to guide us on our voyage through time to the port of eternity. That chart and compass is the Bible. If you steer your course according to this Book, you steer safely. If you steer your course by anything else than this Book you steer to certain shipwreck. If you steer your course according to your feelings, according to the speculations of some petty philosopher or theologian, according to the dreams of poets or the brilliant but sophistical reasoning of some gifted infidel, if you steer by anything else in the world but by the sure declarations of the Only Book of God, the Bible, you will steer your vessel onto the rocks, and you will go down into eternal gloom and darkness. Any hope of salvation and of eternal life that is not founded on the clear, unmistakable teaching of God's Word, is absolutely worthless. Any hope that is founded on the Bible is a sure hope. Any hope that is not founded on the Bible is absolutely worthless.

In one of my pastorates a young married couple had entrusted to them by the Heavenly Father for a brief period, a sweet little child. Then God in His infinite wisdom, and a wisdom in this case which was not altogether inscrutable, and in His tenderness and love, took from these parents that little child, to be with Himself. Their hearts were deeply moved, and in the hour of their sorrow I went to call upon them, taking advantage of their tenderness of heart, and pointed them to that Saviour with whom their child was now safely at home. They both professed to accept Jesus Christ. But after a little while had passed and the first keenness of their sorrow had gone, they began to drift back again into the world. I called upon them to speak with them. Only the wife was at home. I began by talking about the little child and how safe and happy that little one was in the arms of Jesus. To all this she gladly assented. Then I turned the conversation and said to her, " Do you expect to see your child again?" " Oh," she said, " certainly; I have not a doubt that I will see my child again." I said, " Why do you expect to see your child again?"

She said, " Because the child is with Jesus, and I expect when I die I shall go to be with Him too." I said, " Do you think you are saved?" " Oh, yes," she said, " I think I am saved." I said, " Why do you think you are saved?" " Because I feel so," she replied. I said, " Do you think you have eternal life?" " Oh, yes," she said, " I think I have eternal life." I said, " Why do you think you have eternal life?" " Because," she said, " I feel so." I said, " Is that your only ground of hope?" She said, " That is all." I said, " Then your hope is not worth that," snapping my fingers. That seemed cruel, but in reality it was kind. I said, " Your hope is not worth anything. Can you put your finger upon anything in the sure Word of God that proves you have everlasting life?" " No," she answered, " I cannot." " Then," I said, " your hope is absolutely worthless." Then she turned on me, which she had a perfect right to do. It is quite right to talk back to preachers. I think it would be well if people did it more—and she began to talk back, and said, " Do you expect to go to heaven when you die?" I said, " Yes, I know I shall." She said, " When you die do you expect to be with Christ?" " Yes," I said, " I know I shall." She said, " Do you think you have everlasting life?" " Yes," I said, " I know I have." Then she put to me my own question, " Can you put your finger on any definite passage in the Word of God that proves you have eternal life?" I replied, " Yes, thank God, I can, John 3:36, ' He that believeth on the Son *hath everlasting life.*' Now," I said, " I know I believe on Jesus Christ, the Son of God, and on the sure ground of God's Word which I find right here, I know I have everlasting life."

I put the question to each one of you tonight. Can you put your finger on any definite passage in the sure Word of God that proves you are saved, that proves your sins are all forgiven, that proves you are a child of God, that proves you have everlasting life? If you cannot, I advise you to stay to the after meeting and find out whether you are saved or not, even though you be a church member. And if you find that you are not saved, as very likely you will, take the step whereby you will be saved tonight. And even if you are saved, find out something definite and explicit in God's Word that proves that you are saved.

6.   In the sixth place, *We should consider this question immediately*. This is a question of too great importance to admit of delay.   There are many tonight who intend to face this question sometime and think it through, but not now. They must attend to business or pleasure or something else first.   That, too, is consummate folly.   The wise man puts first things first, and eternal matters are certainly the matters of first importance.   God says, " Seek ye *first* the kingdom of God and His righteousness."   This question is of too vast importance to put it off for a single day; for not one of us knows " what a day may bring forth."   Suppose some day when you were out on the Atlantic Ocean you were walking the deck a little after the noon hour on a bright, sunny day. The captain of the vessel comes along and walks with you, and you say, " Captain, where are we?   What is our exact latitude and longitude?" and the captain replies, " I don't know."   You take out your watch and say, " Why, captain, it is after noon.   Did you not take an observation on the sun today at the noon hour?"   " No."   " Well, when do you expect to take an observation?"   " Oh, I don't know, perhaps tomorrow."   Any captain who would make such a reply would lose his commission at the first port of entry.   By tomorrow the boat might be on the rocks, and by tomorrow you may be in hell.

No, no, a question like this admits of no delay.   Find out tonight where you are, and if you are not saved, get saved tonight.

II.   Suggestions to Consider

Before I close, let me give you a few suggestions as to the alternatives that you must face.

1.   First of all, *Are you saved*, or *Are you lost?*   You are certainly one or the other.   Unless you have been definitely saved by a definite acceptance of a definite Saviour, Jesus Christ our Lord, you are definitely lost.   There are just two classes of persons in this world, saved sinners and unsaved sinners, and if you are not a definitely saved sinner, you are a definitely lost sinner.   Are you saved, or are you lost?

2.   In the second place, *Are you on the road to heaven* or

Are you on the road to hell? You are certainly on one or the other. Our Lord Jesus Christ tells us distinctly in the Sermon on the Mount, in Matt. 7:13, 14, that there are just two roads, " the broad road " that " leads to destruction," and " the narrow road " that " leads to life." On which road are you tonight? It is true there are two sides to the broad road that leads to destruction. There is the vile, disgusting, immoral, vicious side of " the broad road," and there is the cultured, refined, moral, attractive side of " the broad road," but these are not two roads, they are only the two sides to the one road, and they both lead to exactly the same destination, Hell. I do not ask you which side of the broad road you are on, the cultured side, the refined side, the attractive side, or the vile, disgusting, vicious, immoral side. That matters comparatively little. I ask you whether you are on that road at all or not. Are you in the narrow way that leads to heaven, or are you in the broad way that leads to hell? Are you on the road that leads up to God, and heaven, and glory, or are you on the road that leads to Satan, and sin, and shame, and everlasting doom?

An English sailor came one night into a mission in New York City. As he passed out of the mission not very much moved by the services, a worker at the door put a little card into his hand. On this card these words were printed, " If I should die tonight I would go to ———." The place was left blank, and underneath was written, " Please fill out and sign your name." The sailor, without even reading the card, put it in his pocket and went to the steamer, went to his bunk and put the card in the edge of his bunk. On the way to Hull, England, he was thrown from the rigging and broke his leg. They took him down and laid him in his bunk, and as he lay there, day after day that card stared him in the face, " If I should die tonight I would go to ———." " Please fill out and sign your name." And one day as he looked at the card, he said, " If I filled that card out honestly, I would have to say, If I should die tonight I would go to hell," but he said, " I am not going to fill the card out that way." And lying there in his bunk he took Jesus Christ, and filled out the card, " If I should die tonight I would go to heaven." He came back from England to New York, went to the mission and handed in the card with his name signed to it, " If I should die tonight I would go to heaven." Suppose you had such a card as that to fill out tonight, " If I should die tonight I would go to ————." What would it be? Heaven or hell? Face the question frankly, and answer it honestly.

3. In the third place, *Are you a child of God,* or *Are you a child of the devil?* You are certainly one or the other. We live in a day in which many superficial thinkers and many popular preachers are telling us that " all men are the children of God." But that is not the teaching of God's Word, and it is not the teaching of Jesus Christ. Jesus Christ says distinctly in John 8:44, in speaking to certain men, " *Ye are of your father—the devil.*" And we are told in I John 3:10, " In this the children of God are manifest, and *the children of the devil.*" And again, we are told distinctly in John 1:12, " But as many as received Him, to them gave He the right to *become children of God,* even to them that believe on His name." So we see that men are not " children of God " until they " become " so by receiving Jesus Christ.

A child of God, or a child of the Devil. Everyone of us here tonight is either one or the other. Which are you?

I was speaking one night in Balarat, Australia, and there sat a long line of educated Chinamen listening to the sermon. I was speaking on the same text as tonight. I came to the point I have come to now, and I said to myself, " I guess I will leave that out. That will not do anybody any good and it may offend somebody unnecessarily." But somehow or other God would not let me leave it out; so I put it in. The next night when I gave out the invitation, among others who came forward were almost that entire line of educated Chinamen. I asked one of them if he would tell the people why he had taken the step and accepted Christ. He arose and said, " I was here last night and heard Dr. Torrey say everyone of us was either a child of God or a child of the Devil. I knew I was not a child of God and therefore I knew I must be a child of the Devil. I made up my mind I would not be a child of the Devil any longer, and therefore I have come forward tonight to take Jesus Christ." I hope some of you educated Americans, and uneducated ones too, will have as much sense tonight as that educated Chinaman had.

4. In the fourth place, If you are a professing Christian, what kind of a Christian are you? *Are you a mere formal Christian or are you a real Christian?* You know there are two kinds. There are two kinds in this building tonight. Are you one of those men or women who call themselves Christians, who go to the house of God on the Lord's Day, go to communion now and then, perhaps teach a Bible Class, or a Sunday School Class on the Lord's Day, but the rest of the week you are running after the theatre, and card party, and dance, and all the frivolities and foolishness of the world; one of the sort of Christians who are trying to hold on to Jesus Christ with one hand, and the world with the other? And it is the right hand you are holding on to the world with, and the left hand that you are holding on to Jesus Christ with. Or, are you a real Christian, one who has renounced the world with your whole heart, given yourself to Jesus Christ with your whole heart, a Christian who can sing, and mean it when you sing it, " I surrender all," a real regenerate child of God? Where art thou? What kind of a Christian are you?

5. Once more, *Are you for Jesus Christ* or *Are you against Him?* You know you are either one or the other, for Jesus Christ Himself says so. He says in Matt. 12:30, " He that is not with Me is against Me."

Every person in this building tonight is either " with Christ " (whole-heartedly, confessedly, openly, out and out for Jesus Christ) or else you are " against " Jesus Christ. Which are you? Are you for Christ or are you against Him. It is a question of tremendous significance, and we all ought to face it honestly. It is folly to seek to dodge it.

In my first pastorate, year after year, for a series of years, there came a gracious outpouring of God's Spirit. In the second or third of these outpourings of His Spirit, a great many of the leading business men of the place were converted. One of the leading business men would not take a stand. He was one of the most exemplary men in the community, most amiable, attractive, upright, a devoted husband and kind father, a constant attendant at church, a member of my Bible Class, and a member of my choir; but he was one of those men who wanted to please both sides. He was identified with friends in business, in the Masonic Lodge, and elsewhere, who were not Christians, and he was afraid he would estrange them if he came out and out, whole-heartedly for Christ. The weeks passed by, and while many of his friends took a stand, he would not. One Sunday morning he was in my Bible Class as usual, and when the session of the school closed he was passing out of my class across the choir platform. He had to pass close to the superintendent of the Sunday School who was an intimate friend, they had been in the Civil War together. As he passed by, this intimate friend turned to him and said, "George?" "Well, what is it, Porter?" he replied, calling the other man by his first name. Then this man said, "George, when are you going to take a stand?" He said, "Ring that bell." Instantly the superintendent stepped up to the bell and rang it, and the congregation going out of the building turned around in surprise, wondering what was going to happen. George stepped to the front of the platform (it was a community where everybody knew everybody else by their first name) and he said, "Friends, I have heard it said time and again during these meetings, 'A man must either be for Jesus Christ, or against Him,' I want you all to know that from this time on, Em (his wife) and I are for Christ." He decided for the whole family without consulting them. And in fact he did decide for the whole family; for a little while later when they stood before the pulpit to receive the right hand of fellowship in the church, he stood there, and his wife stood there, and his father-in-law, his brother-in-law and his sister-in-law, every member of the family who was not already in the church, excepting his little daughter, who, he thought, was too young to come, and she came later. Oh, men and women, follow his footsteps tonight. Decide for Christ tonight. Say right now, "As for me and my house, we will accept Jesus Christ." There are many of you here tonight whose sympathies for years have been with the church of Jesus Christ, but you have never been man enough or woman enough to take an open stand. Now, say, "As for me and my house, we are for Christ."

Where art thou? Put this question to yourself. Where art thou? Where do you stand tonight? Do not try to evade the question, or to obscure it, or to drive it out of your mind. If you do, you are playing the fool's part. You've got to face it sometime, whether you will or not. Better face it tonight while there is time to repent and change your course, if you are traveling the wrong way.

Some of us here tonight honestly do not know where we stand. You do not know whether you are saved or whether you are lost. You do not know whether you are on the road to heaven or on the road to hell. You do not know if you died tonight, whether you would go to heaven or to hell. You do not know whether you are a child of God, or a child of the Devil. You do not know whether you are merely a professing Christian, or a real Christian. You do not know whether you are for Christ, or against Him. I beseech of you, find out before you leave this building tonight.

But many of us do know. We know that we are saved. While we know that we have sinned, sinned grievously, we know our sins are all forgiven, all blotted out, and that we are justified from all things through the atoning death of Jesus Christ. We know that God has put to our account His Own perfect righteousness in Christ Jesus. We know that we are on the road to heaven. We know that if we died tonight, we would go straight to heaven. We know that we are children of God. We know we have eternal life. We know that we are real Christians. While we make no foolish pretense that we are perfect, we know that with our whole heart we belong to Jesus Christ. We know we have been born again and are new creatures in Christ Jesus, that " Old things have passed away," and that " All things have become new." We know that we are for Jesus Christ with our whole heart's affection and with all our strength.

Then, alas, some of us know we are lost. You are under no illusions. You know you are on the road to hell. You know if you died tonight you would go to hell and stay there for all eternity. You know that you are a child of the Devil. You know that though you may be a professing Christian that you are not a real Christian. You know that you are against Jesus Christ, against the One Who loved you and gave Himself for you, against the One Who, though He was rich, yet for your sake, became poor, that you, through His poverty, might become rich. You know you are against the One Who was wounded for your transgressions, and bruised for your iniquities, and upon whom the chastisement of your peace was laid. Oh, men and women, change, and come over the line tonight. Change before you leave this building. Change right now. Turn your back on sin right now. Turn a deaf ear to all the damning lies of infidelity and " the New Theology " right now. Accept Jesus Christ right now. Let the Holy Spirit make you a new creature in Christ Jesus right now.

There is one consideration, that makes this question, Where art thou? of immense importance and consequence, that is, the fact that where you are tonight may determine where you will spend eternity. For many of you beyond a doubt, where you are tonight will determine where you will spend eternity. The road you are on when you leave this building tonight will be the road you will still be on forever, throughout the endless aeons of eternity, heavenwards or hellwards forever and ever.

A story is told of the elder Dr. Forbes Winslow of London, the eminent pathologist in diseases of the mind. A young French nobleman came to London, bringing letters of introduction from leading Frenchmen, among others one from Napoleon III, who was at that time Emperor of France. These letters introduced him to Dr. Forbes Winslow, and solicited Dr. Forbes Winslow's best offices for the young man. He called on Dr. Forbes Winslow and presented his letters, and Dr. Forbes Winslow said, " What is your trouble?" He replied, " Dr. Winslow, I cannot sleep. I have not had a good night's sleep for two years, and unless something is done for me I shall go insane." Dr. Winslow said, " Why can't you sleep?" " Well," said the young man, " I cannot tell you." Dr. Forbes Winslow said, " Have you lost any money?" " No," he said. " Have you lost friends?" " No, I have not lost any friends recently." " Have you suffered in honour or reputation?" " No, not that I know of." " Well," said the doctor, " Why can't you sleep?" The young man said, " I would rather not tell you." " Then," the doctor said, " if you cannot tell me, I cannot help you." " Well," he said, " if I must tell you, I will. I am an infidel. My father was an infidel before me, and yet in spite of the fact that I am an infidel and that my father was an infidel before me, every night when I lie down to sleep I am confronted with the question, 'Eternity, and where shall I spend it?' All night the question rings in my ears, 'Eternity, and where shall I spend it?' If I succeed in getting off to slumber my dreams are worse than my waking hours, and I start from my sleep again in terror." Dr. Winslow said, " I can't do anything for you." " What!" said the young Frenchman, " have I come all the way over here from Paris for you to treat me and you dash my hopes to the ground? Do you mean to tell me my case is hopeless?" Dr. Forbes Winslow said, " I can do nothing for you, but I can tell you of a Physician Who can," and he walked across his office, took up his Bible from the centre table, opened it at Isa. 53:5, 6, and began to read, " He was wounded for our transgressions, He was bruised for our iniquities: the chastisement of our peace was upon Him; and with His stripes we are healed. All we like sheep have gone astray; we have turned every one to his own way; and the LORD hath laid on Him the iniquity of us all." Then looking at the Frenchman, he said, " That is the Only Physician in the world who can help you." There was a curl of scorn on the Frenchman's lips. " Dr. Winslow," he said, " do you mean to tell me that you, an eminent scientist, the most eminent pathologist in diseases of the mind of the day, that *you* believe in that worn-out superstition of the Bible and Christianity?" " Yes," said Dr. Winslow, " I believe in the Bible; I believe in Jesus Christ; and believing in the Bible and believing in Jesus Christ has saved me from becoming what you are." The young fellow stopped and thought, then he said, " Dr. Winslow, if I am honest I ought at least to be willing to consider it, ought I not?" " Yes, certainly." " Well," he said, " will you be my teacher?" And the eminent physician became a physician of the soul, and sat down with his open Bible, and for several consecutive days showed the young Frenchman the way of life. At last the light dawned upon him. He saw Jesus Christ as the Divine Saviour, Who had borne his sins in His Own body on the cross. He put his trust in Him, and went back to Paris with a mind at rest, and able to sleep at night, for he had solved the great question of, Eternity and where he would spend it. He knew he would spend it with Christ in the Glory.

Ah, that is the question of questions, " Eternity, and Where Shall I Spend it?"

Men and women, where will you spend eternity? Thank God I know where I shall spend eternity. I will spend it with Christ in the Glory. You take Him tonight as your personal Saviour, surrender to Him as your Lord and Master, begin to confess Him as such before the world, and strive from this time on to live to please Him in everything each day, and you, too, will know where you will spend eternity. You will spend eternity with Jesus Christ in the Glory. Will you then take Him tonight?

VI

WEIGHED IN THE BALANCES OF GOD

" Tekel; thou art weighed in the balances, and art found wanting."—DANIEL 5:27.

ANYONE who loves the drama should read the Bible. The Bible is the most dramatic book that was ever written. There is nothing to compare with it in Æschylus, or in Sophocles, or in Euripides among the ancients, or in Shakespeare among the moderns, or in any of the most skillful writers of modern scenarios, in striking situation, in graphic delineation and in startling denouement. One of the most dramatic scenes in the Bible is Belshazzar's feast, pictured in the fifth chapter of the book of Daniel. The destructive critics for many years ridiculed the story of Belshazzar, saying that such a person as Belshazzar was unknown in Babylonian history; but, as in so many instances, further investigation proved that the Bible was right and the critics wrong. These criticisms arose from the pitiable ignorance and not from the superior knowledge of the critics. Belshazzar's name (spelled Belsharruzur) was found in one of the tablets of Nabonidus his father, dug up by Sir William Rawlinson at Mugheir.

Belshazzar was not the supreme king of Babylon; Nabonidus his father was the supreme king of Babylon; but he had associated Belshazzar with himself upon the throne. An indication of his secondary position is found in this very chapter (thus illustrating the minute historical accuracy of the Bible account), when Belshazzar offered to make Daniel the *third* ruler in the kingdom, that is, next to himself. But Nabonidus and his armies had been shut out of Babylon by the forces of Cyrus. And now Belshazzar is in supreme command within the city walls. Puffed up by the pride of his newly gotten power, he determines upon a great banquet for the leading lords and ladies of the realm. The far-famed palace of Babylon is ablaze with light. The great banqueting

hall is spread for upwards of a thousand guests. The long
tables are brilliant and dazzling and bewildering with cups
and tankards and plates and salvers of silver and of gold that
reflect back the light that falls upon them from countless
candelabra. The air is heavy with the fragrance of spices,
perfumes, and incense, and tremulous with the music of the
dulcimer, the harp and the sackbut. In and out between the
tables the hired dancers weave through the contortions and
distortions of the oriental dance. Back and forth across the
table fly jest and repartee. As the night advances the revelry
increases. In the midst of the mad merriment a strange and
daring and blasphemous conceit enters the mind of the royal
entertainer, as the fumes of the wine mount to his brain. He
calls to him the chief steward and whispers in his ear some
secret command, and the chief steward, followed by a host
of retainers, disappears from the banqueting hall. The guests
are all agog with curiosity to know what this mysterious man-
date may be. Their curiosity is soon gratified, for the chief
steward and his followers soon return, bearing in their arms
the golden and silver vessels which had been dedicated by
Solomon to the worship of God in the temple at Jerusalem, but
which Nebuchadnezzar had carried away when he sacked the
city, and which Belshazzar now desecrates to adorn a heathen
debauch. The king commanded that the golden goblets be
filled with Babylonian wine and passed down the long banqueting tables. As the guests drink from God's goblets the
fumes of the wine pervade their brains and the revelry becomes wilder and wilder. Faster and faster fly jest and
repartee across the table, louder and louder thrum the instruments, swifter and swifter fly the feet of the hired dancers,
until all is a scene of wildest and most shameless revelry.

But suddenly a silence as of death falls upon the banqueting hall; for Belshazzar, lifting his eyes from the table is
startled to see writing on the plaster of the wall " over against
the candlestick," the armless fingers of a man's hand, inscribing
mystic characters in letters of fire. The king's countenance
changes from boisterous revelry to abject fear, his thoughts
trouble him; and in the graphic language of the Bible, " The
joints of his loins were loosed, and his knees smote one against
another." With difficulty the king pulls himself together and

cries hoarsely, " Bring in hither the enchanters, the Chaldeans, and soothsayers. Whosoever shall read yonder writing, and show me the interpretation thereof, shall be clothed with royal purple, and have a chain of gold cast about his neck in token of his authority, and shall be proclaimed next to myself, the third ruler in the kingdom." Into the banqueting hall stalk the wise men of the East, magnificently appareled, with heads erect, with stately carriage, high expectation of large emoluments to be received for the practise of their secret hearts illuminating every countenance. The king turns towards them and pointing to the writing on the wall shouts, " Whoever of you shall read yonder writing and make known to me the interpretation thereof, shall be clothed with royal purple and have a chain of gold about his neck in token of his authority and shall be proclaimed next to myself, the third ruler in the kingdom." For but a moment the magicians study the writing on the wall and then expectation gives way to fear, and utterly abashed and dismayed they depart from the banqueting hall. Again, terror seizes and freezes the soul of Belshazzar. Again the king's countenance is changed, again his thoughts deeply trouble him, again " the joints of his loins are unloosed and his knees smite one against the other " in utter terror.

The queen-mother, wife of Nabonidus, daughter of Nebuchadnezzar, mother of Belshazzar, hearing of the discomfiture of her royal son, comes into the banqueting hall and seeks to reassure him. " O king," she calls, " live forever; let not thy thoughts trouble thee, nor let thy countenance be changed. There is a man in thy kingdom in whom is the spirit of the holy gods; and in the days of thy father, light and understanding and wisdom, like the wisdom of the gods, were found in him; and the king Nebuchadnezzar thy father, the king, I say, thy father, made him master of the magicians, enchanters, Chaldeans, and soothsayers; forasmuch as an excellent spirit and knowledge, and understanding, interpreting of dreams, and showing of dark sentences, and dissolving of doubts, were found in the same Daniel. Now let Daniel be called, and he will show the interpretation." Daniel is summoned before the king. Into the royal presence comes the holy prophet of God. The king cries to Daniel, " Art thou that

Daniel, who art of the children of the captivity of Judah, whom
the king my father brought out of Judah? I have heard of thee
that the spirit of the gods is in thee, and that light and understanding, and excellent wisdom are found in thee . . . If thou
canst read the writing, and make known to me the interpretation thereof, thou shalt be clothed with purple, and have a
chain of gold about thy neck, and shalt be the third ruler in
the kingdom." With noble pride Daniel disdains the prof-
fered gifts. "O king," he says, "let thy gifts be to thyself,
and give thy rewards to another; nevertheless I will read the
writing unto the king, and make known to him the interpretation thereof." But before doing so Daniel proceeded to
sternly rebuke the blasphemous pride of the king. He calls
to his mind how God had humbled the pride of Nebuchadnezzar, his grandfather, how he had deposed him from his
kingly throne and taken his glory from him, and driven him
from among the sons of men to wander with the wild asses,
to feed on grass like oxen until he learned "that the Most
High God ruleth in the kingdom of man, and that He setteth
up over it whosoever He will." Then, turning to Belshazzar, he
witheringly exclaims, "And thou His son, O Belshazzar, hast
not humbled thy heart, though thou knowest all this, but hast
lifted up thyself against the Lord of Heaven; and they have
brought the vessels of His house before thee, and thou and
thy lords, thy wives and thy concubines have drunk wine from
them; and thou hast praised the gods of silver and gold, of
brass, iron, wood, and stone, which see not, nor hear nor
know; and the God in whose hand thy breath is, and whose
are all thy ways, hast thou not glorified. Then was the part
of the hand sent from before him, and this is the writing that
was inscribed: MENE, MENE, TEKEL UPHARSIN. This is the
interpretation of the thing: MENE; God hath numbered thy
kingdom, and brought it to an end. TEKEL; thou art weighed
in the balances, and art found wanting. PERES; thy kingdom
is divided, and given to the Medes and Persians."

Then commanded Belshazzar, that the royal garment of
purple be brought and placed upon Daniel, that a chain of
gold be thrown about his neck, and that proclamation be made
concerning him, that he should be the third ruler in the kingdom. Strangely enough, and yet true to human nature, the

wild revelry goes on; they try to drown their fears in deeper potations of the maddening wine. Faster and faster fly jest and repartee across the table, louder and louder thrum the instruments, swifter and swifter fly the feet of the dancers, until all is one wild orgy and tumult.

But, hark! What is that sound upon the streets of Babylon? Tramp, tramp, tramp, of heavy feet approaching the palace. What does it mean? The forces of Cyrus have turned the Euphrates from its ordinary bed, and are marching through the dry channel, and " through the two-leaved gates," into the city and upon the palace. Tramp! tramp! tramp! louder and louder grows the sound of the soldiers' feet. There is a terrific pounding at the palace gates, the warders flee, there is a thunderous crash and the soldiers swarm through, and now at the very doors of the palace the tumult increases. Up the stairway is heard the tramp, tramp, tramp of heavily armed men. Belshazzar and his guests look up in terror, some fly to the doors and try to hold them shut, but it is too late. With a mighty crash the soldiers of Media and Persia throng the room. Swords flash in air, Belshazzar looks up, a glittering sword falls and Belshazzar is a corpse; for, " in that night was Belshazzar the king of the Chaldeans slain." I call your attention to just one word of the mystic four upon the wall, " TEKEL," " Thou art weighed in the balances and art found wanting."

In whose balances was it that Belshazzar was weighed? IN THE BALANCES OF GOD. Not in the balances of his own estimation of himself, Belshazzar would never have been found wanting there. Not in the balances of human philosophy, Belshazzar would not have been found wanting there. Not in the balances of public opinion in Babylon, Belshazzar would never have been found wanting there. Public opinion in Babylon with universal acclaim would have proclaimed Belshazzar, " The Coming Man." No! IN THE BALANCES OF GOD. And God is weighing each one of us here tonight in those same balances. How much do you suppose that you weigh in the balances of God? I do not ask you how much you weigh in the balances of your own opinion of yourself. That is of no moment whatever, for the man who thinks best of himself, is the man of whom God thinks worst. I do not ask you how much you weigh in the balance of public opinion. That is of no moment, for our Lord Jesus Himself has declared that " that which is highly esteemed among men is an abomination in the sight of God " (Luke 16:15). No, I ask you how much do you suppose you weigh in the balance of God. Ha! if most of us knew how little we weighed in the balance of God we would be filled with deepest shame and utter horror tonight.

But can we tell how much we weigh in the balances of God? Yes, we can tell exactly how much we weigh in the balances of God, for God Himself has given us in His own book, the Bible, the weights by which He weighs us, one and all, and I am going to take some of these weights by which God weighs us, and weigh you with them tonight.

I.   THE TEN COMMANDMENTS

Let us turn first to the Ten Commandments, the foundation weights of the law of God, the weights whose validity is acknowledged in every land, " the Ten Words " God Himself wrote on the tables of stone; or as we ordinarily term them, the Ten Commandments. We shall not have time to consider them all, but enough to make us all realize how little we weigh in God's balances.

1.   Let us look first of all at the first commandment, Ex. 20:3: " Thou shalt have no other gods before me." How much do you weigh, weighed by this first one of the Ten Commandments?   Many of you will say, " I am all right weighed by that law, whatever other commandment I may have broken, I have never broken that one, I am no idolater, and I have no other god beside the God of the Bible."   Are you perfectly sure about that?   What is a man's god?   A man's god is the thing that a man thinks the most of.   If a man thinks more of money than of anything else, then money is his god.   If a man thinks more of pleasure than of anything else, then pleasure is his god.   If a man thinks more of honour and power than anything else, then honour and power are his gods. How many a man today makes a god of his money, for money he sacrifices his health, his conscience, his honour, his manhood.   How many of you men here tonight, this very week that is just past have done things in your business for which

your conscience condemned you, because there was money in them.   Money is your god, you have broken the first of God's commandments.   Many a man in this audience tonight has just as truly worshipped the Almighty Dollar as if he had a dollar hung up in his bedroom, and knelt down nightly and said his prayers to it.   Many of you here tonight are rejecting and trampling underfoot the Lord Jesus Christ Himself, the Son of God who died on Calvary's cross for you because it would cost you money to accept and confess Him.   Beyond a peradventure money is your god.

Then with some of you alcoholic stimulants are your god. For strong drink you sacrifice your physical strength, your manhood, your business ability, the affection of your wife, and the respect of your children.   Ah! this awful monster-god, Alcohol, has thousands of worshippers in Los Angeles.

With others of you pleasure is your god, for one pleasure or another of this world you sacrifice your time, your opportunities for mental improvement, your highest influence in society and the church and the favour of God.   Pleasure is your god.   Venus, the goddess of pleasure, has many a worshipper in Los Angeles today as truly as in Rome of old.

With many of you *social position* is your god.   Major Whittle was once in the city of Washington and went to call upon a friend with whom in by-gone days he had been intimately associated in Christian work, and who was now high in the Government of the United States.   This old friend welcomed the Major very cordially, and entertained him at his home.   One day he was showing Major Whittle about his beautiful Washington home.   As they went from room to room they entered a room, very large and beautifully decorated.   Major Whittle looked around and then said, " What is this room for?"   The friend looked down and tried to avoid answering the question.   But Major Whittle was not a man easily put off, and he repeated his question, " What is this room for?"   " Well, Major," the man replied, " if you must know, this is a ballroom."   The Major turned his eyes on his old-time associate in Christian work, and said with deep feeling, " Do you mean to tell me that you have fallen so low in the moral scale that you have a ballroom in your home?"   The man dropped his eyes and said,

" Major Whittle, I never thought I would come to this, but
here we are in Washington society and my wife and daughter
say that this is what is necessary to maintain our social position, and I have yielded." Social position was his god. Right
dearly did he pay for it before he got through and right dearly
did that wife and daughter pay for it before they got through.
But let us apply the law to ourselves. How much do you
weigh by this law of God? Is there anything that you put
before God, is there anything that you love more than you
love God? Ah! many of us will have to confess tonight, that
weighed by this very first of the Ten Commandments, *we are
found wanting*.

2. We must omit for lack of time the second commandment, though it is well worth our study and there are many
who are breaking it today. Let me read you the third commandment, " Thou shalt not take the name of the Lord thy
God in vain; for the LORD will not hold him guiltless that
taketh His name in vain." How much do you weigh by that
law of God? There are many who think lightly of this law,
they will say to you, " But I am not a very bad man, I don't
steal, I don't commit adultery, I have never killed anybody.
Oh, I do swear occasionally," as if that were not a matter of
any great consequence, God does not so regard it. God has
laid especial emphasis upon this law. Listen again: " Thou
shalt not take the name of the Lord thy God in vain; for *the
Lord will not hold him guiltless that taketh His name in vain.*"
There is no sin that more clearly shows that the very foundations of upright character are honeycombed, than this sin of
profanity. What is the only solid foundation for upright
character? Reverence for God. When a man's reverence
for God is gone, then the very foundations of character are
gone. Under sufficient temptation the profane swearer will
commit any sin or crime. When a man swears profanely,
reverence for God is manifestly gone, and you can't trust him
anywhere. I would not trust a profane swearer in any place,
he will commit any sin or crime under sufficient temptation.
A profane swearer will steal. I would not trust him with my
pocketbook. Indeed, he is already stealing, he is robbing
God of the reverence which is His due, and a man who will
rob God will rob his fellow man. A man must necessarily

sink very low in the moral scale, before he can swear profanely. A few moments thought will prove that. Is it not necessary that a man sink very low in the moral scale, before he will speak disrespectfully of his own mother? How many men you and I have known, who have sunken very low in their character and conduct, but they had not gone so low that they would speak disrespectfully of their own mother, or permit anyone else to do so. But the man who speaks disrespectfully of God has sunken far below the level of a man who applies the most opprobrious epithets to his own mother. There is not a more contemptible sinner on earth than the profane swearer, nor a more utter fool. When I was in the city of Nashville, I was walking down the principal business street one morning and a man drove by behind a racehorse. He saw me on the sidewalk and drove up to the gutter and hailed me. He said, " Are you not Dr. Torrey?" " Yes." " Well, I want to say that you have stopped my profane tongue." Another man met me in Nashville in a hotel and said, " I have been coming to Nashville for many years, going into the hotels and in and out of the stores. Every former time that I visited Nashville I heard profanity on every hand, but on this trip since your visit I have not heard a profane word." A saloon keeper was reported to have said, " Everybody is going crazy over these Torrey meetings. They are all going to the Reimer Auditorium. Even my own wife has gone crazy. To tell the truth I have gone somewhat crazy myself, Dr. Torrey has at least stopped my profane tongue." I would that I might stop forever every profane tongue in this audience tonight. How much do you weigh, weighed by this law of God?

3. Let me simply read the fourth and fifth commandments though they much need dwelling upon in this day in which you and I live: " Remember the Sabbath day, to keep it holy. Six days shalt thou labour, and do all thy work; but the seventh day is a sabbath unto Jehovah thy God; in it thou shalt not do any work, thou, nor thy son, nor thy daughter, thy man-servant, nor thy maid-servant, nor thy cattle, nor thy stranger that is within thy gates: for in six days Jehovah made heaven and earth, the sea, and all that in them is, and rested the seventh day: wherefore Jehovah blessed the sab-

bath day, and hallowed it. Honour thy father and thy
mother, that thy days may be long in the land which the Lord
thy God giveth thee."

Now let me read you the sixth commandment: " Thou shalt
not kill." How much do you weigh, weighed by that law of
God? Many of you, doubtless, will say I am all right weighed
by that law, whatever else I have done I certainly have not
murdered anyone." Are you sure? " Certainly," you say,
" I am sure. Do you think you have any murderers in this
audience tonight?" Indeed, I do. Remember that there are
other ways of killing people besides killing them the way they
did Earle Remington, a week ago Thursday night, by piercing
his heart with a stiletto, and shooting him through the heart.
There are other ways of killing people besides administering
poison to them or beating them to death with a hammer.
Many a husband kills his wife by slow torture, by his neglect,
by his unkindness, and by his unfaithfulness to her. Ah!
how many a woman there is in Los Angeles tonight with a
broken heart, dying by inches. Her husband is faithless. He
thinks she does not know it; but a woman always knows,
though she may not even whisper it, not even to him. We go
out into our cemeteries and see the white tombstones at the
head of the graves of some women who have died too young,
and we read all sorts of legends on them as to how they died,
but if the truth were told, in many instances it would read,
" Killed by an unkind (or faithless) husband."

I met one day in the city of Minneapolis in the store of a
mutual friend, a very brilliant lawyer, who was going down
rapidly through drink. He was a little intoxicated this morning, as I spoke to him. I said, " John, you ought to take
Jesus Christ as your Saviour." He replied, " Torrey, I don't
like you, you are too narrow, I am a new theology man," and
then he mentioned some leading New Theology men with
whom he agreed. " I believe in the larger hope," he continued, " I do not believe that any man is going to an everlasting Hell." Then turning to me, he said, " Torrey, tell
me honestly what you think would become of me if I should
drop down dead right here now." I looked him straight in
the eye, and said, " John, you would go straight to Hell, and
you would deserve to." He flared up and said, " What have

I done?" I said, " I will tell you what you have done, you've got your wife's heart right under your heel, and you are grinding the very life out of it," and he could not deny it. And then, I said, " John, you are doing something worse than that, you are trampling under foot the glorious Son of God who died on Calvary's cross for you." And he couldn't deny that either.

A son can kill a mother by his wild and reckless and wayward life. I was once stopping in a beautiful home in the East, there was everything that money could buy, and one would naturally have thought that the woman who was at the head of that home, would have been radiantly happy. But I discovered that at night when all the household was asleep she would rise and walk the halls in agony, she could not sleep, her heart was breaking. She had a wayward boy in New York City, hiding from justice, she knew not where he was. Some months afterward I stood by the grave into which that mother had been lowered, and that son stood beside me, and they said she died of paralysis, but I said in my heart, she was murdered and this son that stands by my side was the murderer. I told this in Melbourne, Australia, in the Town Hall, twenty-one years ago, and no sooner had the words fallen from my lips than a man sprang to his feet in the back part of the hall, and came rushing down the aisle with his hands flung in the air, shrieking, " I have killed my mother! I have killed my mother!" I pointed to a side room and asked Father Kent, a Godly Anglican clergyman, to go in there with him. After the meeting was over I went in. He was still on his knees. " Oh!" he sobbed, " I have killed my mother, and that is not all, I have blasphemed the name of Jesus Christ from the infidel platform in this city. Is there any hope for me?" I told him that there was, and he found salvation that noon in Jesus Christ.

Then there is another form of murder too shocking to describe, and yet, alas! so common in Los Angeles. Heartless mothers, more cruel than a female man-eating tiger, killing their own unborn children to escape the responsibilities and the glories of woman's highest calling, motherhood. And men who call themselves doctors aiding and abetting in this infamous work. Such a doctor may put M. D. after his name (medical doctor), but he ought to write it D. M. (damnable murderer). I said this in a certain city, and a doctor's wife was very indignant, but by her anger she did not disprove the truth of what I had said, but simply exposed a culprit. How much do you weigh, weighed by this solemn law of God? Have you ever killed anybody?

4. Listen now to the seventh commandment: "Thou shalt not commit adultery." This is a law upon which one can not wisely dwell in a mixed audience like this, and yet how sorely it needs to be dwelt upon here in our city, yes, and in our whole land and in every other land in this awful day of rapidly growing impurity in which we are now living. How much do you weigh, weighed by that law of God?

How utterly this law of God is disregarded, especially here in southern California. There is no class of sins of which God has expressed His sternest disapproval more clearly than He has of this, by attaching to them the most awful and immediate penalties. Anyone that has committed any of the sins covered by this commandment has brought a swift curse, and oftentimes many curses, upon his own head.

The vilest, meanest, most contemptible, most despicable man that walks the earth is the man who steps in between another man and the affections of his wife. I do not wonder that they shoot him down like a dog. I do not believe in thus shooting them down, for I do not believe in taking the law in one's own hand under any circumstances; but the man who is thus shot down gets only what he merits. He has lived like a dog and like a dog he dies. The vilest woman that walks the earth, the lowest, the most disgusting creature that walks the earth, no matter how fair her face may be, is the woman who steps in between another woman and the affections of her husband, and it does not make her one whit less vile that she does it under the countenance of loose divorce laws. Of course, there is pardon for her, and complete salvation and eternal life for her, if she repents and accepts Jesus Christ, just as there is for all sinners. Thank God! I have seen many such women saved, and some of them become the purest and noblest of saints; but, nevertheless, she is vile, vile, vile, unspeakably vile. And when men and women commit this sin they pay an awful price in this life to say nothing of the eternal Hell to which they are hurrying on.   More suicides come from adultery and kindred sins than from any other cause.   Indeed, whenever a woman commits suicide the first question that is always asked and the first point that the authorities always investigate is, as to whether or not she has gone astray.   In ninety-nine cases out of a hundred it is taken for granted that she has.

The curse of God follows the adulterous pair, and the one who is illicitly loved, becomes a bitter curse and the cause of agony.   How often have I seen that illustrated.   How much do you suppose you weigh, weighed by this law of God? Remember, Jesus Christ applies the law not only to the outward act but to the secret thought of the heart.   Read Matt. 5:28: " But I say unto you, that every one that looketh on a woman to lust after her hath committed adultery with her already in his heart."   How much do you weigh, weighed by this law of God?

5.   Listen now to the eighth commandment, " Thou shalt not steal."   How much do you suppose you weigh, weighed by that law of God?   " Well," you say, " I have certainly never broken that law of God, I have never stolen anything in my life."   Are you sure?   You say, " Do you think you have any thieves in this audience tonight."   Yes, hundreds of them.   Stop and think, What is it to steal?   To steal is to take money or property from another without rendering to that other a sufficient equivalent in property or money in return.   For example: anyone who sells goods to another by misrepresentation and sells them for more than their real value is a thief.   Anyone who buys goods from another and does not give to the one from whom he buys them a full equivalent in money for the goods bought, is a thief.   Every employer of labour who takes advantage of his employees' necessities, and does not render to that employee in good, honest wages, a full equivalent for the labour performed, is a thief.   Every working man who shirks his work and lies down on his job, or in any other way does not render to his employer a full equivalent in honest labour performed for the wages received, is a thief.   All these men are thieves, just as much as any man behind prison bars at San Quentin is a thief.   Everyone who gambles and wins is a thief, for he receives money or

property for which he has rendered no adequate equivalent. Every time you bet on a game of cards, on a horse race, or an automobile race, or on election, or anything else and win, you are a thief. And it may be only two cents, or it may be two thousand dollars that you win, the principle is just the same; and you are as truly a thief in the one case as in the other. Every man who gambles and wins is a thief and every man who gambles and loses is a fool; therefore, every gambler is either a thief or a fool or both. I said this one night in the Royal Albert Hall in London. The boxes were filled with people from the West End where the Royal Albert Hall is located. Many of them were dressed in full dress, coming right from dinner. A man in full dress sprang to his feet in one of the boxes in hot anger, to dispute what I had said. I let him talk, and then before the crowd I proved to him that what I had said was true, that by gambling and winning, he was getting from others money and property without rendering to them an adequate equivalent, and that he was, therefore, just as much a thief in the sight of God as any man in jail. Another man wrote me while we were still holding meetings in the Royal Albert Hall, he wrote a very indignant letter, saying that he heard me say that every one who gambled and won was a thief, and added that he gambled and won and that he was not a thief, and he demanded that I take it back publicly, and threatened that if I did not he would shoot me, or do something else of that kind. But I took his letter to the Royal Albert Hall and *read it*, but I refused to take it back, for it was true; and I am not dead yet.

6. Listen to the *ninth* commandment, " Thou shalt not bear false witness against thy neighbour." How much do you weigh, weighed by that law of God? Do you say, " I have never broken that law of God, I never bore false witness against anybody, I never was in court in my life to bear witness at all?" Does the commandment say anything about court? Is court the only place where we bear testimony about others? Every time you speak evil of another you are bearing witness against them; and if the evil that you speak is false, if it is at all exaggerated or distorted, you have broken this law of God.

I have far more respect for an ordinary thief than I have

for a gossip and a slanderer; for all the thief steals is your pocketbook, but the slanderer and the gossip steal that which is above price, your reputation and the respect in which you are held by others. Oh, you gossips, you unvarnished children of the Devil, that go about blackening the reputations of others, as you tell your foul stories! Some of you say, "Did you hear that awful story about Mrs. Smith, I was so sorry to hear it." You lie! You know you lie! you were glad to hear it. If you had been sorry to hear it, you would have kept it to yourself. And then, you that exaggerate and add to the story that you tell, you also break this law of God. "But," you say, "I thought it was true." Does that make it true? Unless we would break this law of God there are four things that we must do: *First,* Never believe anything that we hear against another, until it is absolutely proven to be true; *Second,* Believe no more than is fully proven; *Third,* When we are compelled to believe it, keep it to ourselves unless plain duty demands that we tell it; *Fourth,* When you must tell it, *tell it exactly as it is.*

7. Listen now, to the *tenth* commandment, "Thou shalt not covet thy neighbour's house, thou shalt not covet thy neighbour's wife, nor his man-servant, nor his maid-servant, nor his ox, nor his ass, nor anything that is thy neighbour's." You will note that the law of God looks not only upon the overt act but upon the secret desire of the heart. It is not enough that you do not steal your neighbour's horse; if you even wish that that neighbour's horse were yours, you have broken the law of God, you have coveted your neighbour's horse. How many a man there is who looks upon his neighbour's beautiful and gifted wife. He would not steal his neighbour's wife if he could (he could not if he would). But you say to yourself, "I wish she were my wife;" you have broken the law of God, you have "coveted your neighbour's wife." How many of us go by a beautiful home belonging to someone else, we would not steal our neighbour's house if we could, but how often we say, "Oh! I wish that were my house." You have broken the holy law of God, you have coveted your neighbour's house. How much do you weigh, weighed by this law of God?

How much do you weigh, weighed by all these Ten

Commandments of God's law, these primary laws of God? Many of you will have to cry out, if you are honest with yourself and God, " I am weighed in the balances of God and found utterly wanting."

II. THE HEAVIER WEIGHTS OF GOD'S BALANCES

But these Ten Commandments are not the heaviest weights in God's law, the heaviest weights with which God weighs us. To find them we must turn to the New Testament.

1. Turn first of all to Matt. 7:12, " All things therefore whatsoever ye would that men should do unto you, even so do ye also unto them: for this is the law and the prophets." This is the so-called " Golden Rule," which Jesus gives as the summary of the law and the prophets. How much do you weigh, weighed by this law of God? Ah! there are so many people nowadays who chatter about the golden rule, and make their boast about the golden rule, and who say, " The golden rule is a good enough religion for me "; but who do not keep it. I was talking to a bluff old sea captain many years ago, and I said to him, " Captain C———, why are you not a Christian?" " Oh!", he serenely said, " The golden rule is a good enough religion for me." I looked him square in the eye and said, " Captain, do you keep the golden rule?" He dropped his eyes; he talked about it, but he did not keep it. Do you keep it? Let me read it to you again, " All things therefore whatsoever ye would that men should do unto you, even so do ye also unto them: for this is the law and the prophets." Please note carefully that it does not say merely " Do not do unto others what you would not have them do unto you." That is purely negative, that is the Confucian golden rule. The Christian golden rule is positive, " Whatsoever ye would that man should do unto you, even so do ye also unto them." Sell goods unto other men just as you would have other men sell goods to you. Do you do it? or are you trying to get the highest prices for the poorest goods? Buy goods of other men the way you would want other men to buy goods of you. Do you do it? or are you running all over town looking for the bargain counters? Pay those who work for you the way you want those for whom you work to pay you. Do you do it? or are you trying hard to get the most work out of men

for the smallest pay?   Work for other men the way you want other men to work for you.   Do you do it? or are you trying to get the largest pay for the smallest amount of work?   Talk about other people behind their back just the way you want other people to talk about you behind your back.   Do you do it?   Say now, how much do you weigh, weighed by the golden rule?

2.   But the Golden Rule is not the heaviest weight in God's love.   Turn to Matt. 22:37-38, "And he said unto him, Thou shalt love the Lord thy God with all thy heart, and with all thy soul, and with all thy mind.   This is the great and first commandment."   How much do you weigh, weighed by that weight?   Put God first in everything, God first in business, God first in politics, God first in study, God first in social life, God first in pleasure, God first in home life, God first in everything. Have you done it?   Have you always done it? If not, you have broken this law of God.   And note what law of God this is, " The *first and great* commandment."   If then you have failed here, you have failed at the most important point.   Keep every other law of God and fail here, and where you fail is infinitely more important than where you have succeeded.   And every last one of us have failed here.

Some years ago I was preaching one night for a Methodist minister in Chicago.   Before the service began he said to me, " I have a young man in my church who wants to study for the ministry.   I wish you would speak with him at the close of the meeting."   After the altar service he brought the young man to me and introduced him.   He had one of the frankest and most open countenances I ever saw.   I said to him, " Your pastor says you wish to study for the ministry." " Yes," he replied.   I said, " Are you a Christian?"   " Why of course I am a Christian," he replied, " I was brought up a Christian and I am not going back on the training of my parents."   I said, " Have you ever been born again?" " What's that?" he said.   I repeated, " Have you been born again?   Our Lord Jesus says in John 3:3, ' except a man be born again he can not see the kingdom of God.' "   He answered, " I never heard of that before in all my life."   I said, " Do you know that you have committed the greatest sin that any man could possibly commit?"   " No," he said, in surprise,

"I never have, you have entirely mistaken my case, I have been very carefully reared." I said to him, "What do you think is the greatest sin that a man can possibly commit?" "Why, murder, of course," he replied. I said, "You are greatly mistaken. Let me show you what God says." And then I opened my Bible to this passage, Matt. 22:37-38. I put it in his hands and asked him to read, and he read: "And he said unto him, Thou shalt love the Lord thy God with all thy heart, and with all thy soul, and with all thy mind. This is the great and first commandment." I said, "Which commandment is this?" He said, "This is the first and great commandment." "Then what must be the first and great sin?" "Why," he replied, "I suppose, not to keep this commandment." I said, "Have you kept it? Have you loved God with all your heart and with all your soul, and with all your mind? Have you put God first in everything, God first in business, God first in politics, God first in study, God first in social life, God first in domestic life, God first in pleasure, God first in everything?" "No," he said, "I have not." I said, "What have you done then?" "I have broken this commandment." I said, "Which commandment is this?" "It is the first and great commandment." I said, "What have you done?" He replied, "I have broken the first and great commandment, I have committed the greatest sin a man can possibly commit, but I never saw it before in all my life." Well, perhaps you never saw it before in all your life, but you see it now. How much do you weigh, weighed by this law of God?

I rest this part of my case here. Need I have any hesitation in saying, that every man and woman here tonight, when put into the balances of God, is found wanting and forever wanting?

III. WHAT MUST WE DO?

What then must we each do? Here is where the Gospel comes in. Up to this point I have preached nothing but law and on the ground of law, there is not one particle of hope for any man or woman in this audience tonight. Nay more, on the ground of law there is not a particle of hope for any man or woman on earth. If there were only law, eternal destruction must be the lot of every child of Adam. It is per-

fectly clear from what we have seen tonight that Paul was
right when he declared, " By the works of the law shall no
flesh be justified in God's sight." (Rom. 3:20.)

But thank God, there is something besides law.   There is
a Gospel as well as law; and the Gospel is of God, just as
much as the law is of God, and the Gospel is as sure as the
law is.   God weighed the whole world in the balances and
found the whole world wanting, and then He provided salvation for an utterly wanting world.   Let me read it to you
from Rom. 3:20-26, " Because by the works of the law shall
no flesh be justified in his sight; for *through the law cometh
the knowledge of sin.*   But now *apart from the law a righteousness of God hath been manifested,* being witnessed by the
law and the prophets; even the righteousness of God through
faith in Jesus Christ *unto all them that believe;* for there is
no distinction; for all have sinned, and fall short of the glory
of God; *being justified freely by* his *grace through the redemption that is in Christ Jesus:* whom God set forth to be a propitiation, through faith, in his blood, to show his righteousness
because of the passing over of the sins done aforetime, in the
forbearance of God; for the showing, I say, of his righteousness at this present season: that he might himself be just, and
the justifier of him that hath faith in Jesus."

God weighed the whole world in the balances and found
the whole world wanting, and then He provided salvation for
a " wanting " world.   He gave His Son to perfectly keep the
law of God, and then to die as an atoning substitute for us
who had broken it.   Listen to Isa. 53:6, " All we like sheep
have gone astray; we have turned every one to his own way;
and the Lord hath laid (Heb. made to strike) on him the
iniquity of us all."   And the moment any one of us forsakes
sin and puts his trust in Jesus Christ as his atoning Saviour,
believes God's testimony about Jesus Christ, that all our sins
were laid upon Him when He died on the cross, and trusts
God to forgive us because Jesus Christ died in our place, *that
very moment we take Jesus Christ into the balance with us,
and the moment we have Jesus Christ in the balance with us,
that moment we can weigh up the heaviest weights of God's
holy law.*

Tonight doubtless some of the more thoughtful ones among

you have said to yourselves, " I wonder if that preacher fancies that he has kept all those laws." No! I know I have not, I have broken God's laws time and time again in the years gone by. How grievously I have broken them, thank God! no one of you will ever know. But I have also believed the Gospel, I believe what God Himself testifies concerning His Son Jesus Christ bearing my sins. *I know that every sin I ever committed was laid on Him and settled when He died in my place on the cross of Calvary.* I unquestioningly and unhesitatingly believe God's word that: " Christ redeemed us from the curse of the law, having become a curse for us; for it is written, Cursed is every one that hangeth on a tree." (Gal. 3:13.) And I have trusted God to forgive my sins on the sole but all-sufficient ground that Christ died in my place; and God has cancelled all my sins. Tonight, I have Jesus Christ in the balance with me, and God can put all the weights of his law in the other pan of the balance, and Jesus Christ and I will weigh them all up.

Men and women you are found wanting tonight. You are weighed in the balances of God and found utterly wanting. Don't try to shut your eyes to that fact. Listen no longer to the siren voices of Christian Science and the " New Theology " and " Liberal Theology," that once sounded to you like the sweetest song, that there is no such thing as sin, or that, if there ever was such a thing as sin, your sin is not very great. There is sin, you know that there is. You are a great sinner, you know that you are. You are so great a sinner that you have broken the first and greatest of God's commandments. You know that you have, YOU HAVE BEEN WEIGHED IN THE BALANCES OF GOD AND YOU ARE FOUND WANTING, UTTERLY WANTING.

But Jesus Christ, your Crucified and Risen Saviour, stands ready to get into the balances with you tonight, yes, right now. And with Jesus Christ in the balances, you will never be found wanting even by the infinitely Holy God. Will you take Jesus Christ with you into the balance tonight? Will you accept Him as your personal Saviour tonight, surrender to Him as your Lord and Master, confess Him as such before the world, and strive from this time on to live to please Him in everything day by day?

The time is fast hurrying on when God will weigh every one of us in His balances, for the last time. Let me repeat it, the time is fast hurrying on when God will weigh every one of us in His balances for the last time! And woe be to the man whom God weighs in His balances for the last time and who has not Jesus Christ in the balances with him. There can be nothing for such a one but eternal woe, and eternal darkness, and eternal despair. If God weighs you in His balances for the last time and you haven't Jesus Christ in the balances with you, you will remember this sermon tonight, and this text. You will remember this audience gathered together here. You will remember everything about this occasion, and you will look back and say, "Oh! if I had only improved that opportunity."

I once heard Mr. Moody tell a story I shall never forget. A man was set to watch a drawbridge. He had orders not to open the draw after a certain time until a special train had passed. The hour came. Boat after boat came up and urged him to open the bridge and let them through. "No, I have my orders to wait till the special passes." At last a friend came up and over-urged him, and he allowed himself to be persuaded. He threw the draw open. No sooner was the bridge well open and the vessels beginning to enter, than he heard the whistle of the special up the track. He sprang to the lever, but he was too late. The train came on with lightning speed. He looked wildly on as it plunged into the open chasm. He heard the shrieks of the injured and saw the corpses of the dead, and went raving mad. He never recovered his senses; but walked up and down the padded cell of the asylum, crying, "Oh! if I only had; oh! if I only had." Had what? Obeyed orders. Men and women, reject Christ for the last time and you will walk up and down the corridors of hell, the eternal madhouse of the universe, wringing your hands, and saying, "Oh! if I only had; oh! if I only had!" Had what? Obeyed God, and accepted His Son as your Saviour. Will you do it now?

VII

THE REAL TRUTH ABOUT THE JUDGMENT DAY

" God now commandeth all men everywhere to repent: because He hath appointed a day, in the which He will judge the world in righteousness by that Man Whom He hath ordained; whereof He hath given assurance unto all men, in that He hath raised Him from the dead."—ACTS 17 : 30, 31.

M Y subject tonight is, The Real Truth About the Judgment Day. You will find my text, indeed, you will find my whole sermon in Acts 17:30, 31, " God now commandeth all men everywhere to repent: because *He hath appointed a day, in the which He will judge the world in righteousness* by that Man Whom He hath ordained; whereof He hath given assurance unto all men, in that He hath raised Him from the dead." The man who uttered these startling words was the apostle Paul. They were spoken to one of the most distinguished audiences that ever listened to a sermon, to an audience composed entirely of the leading philosophers of the day, assembled in the greatest centre of culture of the day, Athens, and at one of the most celebrated centres of thought and philosophy of any day, the Areopagus. Speaking to this exceptionally intelligent audience in this place famed through the centuries, Paul declared to them that there was a final day of judgment coming for every member of the human race. He declared furthermore that the coming of that day was not a matter of human speculation but of Divine announcement, and that God had backed up His announcement by a present-day fact, the resurrection of Christ Jesus from the dead.

These words that God spoke through the apostle Paul present to us the five great divisions of our subject tonight. First, The Certainty that there is to be a Judgment Day; Second, The Persons who are to be Judged in that day; Third,

126

The Basis of the Judgment pronounced upon that Day;
Fourth, The Judge Who shall preside at that Judgment;
Fifth, The Issues of the Judgment Day.

I. THE CERTAINTY THAT THERE IS TO BE A JUDGMENT DAY

First of all, then, let us consider the Certainty of that coming Judgment Day.   There are two events in the future which
are absolutely certain.   In the first place, it is absolutely certain that Jesus Christ is coming back again to receive His
people unto Himself and to reward them according to their
works; and in the second place, it is absolutely certain that
Jesus Christ is coming again to this earth to judge the whole
inhabited earth.   I am asked almost every day, " What will
be the outcome of these appalling international entanglements
in Europe," and I always reply, " I do not know."   Men often
come to me with the question, " What will be the outcome of
these great combinations of labouring men on the one hand
to resist the encroachments of capital, and of these great combinations of capital on the other hand to control both our commercial and our political life," and again I reply, " I do not
know."   But, I will tell you what I do know, and it is infinitely more important: I know that some day Jesus Christ,
our Lord, will come back again and receive His waiting and
faithful people unto Himself, and I also know that there is
to be a Judgment Day for the world, and that Judgment Day
is the subject of our thought tonight.

It is absolutely certain that there is to be a Judgment Day.
As our text reads, " God hath appointed a day, in the which
He will judge the world in righteousness."   It is absolutely
certain that there will be that Judgment Day.

Last Sunday night our subject was, Something tremendously
important that is absolutely certain.   That absolute certainty
was that if we sinned, our sin would find us out, that we
would suffer for that sin, and suffer for every sin we committed.   But there is another absolute certainty, and that is,
that there is to be a Day of Judgment.

Men who are living in sin, and men who are proudly boasting that they are possessors of " the Modern Mind," and who
often at least suggest that they have a monopoly on " the
Modern Mind," may laugh at the thought of a coming Day

of Judgment, but they cannot laugh it away. In the days of Noah men laughed at Noah's predictions that there was to be a flood, but the flood came and swept them all away in spite of all their laughter. In the days of Lot the men of Sodom laughed at the idea that God would rain fire and brimstone out of heaven, and destroy Sodom and Gomorrah and the other cities of the plain, but the fire and brimstone fell just the same, and those cities were blotted out, and today their ruins lie beneath the bitter waters of the Dead Sea. In the days of Jeremiah the people of Jerusalem scoffed at Jeremiah's predictions that Nebuchadnezzar would come and lay Jerusalem in the dust and destroy their temple, but it all came to pass to the very letter just as God said it would and just as Jeremiah believed and predicted. In the days of Jesus Christ Himself, men laughed at the predictions of the Son of God that the armies of Rome under Titus and Vespasian would come and besiege Jerusalem, and lay Jerusalem's walls even with the ground, and that such calamities would overtake that city and its population as the world had never seen in all its history; but historians outside of the Bible tell us that it all came to pass to the minutest particular just as Christ predicted, that Jerusalem was overtaken with the most appalling siege in the world's history, when the streets of the city ran with blood, when the people gaunt and starving stalked the streets, when mothers ate their own children in the straitness of the siege, and when a million people perished in the awful judgment that came upon the city that had rejected and crucified its rightful king, Jesus.

All of God's predictions concerning judgment on individuals and nations in times past have come true to the very letter, in spite of all the false hopes that have been held out by false prophets and self-sufficient philosophers and the blind optimists of the day. And if we are to judge the future by the past, and there is no other intelligent way to judge it, God's predictions about the future with regard to judgments on individuals and nations will also come true to the very letter, in spite of all the false hopes held out by our modern false prophets, by the liberal preachers and " men of modern mind " and senseless optimists. It is absolutely certain that there is to be a Judgment Day for the world.

I say it is absolutely certain that there is to be a Judgment Day for the world. Why do I say so?

1. First of all, I say *it is absolutely certain that there is to be a Judgment Day because Jesus Christ says so, and everything Jesus Christ says is absolutely certain.* There are many in our day who are willing to accept anything Jesus Christ says even though they may be more or less skeptical about some other parts of the Bible. Well, personally, for perfectly good and sufficient reasons, I believe every part of the Bible, but we do not need to discuss that tonight, for *Jesus Christ Himself* declares that there is to be a Judgment Day, and that He Himself is to be the Judge, and I am ready to bank on anything and everything Jesus Christ says. I am ready to risk all my hopes for time and eternity on any plain statement of Jesus Christ. Every really intelligent and truly wise man will bank on anything and everything Jesus Christ says. Any man or woman who would listen to anyone who contradicts Jesus Christ, any one who, for any reason, doubts any statement of Jesus Christ, is a fool; and the final outcome will prove that he is a fool. Now, Jesus Christ says that there is to be a Judgment Day and that He is to be the Judge. These are His words. You will find them in John 5:22-29, " For neither doth the Father judge any man, but He hath given all judgment unto the Son; that all may honour the Son, even as they honour the Father. He that honoureth not the Son honoureth not the Father that sent Him. Verily, verily, I say unto you, He that heareth My word, and believeth Him that sent Me, hath eternal life, and cometh not into judgment, but hath passed out of death into life. Verily, verily, I say unto you, The hour cometh, and now is, when the dead shall hear the voice of the Son of God; and they that hear shall live. For as the Father hath life in Himself, even so gave He to the Son also to have life in Himself: and He gave Him authority to execute judgment, because He is (the) Son of man. Marvel not at this: for the hour cometh, in which all that are in the tombs shall hear His voice, and shall come forth; they that have done good, unto the resurrection of life; and they that have done evil, unto the resurrection of judgment."

2. In the second place, I say that *it is absolutely certain*

that there is to be a Judgment Day, and that Jesus Christ is to be the Judge, because the absolutely certain fact of the resurrection of Jesus Christ in the past points forward with unerring finger to an absolutely certain Judgment Day in the future. It is absolutely certain that after Jesus was nailed to the cross, and died, and His body was taken down and laid in Joseph's tomb, that God raised that body of Jesus Christ from the dead. The resurrection of the body of Jesus Christ from the dead is the best proven fact in history. I have not time to go into that tonight, but I have time and time again from this platform, shown in my addresses (as I have also shown in my books), that the evidence for the resurrection of Jesus Christ is so overwhelmingly convincing that no candid man, that is, no man who really wishes to know the truth and is willing to obey the truth whatever it may be, can sit down and thoroughly examine the evidence of the resurrection of the body of Jesus Christ from the dead, and come to any other conclusion than that His body was raised from the dead, just as is related in the four gospels and in the Acts of the Apostles and in the fifteenth chapter of the First Epistle to the Corinthians.

The resurrection of Jesus Christ from the dead is not a theological fiction; it is not a poet's dream; it is not a romancer's fancy; it is an established fact of history. Well, that absolutely certain historical fact of the resurrection of Jesus Christ in the past points forward with unerring finger to the absolute certainty of a Judgment Day in the future in which He Whom God raised from the dead is to be the Judge.

" How," someone may ask, " does the resurrection of Jesus Christ in the past, prove that there is to be a Judgment Day in the future?" In this unmistakable way: when Jesus Christ was here upon the earth He claimed, as I have already shown you in the passage from the fifth chapter of John, that there was to be a Judgment Day, and that He was to be the Judge. Men hated Him with bitterest hatred for making that claim, and the other claim involved in it, the claim that He Himself was Divine. They put Him to death for making these claims, but before they put Him to death He said in effect, " My Father, Jehovah God, will set His seal to the claim for making which you put Me to death, by raising Me from the dead

on the third day." The hour which He had proclaimed for
His resurrection came, the breath of God swept through that
sleeping body, and God raised Jesus Christ from the dead,
and by thus raising Him, God, in an unmistakable way, set
His seal to Christ's claims, and said in accents that cannot
be mistaken, and that are a message direct from heaven to all
ages, "There is to be a Judgment Day, and this, My Son, is
to be the Judge."

If there is any man here tonight who flatters himself that
there is to be no Judgment Day; if there is any man here tonight who fancies he can go on in sin, and never be called to
strict account for it; if there is any man here tonight who
imagines he can go on trampling under foot the Son of God,
day after day, week after week, and month after month, and
year after year, and not have to suffer for it, listen, man, that
hope of yours is utterly baseless. In the light of the Resurrection of Jesus Christ from the dead it is absolutely certain
that there is to be a Judgment Day and you will have to answer for your outrageous offenses against God and against the
Christ who is Himself to be the Judge on that day. It is
absolutely certain that there will be a day in which Jesus
Christ will judge you and judge the world in righteousness.

II.   The Persons Who Are to be Judged

Now let us consider who are the persons who are to be
judged upon that Judgment Day that is surely coming, and
ever more and more swiftly drawing nigh. Who are they?
Our text answers the question with unmistakable plainness.
Listen again, "God hath appointed a day, in the which He
will judge the world in righteousness." The Greek word here
translated "world" means "the inhabited earth." That judgment is to be a judgment of the whole world, the whole inhabited earth. It will be no class judgment. Every man and
woman upon this earth when the Lord Jesus comes will have
to face Him as Judge on that day. Of course, all who have
received the Lord Jesus Christ as their Saviour, and surrendered to Him as their Lord and Master, and confessed Him
as such before the world, and who are living to please Him,
will have been caught up to meet Him in the air; but all the
rest, everyone still living on earth, will have to face the Judge

in that day. There will be no escaping that day. Men often escape human courts. There is many a thief that has never been arrested. There is many a murderer that remains un-hung. But when God sends forth His officers to gather the people for that Judgment Day, everyone will have to come, and he will have to stay right there until his case is settled. Men have often escaped me when I am preaching. When the preaching becomes too pointed they get up and go out, and thus escape me. Or they remain and laugh, and whisper to someone else, and thus they escape me and the truth, but you cannot escape God in that way on that day. You will have to come there, and you will have to stay there until your case is decided. God is going to judge the world in righteousness. There will be one meeting at which every man and woman on earth will have to be present. How you would rejoice if every infidel in Los Angeles were at this meeting tonight. But most infidels would not dare to come to this meeting. But there will be a meeting at which every infidel will have to be pres-ent, there will be a meeting at which every hypocritical church member will be present, there will be a meeting at which every impenitent sinner will be present, the meeting with Jesus Christ at the Judgment Bar of God.

That man who is sitting in this meeting tonight trying to make light of everything I am saying, listen, you will be at that meeting and you will not make light of it. You will be there face to face with Jesus Christ. That woman in this audience who has come to this meeting for any purpose but a holy one, and who is probably not paying much attention to what I am saying, at that meeting with Jesus Christ at the Judgment Bar of God, you will pay the closest and most pain-ful attention.

III. The Basis of the Judgment to be Pronounced on that Day

Now let us consider what is to be the basis of the judgment that is to be pronounced on that day.

1. In the first place, *The basis of the judgment is to be, " The things done in the body."* We read in Second Corin-thians, chapter five, verse ten, " For we must all be made manifest before the judgment-seat of Christ; that each one

may receive the things *done in the body*, according to what he hath done, whether it be good or bad." " The *things done in the body*," are the basis of that judgment. There are many preachers in this day who tell us a man can live in sin all his days, and die in sin, and can then have another probation, another chance to repent; that even after death he may repent, and turn to God, and accept Christ, and be saved. But when they say it they contradict the Word of God. The Old Book does not hold out any such hope. It says that " Each one (shall) receive the things *done in the body*," that is, done in the life that now is, done this side of the grave, done before we shuffle off this mortal coil. The issues of eternity are determined in the life that now is; they are determined by " the things done in the body."

That man who tonight is living in drunkenness, who is squandering his time, and his money, and his manhood in a life of dissipation, you will have to answer for that in that day. That woman who tonight is living a life of frivolity, and foolishness and fashion, living a life of pleasure and self-gratification, instead of living for the God Who made her and for the Christ Who died for her; you will have to answer for that, in that day. That man who professes to be a Christian, but who lives just like the world; you will have to answer for that, in that day. That man who has made gold his god, overreaching his neighbour in business, oppressing his employees, turning a deaf ear to the cry of the widow and orphan at home, and the heathen abroad; you will have to answer for that in that day. That man who knows the truth, but will not heed it, and accept Jesus Christ as his Saviour, and surrender to Him as his Lord and Master, and confess Him as Such before the world, because he fears it will hurt him in business or in politics or in some other way; you will have to answer for that, in that day. That man who is a libertine, living in lust, living like a beast, scattering ruin wherever he goes; you will have to answer for that, in that day. " The things done in the body "—they will all come up, even the things you have forgotten.

There is a man here tonight who years ago did a base and nefarious deed, and tonight he is very comfortable in the thought that no one on earth knows of it. Man, the whole

world will know about it in that day unless you repent, and
Jesus Christ will know about it and pass eternal judgment
upon it.   There is a woman here tonight who had a very black
page in her past history, but of late years she has found comfort in the thought concerning that black page, in that no one
now lives who knows anything about it, that it is all forgotten, that there is no one still alive to bring it up.   Listen!
The whole world will know about it in that day unless you
repent and turn to Christ; and Jesus Christ Himself will
bring it up, and what then?   Eternally damned!

2.   In the second place, *The secret things will be judged.*
In Rom. 2:16, we read, " In that day (when) God shall *judge
the secrets of men,* according to my Gospel, by Jesus Christ."
The secret things, the things done in the dark, the things done
under cover of night, the things done when nobody saw—but
God; all will be brought to light in that day.

I heard many years ago of a woman in Wales who killed
a man by driving a nail into his skull, and then so successfully covered up the wound that there was no suspicion cast
upon her.   Years passed, and the woman flattered herself that
she never would be found out, but one day the grave-digger
was at work in the cemetery, and threw up this man's skull,
and there was the hole in it and the nail in the hole.   I do
not know that he suspected the woman, but he took the skull
to her and said, " Look there!"   She threw up her hands and
cried, " My God!   Found out at last!"   It will all be found
out at last.   The secret things, yes, even the thoughts and
imaginations of the heart.   Oh! You men here tonight who
are boasting of your morality, and think you need no atoning
Saviour, how would you like to have the thoughts, and fancies, and the desires, and imaginations of even the last twenty-
four hours photographed and thrown upon a screen before
this audience tonight?   Listen!   The whole world will see
these secret things in that day, not the secret things of twenty-
four hours only, but of your whole lifetime; unless you repent
and accept Jesus Christ, and thus get your sins covered.   You,
my fair and fine lady, you who have boasted of your purity
and nobility of character, a nobility that you fondly fancy
is greater than that of others, and think that you ought to
be saved because of your exceptional goodness; how would

you like to have the hidden things of the chambers of your imagery and your unuttered desires photographed, and thrown on a screen before all this audience tonight? Listen! The whole world will see them all in that day, unless you repent and receive Jesus Christ, and have it all covered by His atoning blood. Yes, the secret things will come to light.

3. The Lord also tells us that, *Our words will be the basis upon which we are judged.* He says in Matt. 12:36, " And I say unto you, that *every idle word that men shall speak,* they shall give account thereof in the day of judgment." Our careless, thoughtless, unstudied words reveal what we really are at heart. In our studied speeches we do not reveal ourselves, what we really are, but what we would like to seem to be; but in our " idle words," our unpremeditated words that we drop accidentally, there is a true revelation of just what is in our hearts. Your impure words, or unkind words, or harsh words, or words of gossip, and slander, or heedless words about God, and Christ, and the Bible; all your heedless, thoughtless words you will give account thereof in the day of judgment.

One night at a meeting in Minneapolis, one of my workers came to me and said, " Here is an infidel; will you come and speak to him?" I went to him, and asked, " Is it true that you are an infidel?" He said, " Yes, I am an infidel." I said, " Why are you an infidel?" He replied, " Because the Bible is full of contradictions." " Full of contradictions?" I said. " Yes," he replied. " Will you please show me one," I asked. " Oh," said he, " it is full of them." " Well," I said, " if it is full of them, you ought, at least, to be able to show me one." " Oh," he replied, " it is just full of them." " Well," I insisted, " please show me one." " Well," he replied, " I do not pretend to know as much about the Bible as you do." " Then," I said, " what are you talking about it for in this way?" Then I looked him square in the eye and I told him what Jesus said of the idle words men speak, " That every idle word that men shall speak, they shall give account thereof in the day of judgment. Now," I said, " this book is God's Word. God is the Author of this Book, and you lightly and thoughtlessly have been slandering the Word of God, and in doing that, you have been slandering God, Himself, the Author of the Book. I want to say to you, sir, that you will have to give account of the words you have spoken to me tonight in the day of judgment." The man turned pale, and well he might.

I want to say to you men here tonight, who are pulling the Word of God to pieces because you have been told that some scientist or scholar says so and so; you men who dare to criticise the Book that God has given to us, and the Book you really know nothing about; you men who are taking up the idle talk of newspapers, and reviews, and books of men who are wise in other directions, but who when they begin to talk about the Bible are talking about something they know nothing about; you who, therefore, are slandering God's Word and the Author of It, you will have to give account thereof, of every word you speak, in the day of judgment. You may well tremble. I wish to say to you men who have been taking the Name of the glorious Son of God, Jesus Christ, our Lord, "in Whom dwells all the fulness of the Godhead," lightly on your lips, and have been saying flippantly, "I do not believe Jesus Christ is Divine in any other sense than that we are all divine; I do not believe that Jesus Christ in any unique sense is the Son of God"; you, who have been trying to rob the glorious Son of God of what is His just due, the Divine honour and worship which are His due, you will have to give account of every word you have said, in the day of judgment.

4. But the great and final basis of judgment in that day will be what we do with Jesus Christ. We are told in John 3:18, 19, "He that believeth on Him is not condemned: but he that believeth not is condemned already, because he hath not believed in the Name of the Only begotten Son of God. And this is the condemnation, that light is come into the world, and men loved darkness rather than light, because their deeds were evil." God sent One down into this world to be our Saviour. The One He sent was His Own and His only Son. In Him was incarnated all the fulness of the Godhead, all His attributes and moral excellencies. Jesus Christ was Truth and Light Incarnate. The rejection of Jesus Christ, the Son of God, Whom God hath appointed to be our Saviour, our King and Lord, is the most daring and damning of all sins. Light has been sent into the world in Him, and men

have loved darkness rather than light because their own deeds
were evil.   There is nothing that so clearly reveals the human
heart as what a man does with Jesus Christ.

As I have said, Christ is God incarnate, the Light and Life
of God, come down into this world, and the rejection of Jesus
Christ, therefore, proves a wicked heart.   What a man is, is
clearly shown by what a man chooses and by what a man
rejects.   And the man who rejects Jesus Christ, however
amiable his traits of character may be in many ways, proves
that at his heart he is bad, utterly bad.   The great question,
therefore, of the Judgment Day will be, " What did you do
with Jesus Christ?"

Oh, I can imagine some people in that day.   I can imagine
that man who sits up yonder in the gallery tonight, trying to
make light of all I am saying; I see him standing before the
Judgment Bar of God, and the throng falls back.   There is
a profound silence.   Then comes rolling forth like the sound
of many waters the majestic voice of the Judge, " What did
you do with Jesus Christ?"

IV. Who is to be the Judge?

We come now to the very important question, Who is to be
the Judge in that day?   Who is to sit as Judge in that great
Judgment Day that is coming?   We have already answered
that question in what has been said: Jesus Christ, Himself,
is to sit as Judge.   Listen to the text again, " God hath appointed a day, in the which He will judge the world in righteousness *by that Man Whom He hath ordained; whereof He
hath given assurance unto all men, in that He hath raised Him
from the dead.*"   Yes, Jesus Christ is to be the Judge.   He,
Himself, also declares that fact.   He says in John 5:22, 23,
" For neither doth the Father judge any man, but He hath
given all judgment unto the Son; that all may honour the Son,
even as they honour the Father."   Yes, beyond a question
Jesus Christ is to be the Judge.   God set the stamp of His
endorsement on Jesus Christ's claim that He was to be the
Judge by raising Him from the dead.

It is not only certain there is to be a Judgment Day; it is
also certain that Jesus Christ is to be the Judge.   That same
Christ Whom you are rejecting tonight is to be the Judge.

That same Christ Whom you are robbing of the honour and
obedience and worship that are His due, is to be the Judge.
That same Christ Whose Deity you are denying, not that you
have any reason for denying it, but simply because you do
not wish to believe it and because you want comfort in your
sin and in your rejection of Him—that same Christ Jesus
Whom you are trampling under foot tonight, will sit as Judge
in that day. That day will be a very dark day for some
people. It will be a dark day for Annas and Caiaphas, who
robbed Jesus of every form of justice, and sent Him unjustly
to all the agony of the cross. Now they stand before the Bar
of Judgment, and Jesus Christ, Whom they so grievously
wronged, sits upon the throne. I can imagine Pontius Pilate
in that day, who knew that Jesus Christ was innocent, and
yet condemned Him to death to please the Jewish mob. Now,
Pilate stands at the Bar of Judgment, and the Christ he so
basely wronged sits upon the throne. I can imagine the soldiers who spat upon Him, and mocked Him, and crowned
Him with thorns; and now the Christ they spat upon, buffeted,
scourged, and crowned with thorns, sits upon the throne, and
they stand before the Judgment Bar. I can imagine Judas
Iscariot, who for thirty paltry pieces of silver sold his Master,
after three years of close association with Him. Now Judas
Iscariot stands before the Bar, and the Christ He betrayed
for the paltry silver, sits upon the throne. Yes, I can imagine
that man, and that woman in this audience tonight, who have
been telling their friends that they do not believe that Jesus
is Divine, and who have been trampling under foot the Son of
God all these years; you who have been resisting all the in-
vitations of mercy for lo, all these many years; now you stand
before the throne, and the Christ you have defamed, slan-
dered, rejected, and trampled under foot, sits as Judge upon
the throne.

V. THE ISSUES OF THE JUDGMENT DAY

Now, please notice for a few moments, the issues of that
coming Judgment Day. What will they be? They will be
final and irrevocable. There will be no possibility of appeal-
ing to a higher court, for that is the Highest Court in the
universe. And there will be no termination of the sentence.

It will be for all eternity. A man is filled with deepest gloom even in this brief life here on earth when he gets a life sentence. Five years, ten years, that is hard, but a life sentence is appalling. But this will be a sentence not merely for the seventy or possibly eighty years of human life here on earth, but a sentence for a never-ending eternity. As the destinies of men are determined in that day, they will be determined for all eternity. Yes, the issues of this Judgment Day will be eternal. The issues will be either eternal joy, and eternal life, and eternal glory, or eternal death, eternal darkness, eternal despair, eternal shame, eternal agony, eternal gloom.

Oh, men and women, I would that I had it in my power tonight to so picture to you that great Judgment Day that every man and woman in this audience would go out from here with the Judgment Day of Christ before them as the great vivid reality that it ought to be; but it surpasses all my powers. There stands the Judgment Throne; its blazing glory, its dazzling magnificence, its overwhelming splendour, I cannot describe. There sits the Christ of God, Christ Jesus, upon that throne. His face is shining with a glory above the glory of the noonday sun, His eyes glow like flames of fire, piercing men through and through. And there you stand before that awful Judgment Bar, with the eyes of the Christ upon you, like flames of fire, piercing you through and through, your whole life laid bare, and your secret thoughts revealed. All is silence. The lips of the Judge begin to move, He is about to speak, to pronounce your eternal destiny. What will the sentence be? Oh, men and women, Repent, *Repent*, REPENT! " God now commandeth all men everywhere to repent: because He hath appointed a day, in the which He will judge the world in righteousness by that Man Whom He hath ordained; whereof He hath given assurance unto all men in that He hath raised Him from the dead."

Repent, *Repent*, REPENT!

VIII

WHAT IT COSTS NOT TO BE A CHRISTIAN

MANY years ago I was talking one evening with an apparently rather frivolous society girl in the city of New Haven when she stopped me suddenly and said, " Don't talk that way, Mr. Torrey, it makes me think, and I hate to think." The world is full of women who hate to think, and it is just as full of men who hate to think. And because they hate to think they go into things blindfolded, and come out with broken hearts and blighted hopes, and blasted lives. It is so in business. How many a man there is in this city tonight who, a few years ago had a business proposition made to him which seemed to promise well on the surface, and instead of sitting down as any thoroughly intelligent business man would, and thinking it all through as to how much he would have to put into that enterprise before he realized upon his investment, what the interest upon his investment would be, and what the ultimate net profit would be, simply because it seemed to promise well upon the surface, and because he hated to think, he put his money into that enterprise and lost it all, and life from that day to this has been a wretched drag for a bare existence, simply because he hated to think.

It is the same way in domestic life. How many a woman there is in this city tonight who a few years ago met a young man who had a handsome face, an athletic figure, attractive and popular manners, and who was master of a thousand and one small arts whereby a young man knows how to gain the admiration and affection of young women, and one night when they were going home together from a dance, or a theatre, or some social function, he made to her a proposition of marriage, and instead of sitting down as any really intelligent young woman would do under the circumstances, and thinking it all through as to whether that young man had the mental and moral qualifications that would fit him to be a com-

panion for life, just because he had a handsome face, an athletic figure, and attractive and popular manners, and because
she hated to think, that young woman accepted his proposition of marriage, and in due time they were married.   And
a few weeks or a few months later she awakened one awful
morning to the fact that she had married a fool, or what was
worse a rascal, and that woman's life from that day to this,
has been wretched beyond description, simply because she
hated to think.

But there is no place where that mistake is made so often
and where it is so fatal as in the matter of being or not being a
Christian.   Men and women go into a Christless life or drift on
in a Christless life day after day, week after week, month after
month, and year after year, without ever sitting down for thirty
consecutive minutes to consider What it Costs Not to be a
Christian, and so they make shipwreck both of time and eternity, simply because " they hate to think."   Tonight I am going
to ask you to do some thinking, some good, hard, honest, earnest thinking.   What I am going to ask you to think about is
this, What it costs not to be a Christian, what it costs to live
and to die without Jesus Christ; and when I get through, if you
think you are willing to pay the price of a Christless life and
a Christless death, I have nothing more to say, but if, when
I get through, you decide it costs altogether too much not to
be a Christian, I am going to ask you to do the only intelligent thing there is to do in the premises, and that is to accept
Jesus Christ and to publicly confess your acceptance of Jesus
Christ right here tonight.   There are many who are saying,
" I do not wish to become a Christian because it costs too
much," but we shall see tonight that it costs infinitely more
not to be a Christian than it costs to be a Christian.

I.   What Do We Mean by a Christian?

What Does it Cost not to be a Christian?   First of all,
what do we mean by a Christian?   The word is used constantly very carelessly, so tonight we shall attempt to define
a " Christian," scripturally and accurately.   What do we
mean by a " Christian?"   By a Christian I understand any
man, woman or child who comes to God as a lost sinner, accepts Jesus Christ as their personal Saviour, surrenders to

Him as their Lord and Master, and confesses Him as such before the world, and strives to live to please Him in everything day by day. Let me repeat that definition, By a Christian I understand any man, woman or child who comes to God as a lost sinner, accepts Jesus Christ as a personal Saviour, surrenders to Him as their Lord and Master, confesses Him as such before the world, and strives to live to please Him in everything day by day.

II. What it Costs Not to be a Christian

What does it cost not to be a Christian?

1. First of all, *Not to be a Christian costs the sacrifice of peace, peace of conscience and peace of heart.* A Christian has peace: As we read in Rom. 5:1, " Being therefore justified by faith, *we have peace with God* through our Lord Jesus Christ," and of course, having peace with God, we have peace in our own hearts. But no one out of Christ has peace. There is not a man or woman in this house tonight out of Christ, who has peace. God tells us definitely in Isa. 57:21, " There is no peace, saith my God, to the wicked," and by the wicked is not meant the criminal, or the vicious, but everyone who has not surrendered his will to God. There is not a man or woman on earth out of Christ, who has peace. You may have pleasure, you may have fun, you may have merriment, you may have gaiety, you may have good times, delightful times, you may succeed for a time in drowning in a measure the deeper voice of conscience in excitement, or pleasure, or money-getting, or in something else, but way down in the bottom of your heart you haven't peace.

Some years ago I was walking down the aisle of a hall where I had been preaching in Chicago. I saw a man still remaining in one of the seats and I dropped into the seat behind him, and leaned over and said, " Sir, why are you not a Christian?" " Oh," he replied with a shrug of his shoulders, " I am very well satisfied as I am." I said, "You haven't peace." " How do you know that, I would like to know?" he asked. I replied, " Because God says so: ' There is no peace, saith my God, to the wicked.' " He dropped his eyes and said, " You are right, sir, I haven't peace." And there is not a man or woman out of Christ in this building tonight who

has peace, and you never will have peace until you accept
Jesus Christ as your personal Saviour, surrender to Him as
your Lord and Master, and confess Him as such before the
world. Out of Jesus Christ peace is an impossibility. Not
to be a Christian costs the sacrifice of peace.

2. In the second place, *Not to be a Christian costs the
sacrifice of joy, of the highest, purest, truest, most satisfying,
and most enduring joy that is to be found here on earth.* I
am not talking about heaven now, but about the joy that
comes to the true believer in Jesus Christ in the life that now
is, and which the one who does not accept Christ altogether
misses. We read in I Pet. 1:8: " Whom not having seen
ye love; on Whom, though now ye see Him not, yet believing,
ye rejoice greatly with joy unspeakable and full of glory."
A true Christian, a real believer in Jesus Christ, has great
joy, " joy unspeakable and full of glory," and he is the only
one who does have " joy unspeakable and full of glory." I
know what some of you are saying to yourselves right now.
You are saying, " I know Christians who haven't ' joy unspeakable and full of glory.' " Let me ask you a question,
" Are they real Christians?" You know there are two kinds
of so-called " Christians." First, there are those who profess
to be Christians but who are not, and there are those who
profess to be Christians and really are. That is to say, there
are those who profess to be Christians but they are holding
on to the world with one hand and holding on to Jesus Christ
with the other hand, and it is usually the right hand with
which they are holding on to the world, and the left hand with
which they are holding on to Jesus Christ. I am perfectly
willing to admit that that kind of " Christians " haven't " joy
unspeakable and full of glory." They have " just enough
religion to make them miserable." But I am not speaking
of that kind of Christians, I am speaking of real Christians,
those who have let go of the world with both hands, and have
taken hold of Jesus Christ with both hands, those who have
made a full surrender to Jesus Christ, and I affirm tonight
that all such Christians have " joy unspeakable and full of
glory," and no one else has. It is at this point that Satan
deceives men and women when they are thinking of accepting
Christ, especially young men and young women. When a

young man or young woman begins to think seriously of accepting Jesus Christ Satan comes and whispers, " Don't accept Jesus Christ; for, if you do, you will have to give up this, and this, and this," and he mentions pretty much everything of which the young man or woman is particularly fond, and then he adds, " It will take all the brightness, and all the sunshine, and all the light-heartedness, and all the joy out of your life to become a Christian." Now this statement of Satan's is a lie. Our Lord Jesus tells us that the Devil " is a liar and the father of it," and this is one of his favourite and most palpable lies. If one would only stop to think he would see at once that it was a lie; for anyone in this world who has two open eyes in his head must see that the happiest people, the most radiantly happy people, the most constantly happy people, are the real Christians. So far from its taking all the brightness and all the sunshine, and all the light-heartedness and all the joy out of life to become a Christian, we never know what real brightness and real sunshine and real light-heartedness and real joy are until we do take Him. Ask anyone who has ever tried the world and afterwards tried Jesus Christ whether he has found a better and more satisfying joy in Jesus Christ than he has in the world, and you will always get the same answer, no matter how unusual and how great his opportunities for enjoying the world may have been, and how completely he may have tasted the joys of the world; with absolute unanimity all those who have tried the world and have really tried Jesus Christ, will tell you that they have found in Jesus Christ a joy immeasurably better, truer, nobler, more satisfying, more enduring, more overflowing than they have ever found in the world. Take my own experience. I tried the world for all there was in it, tried it with such opportunities for trying it as very few men or women enjoy. I know practically everything this world has to give, and then I tried Jesus Christ; and my testimony is the same as that of every other person who has ever really tried the world, and then tried Jesus Christ. I have found in Jesus Christ a joy that is immeasurably deeper, higher, purer, more satisfying, more enduring, more wonderful and glorious in every way than I ever found in the world. When you have the absolutely unanimous testimony of all competent witnesses, that is of all who have had personal experience, if you are an honest and reasonable man you are bound to believe; therefore, it does not admit of a moment's intelligent question that there is a far better joy in Jesus Christ than any this world has to give.

It is strange how anyone can be deceived by the Devil's lie that it takes all the joy and sunshine out of life to accept Jesus Christ and surrender to Him.   But yet Satan does succeed with countless thousands in deceiving them at that very point.   He deceived me at that point for several dark, bitter years.   As a young boy I was brought face to face with the question, would I accept Jesus Christ?   There was a large room in the third story of our country home where we used to put the old books out of our library and I loved to go into that room alone, sit on the floor and gather around me some of those old books, rummaging through them.   One day I picked up a book that belonged to my mother, the covenant of the church of which she was a member.   I wondered whether I could not be a Christian and so I began to read that book.   When I read the first thing I said, " Why I could say Yes to that," and the next, " I could say Yes to that," and the next, " I could say Yes to that," and I was getting along finely—until I came to something to the effect that if I became a Christian I must be willing to go wherever God told me to go, and to do anything God told me to do, and to be anything God told me to be.   I closed the book and flung it across the room and said, " Never, just as like as not God would tell me to be a preacher," and I had made up my mind to be a lawyer as so many in my father's family had been before me.   I settled it then and there that I would not be a Christian.   Then I went in for a life of pleasure.   I had every opportunity that this world affords for finding it.   My father was rich, we had a beautiful home, great grounds, and lawns and gardens, and barns and stables and horses and carriages, and servants and pretty much everything that money could buy.   Furthermore I was sent off to Yale College when I was only fifteen years of age.   Now, you take a young fellow in Yale with a rich father back of him who sends him all the money he asks for, and never asks him how he spends a penny of it (it would have been a good thing for me some-

times if he had asked me), and who learns easily and can
stand well in his classes without doing much studying, if any
man on earth can have a good time he can. And I went in
for a good time. Did I find it? I did not, I found disappointment, and wretchedness, and gloom. Then I plunged
more deeply into the dissipations of this world to find joy.
Did I find it? I did not, I found utter bitterness, disappointment and despair, until one awful night, still a very young
man, but life already burned out, I sprang out of my bed in
the dark in the middle of the night in great agony, the agony
of a great and nameless horror, and rushed to my washstand
drawer and drew it open to take out the instrument that would
put an end to the whole miserable business. I could not find
it. I don't know to this day why I could not find it, for I
am confident it was there, except that God would not let me
find it—and I sank down on my knees before that open drawer
and I said, " Oh God, if You will take this awful burden off
my heart I will preach the Gospel." I did not hope to find
joy. I hoped I might get rid of some of my misery. To my
utter amazement, however, by that step and the steps that
followed it I found a joy deeper and purer and more satisfying than I dreamed was possible, and for many, many long
years that joy has been getting better every year. Oh, men
and women, especially young men and women, if you wish
to find the purest, deepest, most satisfying, most enduring,
most exceeding and glorious joy that is to be known this side
of heaven, take the Lord Jesus Christ, and take Him tonight.

3.   In the third place, *Not to be a Christian costs the sacrifice of hope.* A Christian has hope. As we read in Titus
1:2, " In hope of eternal life, which God, who cannot lie,
promised." See how sure that hope is resting upon the Word
of God, " Who can not lie." See how magnificent it is,
" HOPE OF ETERNAL LIFE." Has the world anything to put
up against that? And you all know that hope for the future
is more important than present possession. " No," a man up
yonder in the gallery says, " I do not know that and I do not
believe it. Give me the present and let the future take care
of itself." Yes, you do believe it. There is not a man in
this building tonight who does not believe that hope for the
future is more important than present possession. " No," that

man insists, " I do not believe it." Yes you do, and I will prove to you that you do inside of five minutes. Suppose you had your choice tonight between being a millionaire with all that millions could buy but no hope for tomorrow, but with the rising of tomorrow's sun and the opening of tomorrow's banks to be proved to be an embezzler, and all your money swept away and you cast into prison to spend the remainder of your life there, or to be penniless tonight, but with the absolutely certain hope that with the rising of tomorrow's sun, and the opening of tomorrow's banks you were to be a millionaire all the rest of your life, which would you choose? " Why," you reply, " I would choose to be penniless tonight but with the absolute certainty that tomorrow and all the rest of my life I would be a millionaire." So would I, but don't you see that proves that you believe that hope for tomorrow is more important than possession today, that hope for the future is more important than present possession? And I would rather be the poorest child of God who walks this earth tonight with the absolutely certain hope that with the rising of eternity's sun, and the opening of eternity's banks, I was to be to all eternity an heir of God and joint-heir with Jesus Christ, than to be the richest man out of Christ that there is on earth tonight but with no outlook for all eternity but to be cast into God's eternal prison house of hell.

When you get right down to it, a man out of Christ has no hope that is at all sure even for the life that now is. " Oh," someone may say, " that is going altogether too far. A man out of Christ may have no hope for eternity but if he has plenty of money, if he is well fixed in this world, he has at least a good hope for many years to come." No, not a hope at all sure. Come with me to New York City. We go up Fifth Avenue to about Fifty-second Street. We stop before one of the finest mansions on Fifth Avenue. We enter the front gate, ascend the steps, ring the bell, and are ushered in. We walk down a long hall to the library at the end of the hall. As we look in we see two men in deep and earnest conversation. One of them is the richest man of his day in America, worth one hundred and ninety-six millions of dollars by an actual inventory of his property taken a few days after the day of which I am now speaking. The other one is one of America's great financiers who is trying to show this one hundred and ninety-six millionaire how to make his one hundred and ninety-six millions two hundred millions by an investment in Balitmore and Ohio stock. As we look in you whisper to me, " I don't know anything about that man's religious convictions, I know nothing about his eternal prospects, but he is well fixed for many years to come as far as this world is concerned. I would like to be in his shoes." You are greatly mistaken, for while we are still looking in the door that one hundred and ninety-six millionaire falls forward out of his chair on to his face on the floor, and when Mr. Garrett picks Wm. H. Vanderbilt from the floor he is a corpse. For all his one hundred and ninety-six millions he had no hope for five minutes. I told this story one day in western Pennsylvania in a men's meeting. There was in my audience a gentleman who was himself several times a millionaire. At the close of the meeting he came to me and said, " I have a country home seven miles out in the country. Won't you come out and spend the night with me? I will bring you back tomorrow to your meetings." I consented. When he got into the carriage he dismissed his driver and drove the span himself. He was rather quiet until we got well out of town, then he turned suddenly to me and said, " Why didn't you tell the rest of that story?" I replied, " The rest of what story?" " The rest of that story about Wm. H. Vanderbilt and Quincy Garrett; it would have proved your point as well as the part you told, for Quincy Garrett died in a madhouse."

Oh, men and women, we are all of us like men and women standing on the seashore, looking out over the broad ocean of eternity, and as we look out over the broad ocean of eternity toward some of us—those of us who have a living faith in Jesus Christ—there come gallant vessels laden with gold and silver and precious stones, with every sail set, wafted swiftly toward us by the breezes of the Divine favour, but toward the rest of us as we stand looking out over that broad ocean of eternity—those of us who are out of Christ—toward us there come no vessels but dismantled wrecks, with no cargoes but the livid corpses of lost opportunities, over which are hovering the vultures of eternal despair, driven madly towards us by the fast rising blasts of the indignation of a Holy and an outraged God. That is what it costs not to be a Christian.

4. In the fourth place, *Not to be a Christian costs the sacrifice of the highest manhood and the highest womanhood.* Have you ever thought of it, everyone of us has fallen away from God's ideal of manhood through sin. As Paul puts it in his graphic and expressive way in Rom. 3:23, " All have sinned, and *fall short of the glory of God."* That is God's ideal of manhood, " the glory of God " reincarnated in your life and mine, and we have all fallen short of it by sin; and the only way back to God's ideal of manhood is by the accept- ance of Jesus Christ and the regenerating and transforming power of God in Him. The best that any man or any woman out of Christ can attain unto, is a mere caricature of God's ideal of manhood or of womanhood. Is there any man here tonight so lost to all that is high, all that is true, all that is really manly that you are willing to be a mere caricature of God's ideal of manhood? Well, that is what it costs not to be a Christian. Is there a woman here tonight who is so utterly lost to all that is high and pure and true and noble and really womanly that she is willing to be a mere caricature of womanhood as God created woman to be? That is what it costs not to be a Christian. And if there were not a single other argument for becoming a Christian, if I were not a Christian, I would come to Christ tonight on that argument alone.

5. In the next place, *Not to be a Christian costs the sacri- fice of God's favour.* We have all lost God's favour by sin and the only way back to God's favour is by the acceptance of the Sin-Bearer Whom God Himself has provided. How plain the Bible is about that. Read John 3:36, " He that be- lieveth on the Son hath everlasting life, and he that *believeth not the Son* shall not see life, but the *wrath of God abideth on him."* It is not so much that the wrath of God is coming upon one who does not receive Jesus Christ in some future awful day of judgment, but the " wrath of God," the burning, intense displeasure of God, rests tonight upon every man and woman in this audience who is out of Christ. " Well," some man will say, " I suppose that is true, but I don't know whether I care so much about that after all. ' The dis-

pleasure of God'? Who is God anyway? Oh," you say, " I suppose that there is a God but He is so far away, so mystical, so shadowy, so unreal that He is no real factor in my life. If I have the favour of my family, the favour of my neighbours, the favour of my employer, the favour of my business associates, the favour of my political constituents, the favour of the men and women with whom I come in constant contact, I do not know as I care so very much whether I have the favour of that far-away Being that you call God or not." Stop a moment and think. When you go out of this building tonight look up toward the heavens, look at those wonderful worlds of light which men call stars, about which the astronomers are telling us such wonderful things in your day and mine, and say to yourself, " The great God Who made those wonderful worlds of light that men call stars, the God Who holds them in the hollow of His hand as they go whirling through space with such incredible momentum, that God loves me, but He is displeased with me." When you lie down to sleep tonight and cannot sleep, perhaps cannot sleep for thinking of this sermon—for I verily believe that there are many of you here tonight who if you do not accept Christ and confess Him before you leave this building tonight, will not get much sleep when you get home,—when you lie there alone and cannot sleep, and the rest of the house is hushed in slumber and you lie there alone—alone with God—looking up into God's face as you lie there, and God looking down not into your face only, but into your heart, say to yourself as you lie there, " Yon great God into Whose face I am now looking up, and Who is looking down not into my face only but into my heart, that God loves me,—but He is displeased with me." Men and women, if I had to face that thought tonight I would not try to sleep until I found peace with God, if there were any way to find it, and thank God, there is.

6.   In the next place, *Not to be a Christian costs the sacrifice of Christ's acknowledgment in the world to come.* The words of our Lord Jesus Christ Himself are perfectly plain about that. Read what He says in Matt. 10:32, 33, " Whosoever therefore shall confess Me before men, him will I confess also before My Father which is in Heaven. But whosoever shall deny Me before men, him will I also deny before

My Father which is in Heaven." That is plain enough, is it
not? Yet we are living in a day of such superficial thought
that there are many who will tell you, yes, even many alleged
" ministers of the Gospel " who will tell you, that if a man has
faith in Jesus Christ in his heart he does not need to confess
Him with the mouth, but God Who looks upon the secret heart
sees that faith, and justifies him on the ground of that faith
which he has in his heart but never confesses. I challenge
any man to show me one single line between the covers of this
Book which properly interpreted in its context will permit of
any such an interpretation. " But," you say, " are we not
saved by faith?" Yes, we are saved by faith, but we are
saved by a real faith, and real faith in Christ always leads to
open confession of Christ. Read what God says in Rom. 10:9,
10, " If thou shalt *confess with thy mouth Jesus* as Lord, and
shalt believe in thy heart that God raised Him from the dead,
thou shalt be saved: for with the heart man believeth unto
righteousness; and with the mouth *confession is made unto
salvation*." Listen again to the words of Jesus Christ Himself, " Whosoever therefore *shall confess Me before men,* him
will I confess also before My Father which is in Heaven. But
whosoever shall deny Me before men, him will I also deny
before My Father which is in Heaven." That is plain enough,
isn't it? And read another utterance of Jesus Christ in
Mark 8:38, " Whosoever therefore shall be ashamed of Me
and of My words in this adulterous and sinful generation, of
him also shall the Son of Man be ashamed when He cometh
in the glory of His Father with the holy angels." That is
plain enough, isn't it? I can imagine that great day when our
Lord Jesus summons all His own before the bar of God.
There they stand in bright and shining array, the Lord Jesus
Christ Himself at the head of that glorious company, and now
the Lord Jesus turns to God the Father, and with a glad wave
of His hand He says, " All these are Mine. They confessed
Me on earth before men. I now confess them before Thee,
My Father in Heaven." But look! look! There on the outskirts of that glorious company stands a man. He hung upon
the outskirts of the Church of Jesus Christ when He was here
upon earth. His sympathies were with the church, his asso-
ciations were largely with the church, his gifts to the church

were generous, very likely his wife was a member of the church. But the man himself, was a coward, he was afraid of others in the lodge or club or union. He was afraid of his business associates or political associates. He never came out and publicly confessed his Lord before the world, and now he thinks that because he has hung upon the outskirts of the church here upon earth he can hang upon the outskirts of the church up there; but now the Lord Jesus Christ turns to him —I do not believe it will be so much in anger as in unutterable pity—and with a sad wave of His hand He says, " Depart, depart, you did not confess Me upon earth before men. I cannot confess thee before My Father which is in Heaven." That is what it costs not to be a Christian, not to be an open, confessed, whole-hearted follower of Jesus Christ.

7.   Just once more, *Not to be a Christian costs the sacrifice of eternal life, and means to perish forever.* How plain the Word of God is about that. Read the words of our Lord Jesus Himself in John 3:14, 15, " And as Moses lifted up the serpent in the wilderness, even so must the Son of Man be lifted up: that whosoever believeth in Him should not perish, but have eternal life." How plain that is. " Believe "— " have eternal life," not believe—" perish." Read John 3:16, " For God so loved the world that He gave His Only begotten Son, that whosoever believeth in Him should not perish, but have everlasting life." How plain that is. " Believe "— have everlasting life, not believe—" perish." Just one more, John 3:36, " He that believeth on the Son hath everlasting life: and he that believeth not the Son shall not see life; but the wrath of God abideth on him." How plain that is. Believe—" have everlasting life," not believe—" the wrath of God abideth on him."

Do you ask me what eternal life means? I cannot tell you. I can tell you what its beginnings are, for I have them already in my heart tonight, but what eternal life means in the full outworking of an endless eternity in personal and intimate fellowship with God, no human language can describe, no human imagination can conceive. But I tell you what to do. Take that moment in your own life whose joy was highest, purest, deepest, most thrilling, most satisfying, most overflowing, most glorious and unutterable, that moment of su-

premest joy that you have ever known in all your life, multiply that by infinity, and carry it out to all eternity, and you
will have some faint conception of what " ETERNAL LIFE "
means.

And now do you ask me what it means to " perish "? I
can tell you that even less than the other. The beginnings
of what it means to " perish," we see in the men and women
who have gone down deepest into sin, in the corruption of their
nature, in the depravity of their character, in their utter and
hopeless bondage, in their degradation and shame and agony
and despair. But what it means to " perish " in the full out-
workings of an endless eternity separated from God, no human
language can describe, no human imagination can fancy. But
I will tell you what to do, take that moment in your own life
whose sorrow was heaviest to bear, whose anguish was keenest, whose agony was most crushing, whose midnight darkness
of shame and anguish and despair were most unutterable,
multiply that blackest midnight of anguish and despair and
shame you ever knew by infinity and carry it out to all eternity, and you will have some faint conception of what it means
to " perish."   And that is what it costs not to be a Christian.

Are you ready to pay this awful cost of not being a Christian, this awful cost of living and dying without Jesus Christ?
If you are not, in a few moments I am going to ask you to do
the only manly and womanly thing there is to do under the
circumstances, stand right up here and avow publicly your
acceptance of Jesus Christ. But before I do that I want you
to consider for a few moments the other side, what it costs to
be a Christian. If you become a Christian it very likely will
cost you the loss of friends who are very dear to you now. I
do not think that many ever came to Christ without losing
some of the friendships of the past. If you become a Christian it will cost you the loss of pleasures of which you are
very fond. I do not think anyone ever became a Christian
without having to give up some of the pleasures of the past.
If you become a Christian it may cost you the loss of money.
The night when I preached upon this subject in the Royal
Albert Hall in London, one of the first men who arose and
who afterwards came down to the front and publicly confessed
Christ, it cost him the loss of half of his income. He said

to me, "If I become a Christian I will have to give up my secret commissions, will I not?" I said, "You certainly will." "Well," he said, "half of my income is from my secret commissions, and if I become a Christian and have to give them up it will cut my income right in two in the middle." But the man became a Christian that night and gave up his secret commissions. Some months afterward in another part of London he came to me and said, "That night that I accepted Christ in the Royal Albert Hall it cost me half my income, but I have never regretted it to this day." If you become a Christian it may cost you the giving up of some of your most cherished ambitions. It did me. It took me out of one profession into another. But here is my question, Are you willing for the sake of a few Godless companions that you are better off without anyway, for the sake of a few unworthy pleasures that never satisfy and cannot last, for the sake of a few hundred dollars or even thousands or millions of dollars, that clutch never so tightly, you cannot take into the grave with you, and which only serve to make a death-bed miserable, are you willing for the sake of things like these, to give up peace and joy and hope and manhood or womanhood and God's favour and Christ's acknowledgment and eternal life, and perish forever? If you are, I have nothing more to say. If you are not, in a few moments I shall ask you to stand up and publicly confess your acceptance of Jesus Christ right here and now.

One night when Dr. MacArthur had finished preaching in the Calvary Baptist Church in New York City, a gentleman came to him and said, "Dr. MacArthur, I wish to ask you a question." "What is your question?" replied Dr. MacArthur. "My question is this, if I become a Christian must I give up my money?" Dr. MacArthur answered wisely, "If you become a Christian and Jesus Christ tells you to give up your money you must be ready to give it up, every penny of it, if Jesus Christ tells you to." The man hesitated a moment and then said, "Dr. MacArthur, I will take a week to think about it." At the close of the week he came back to Dr. MacArthur. There was a look of awful determination on his face. He said, "Dr. MacArthur, I have settled it. I will hold on to my money till death, and if Christ and Heaven must go, they must

go." That was a terrible decision, but it was an intelligent
one. Are you willing to say that tonight, " I will hold on to
my money till death, I will hold on to my Godless companions
till death, I will hold on to my worldly pleasures till death,
I will hold on to my personal ambitions till death, I will hold
on to my sin till death, I will hold on to this, or that that
stands between me and Jesus Christ till death, and if Christ
and Heaven must go, and peace must go, and joy must go, and
hope must go, and manhood or womanhood must go, and
God's favour must go, and Christ's acknowledgment must go,
and eternal life must go, and eternal death come, let them go
and let it come "? Are you willing to say that? That is
what you do say practically if you go out of this place tonight
without accepting Jesus Christ.

On the night I spoke on this subject in the Royal Albert
Hall in London there sat on the platform a distinguished
colonel in the British Army. He had a brilliant military
record, but he was not a Christian (though he was a Church
member). Indeed, he was far from being a Christian. His
friends had induced him to come to hear me that night by
promising him a seat on the platform where no one would be
likely to speak to him. Just to the left of the raised platform on which I stood sat Lord Kinnaird, chairman of our
committee. Next to him sat the Marquis of Wimburne, next
to him sat Bishop Taylor-Smith, Chaplain-General of His
Majesty's forces, and next to him sat this dashing English
colonel recently returned from the Boer War. As I spoke
upon the subject upon which I am speaking tonight he became interested, and more and more interested as I proceeded.
When I reached the conclusion of my sermon he was all interest, and no sooner had the invitation for everyone to stand
who would then and there accept Jesus Christ as their personal Saviour, and surrender to Him as their Lord and Master,
and confess Him as such before the world, and strive to live
from that time on to please Him in everything from day to
day, fallen from my lips than Col. Horace Beauchamp, afterwards Sir Horace Beauchamp, sprang to his feet and stood,
as the London papers described it the next morning, " like
the brave soldier he was," and as the papers also said the next
day, " he had scarcely risen when three hundred men sprang

to their feet all over the Royal Albert Hall and followed the dashing colonel into the breach." Within a week he was witnessing for Christ throughout London. When the late war broke out he went to the front and fell leading a desperate charge at Gallipoli.

Who of you tonight will take here right now the stand the brave colonel took that night?

IX

THE MOST IMPORTANT QUESTION THAT ANY MAN EVER ASKED OR ANSWERED

" What then shall I do with Jesus which is called Christ?"
—MATTHEW 27 : 22.

MY subject tonight is, The most important question that any man ever asked or answered. You will find that question in Matt. 27:22, " What shall I do then with Jesus which is called Christ?" I say that this is the most important question that any man ever asked or answered; for if we do the right thing with Jesus Christ we shall get everything that is worth having for time and for eternity, but if we do the wrong thing with Jesus Christ we shall lose everything that is worth having for time and for eternity.

Let me call your attention to some of the things that depend entirely upon what one does with Jesus Christ.

I.   OUR ACCEPTANCE BEFORE GOD

First of all, *Our acceptance before God depends entirely upon what we do with Jesus Christ.* If you accept Jesus Christ God will accept you, no matter who you are, what you have been or what you may have done in the past: on the other hand, if you reject Jesus Christ, God will reject you, no matter what else you may do, no matter who you are, no matter what you have been or what you may have done in the past. Our acceptance before God depends solely and entirely upon what we do with Jesus Christ. The Word of God makes this as plain as day: we read in John 3:18, " He that believeth on Him is not condemned: but he that believeth not is condemned already, because he hath not believed in the name of the only begotten Son of God." Here we are told that the one that " believeth on Him " (no matter who he is or what he has done) is not condemned, but that the one " that believeth not " is condemned already (no matter who he is or what else he may have done). There is just one reason for

157

his condemnation, " *because he hath not believed* in the name of the only begotten Son of God." Nothing could make it plainer that our acceptance before God depends entirely on what we do with Jesus Christ, that if we accept Jesus Christ, God will accept us, and if we reject Jesus Christ, God will reject us.

Our acceptance before God does not depend upon our own good works. In order to be accepted before God on the ground of our own good works our works must be absolutely perfect, for God is a perfect God and nothing but perfect works can satisfy a perfect God. If anyone of us should perfectly keep the law of God from the hour of our birth to the hour of our death we would be accepted before God on the ground of our own good works. But not one of us has ever done it; so no man is accepted before God on the ground of his own good works. We are told over and over again in God's own Word that " *by works of law* shall no flesh be justified in His sight." (Rom. 3:20, see Greek.) All that the law does for us is to bring us to a consciousness of sin, a realization that we have broken the law of God (Rom. 3:20).

The law of God demands absolutely perfect obedience: the moment any man breaks the law of God at any point that moment acceptance before God on the ground of good works becomes an impossibility. As we read in Gal. 3:10, " As many as are of works of law are under the curse: for it is written, Cursed is everyone who continueth not *in all things* that are written in the book of the law, to do them." If a man should keep the law of God a hundred years and then break it at any point he would be under the curse of the broken law of God; and everyone of us has already broken the law of God, and therefore every one of us is under the curse of the broken law of God, as far as our works are concerned. So, acceptance before God on the ground of works is an absolute impossibility. Of all the men who have ever lived upon this earth or who live upon it now, not one single man ever has been or ever will be accepted before God on the ground of his own good works. Men oftentimes say to me, " My life is just as good as that of such and such a Christian and therefore if he is saved I ought to be." Now, if salvation were by works, that would be a perfectly good argument; but as no man is saved by works, Christian or non-Christian, the argument falls to the ground. The Christian man is not saved by his works, neither is the unchristian man; and though it were true that your works were just as good as those of the Christian they would not save you, for he is saved, not by his works but through his acceptance of Jesus Christ, and that is the only way that you can be saved.

No man is saved by his own good character. In order to be saved by our own good character our character must be absolutely, flawlessly holy; for God is an infinitely Holy God and nothing but absolute perfection will satisfy an infinitely Holy God, and not one of us ever has maintained a flawlessly holy character. We hear a great deal in these days about "*salvation by character*," but such a thing is an absolute impossibility. We are not " saved *by* character ": we are saved *to* character: that is to say, a holy character is not the ground upon which we are saved, it is the result of our having been saved.

There is but one ground upon which any man is saved and that ground is the atoning death of Jesus Christ on the cross of Calvary where our sins were laid upon Him and settled forever. There is but one condition upon which any man is saved and that one condition is, believing on Him Who made the perfect atonement on the cross of Calvary. Paul puts it very plainly in Rom. 3:22-26, " For all have sinned, and fall short of the glory of God; being *justified freely* by His grace through the redemption that is in Christ Jesus: Whom God set forth to be a propitiation, through faith, in His blood, to show His righteousness because of the passing over of the sins done aforetime, in the forbearance of God; for the showing, I say, of His righteousness at this present season: that He might Himself be just, and *the justifier of him that hath faith in Jesus*." Paul puts the same thought in another way in the next chapter, Rom. 4:5, " But *to him that worketh not, but believeth on Him that justifieth the ungodly, his faith is reckoned for righteousness*." The moment any man believes on Jesus Christ, receives Jesus Christ as his personal Saviour, and surrenders to Him as his Lord and Master, that moment his sins are all blotted out and all the perfect righteousness of God in Jesus Christ is put to his account. If the vilest man or woman in this city should come into this building to-night and should here and now accept Jesus Christ as their personal Saviour, that moment their sins would all be blotted out and their record would be as white in God's sight as that of the purest angel in heaven.

Some years ago I was preaching one morning in the city of Chicago on Rom. 8:1, " There is therefore now no condemnation to them that are in Christ Jesus," and I made this remark, " If the vilest woman in Chicago should come into this building this morning and should here and now accept Jesus Christ as her personal Saviour, the moment she did it every sin she ever committed would be blotted out, and her record would be as white in God's sight as that of the purest woman in the room." Unknown to me, one of the members of my own congregation had gone that morning down into a vile den of iniquity and invited a woman who was one of the lowest of outcasts to come and hear me preach. The woman replied, " I never go to church. I would not be welcome at church," to which the woman who was a saint replied, " You will be welcome at our church," which, thank God, was true. " No," the woman said, " I never go to church. Church is not for the likes of me." Then the woman who was a saint said, " If you will go with me, I will go with you." " No, no," the other repled, " that would never do. The policemen know me and the boys on the street know me and sometimes they throw stones at me, and if they saw you walking up the street with me they would think you were just such as I am." To this the saintly woman, who had the spirit of the Master, replied, " I don't care what they think of me. If you will go with me, I will go with you." But the other one still refused. As the woman who was a saint kept urging her, finally she consented to this arrangement, that the woman who was a saint should go a few steps ahead and the woman who was a sinner should follow closely behind her. So on up LaSalle Avenue they came, the woman who was a saint a few steps ahead and the woman who was a sinner a few steps behind. Block after block they walked until they reached the corner of Chicago Avenue, where the Moody Church was then located. The woman who was a saint went up the stairs, opened the door, passed into the auditorium and took a seat. The woman who was a sinner timidly followed, fearfully opened the door, looked in, saw a vacant seat in the last pew underneath the gallery, stole in and dropped into that seat. She had been in but a few moments when I made the remark I just quoted, " If the vilest woman in Chicago should come to this church this morning and should here and now accept Jesus Christ as her personal Saviour, the moment she did it all her sins would be blotted out and her record would be as white in God's sight as that of the purest woman in the room." My words went floating down over the heads of the audience and dropped into the heart of the woman who was a sinner as she sat in the last seat under the gallery. She believed it, she saw Jesus Christ hanging upon the cross and all her sins laid upon Him and settled forever, she put her trust in Him, and instantly her sins were all blotted out, and the perfect righteousness of God was put to her account and her record was as white in God's sight as that of the purest woman in the room. When the service was over, as I stepped down from the platform this woman came walking up the aisle with the tears streaming down her cheeks, to thank me for the blessing she had received that morning.

I repeat that statement here tonight: If the vilest woman in this city (or the vilest man) should come into this building tonight and should here and now believe God's testimony about Jesus Christ, that all their sins were laid upon Him and settled forever, and should here and now put her trust in Jesus Christ as her own atoning Saviour, the moment she did it every sin she ever committed would be blotted out and all the perfect righteousness of God in Jesus Christ would be put to her account, and her record would be as white in God's sight as that of the purest woman in the room. If you accept Jesus Christ, God will accept you, but if you reject Jesus Christ, God will reject you. Will you accept Him tonight?

II. Our Finding Peace of Conscience Depends Entirely on What We Do With Jesus Christ

In the second place, *Our finding peace of conscience depends entirely on what we do with Jesus Christ.* As we read in Rom. 5:1, " Being therefore justified by faith, *we have peace with God* through our Lord Jesus Christ." The world

is full of men and women who are seeking peace of conscience,
but the great mass of men are seeking peace of conscience in
ways that peace of conscience was never found. Many are
seeking peace of conscience by turning over a new leaf and
leading a better life, but no man ever found peace of conscience in that way. Many are seeking peace of conscience
by saying many prayers and doing many penances, but not
one man or woman in all this world's history ever found true
peace of conscience in that way. Many are seeking peace of
conscience by doing good works, by giving to the poor or to
the work of the church. That accounts for many of the large
gifts that rich men are giving today. They have done wrong.
Very likely they have accumulated their wealth by crooked
practices and their consciences trouble them and they fancy
if they give a part of their ill-gotten wealth to the poor or to
the church they will find peace of conscience. But no one
ever found peace of conscience through his gifts, whether they
were small or great.

There is but one ground upon which any man ever found
true and lasting peace of conscience, and that ground is the
atoning death of Jesus Christ upon the cross of Calvary, and
there is only one condition upon which any man or woman
ever found deep and lasting peace of conscience, and that is
the condition of believing on and accepting as their own personal Saviour the One Who bore their sins in His Own Body
on the cross of Calvary. The moment anyone truly believes
on Jesus Christ, that moment he finds peace, but if one will
not believe on Jesus Christ there is absolutely nothing else he
can do that will bring him peace.

Years ago there was a very brilliant student in a German
university, a student of philosophy, but he was leading a
worldly, reckless life. One time as he was riding through a
forest with another student, a thunder-storm came up and a
flash of lightning instantly killed his fellow-student. That set
him to thinking, but he did not give up his careless life even
yet. Some time afterward, as he was going through the forest
again, his sword hanging by his side after the manner of the
students of that day, somehow or other the sword pierced an
artery in his leg and he nearly bled to death before help could
be secured. That set him to thinking still more deeply. He

gave up his reckless life. He entered upon a religious life. After the custom of the day, he went into a monastery to lead a " religious " life as a monk. He subjected himself to all manner of austerities. He would spend long nights and days in vigils and in fastings. Sometimes his fellow monks would find him lying unconscious on the stone floor of his cell, overcome by the severities to which he subjected himself, but still he did not find peace. He started on a long pilgrimage from Germany to Rome on foot, but he did not find peace. At Rome he started to go up the Scala Pilati on his knees, hoping by this penance to find peace. Wearily he toiled up the long stairway, but before he reached the top a verse in the chained Bible that he had read in the monastery came to his mind, " The just shall live by faith." He saw Jesus Christ on the cross bearing all his sins, put his trust in Him as his personal Saviour, sprang to his feet and came bounding down the steps with a heart full of peace, and shook all Europe and the world by preaching Justification by faith by simple faith in Jesus Christ,—Martin Luther.

I had a very dear friend. Before he became my friend he had led a reckless life. He had been one of the most notorious professional gamblers in the South. He had one gambling house in Atlanta and another in Nashville. One night as he sat at the gaming table the man across the table accused him of dishonesty at the cards. Quick as a flash he drew his revolver and fired it across the table. The bullet entered the other man's throat and he fell back from the table to the floor. Instantly the man who afterwards became my friend sprang up from his chair, ran around the table, lifted the other man's head from the floor on to his own knee, took out his handkerchief and tried to staunch the flow of blood as it gushed out from the wound. But it was too late, the wound was mortal and the other man died. The man who is now my friend was arrested, tried for murder, but acquitted on the ground that he shot the other man in self-defense. But though acquitted by a human court he was not acquitted before the bar of God and not acquitted before the bar of his own conscience. He became a haunted man. He tried in every way he could think of to find peace. He gave up his gambling and entered upon an honest life, but he did not find peace. He took up honest

work, but he did not find peace. He even went so far as to
unite with the church, but he did not find peace. He endured
two years of awful agony. One night he was in his room
alone, kneeling in prayer, and he cried to God, " Oh, God, will
nothing ever cleanse my conscience from the memory of the
awful thing I have done?" Just then the strains of the old
familiar hymn came running through his mind,

> " What shall wash away my stain?
> Nothing but the blood of Jesus;
> What will make me whole again?
> Nothing but the blood of Jesus."

He saw Jesus Christ upon the cross paying the penalty of
his sin. He put his trust in Jesus Christ then and there, and
he found peace; and for years Stephen Holcomb went up and
down this land preaching peace through simple faith in Jesus
Christ. There are some of you here tonight whose consciences
are tortured by memories of sins committed in the past. What
would you not give for peace? Listen! You may have peace
tonight. No matter how black or how great your sin, you
may have peace right now. But there is only one way to get
it, by believing God's testimony about Jesus Christ that your
sins were all laid upon Jesus Christ and settled forever, and
trusting God to forgive you because Jesus Christ died in your
place. The moment you will thus put your trust in Jesus
Christ, that moment you will find peace. And there is no
other way in which you can find peace. Any man's finding
peace of conscience depends entirely upon just one thing, his
accepting Jesus Christ. If you accept Jesus Christ you will
find peace, no matter who you are, no matter what you have
done, no matter how many and how black your sins may have
been, no matter what else you may do or may not do. But
if you reject Jesus Christ there is no other thing you can do
that will bring you peace.

III. OUR FINDING JOY THAT IS DEEP AND SATISFYING AND
LASTING DEPENDS ENTIRELY UPON WHAT WE DO
WITH JESUS CHRIST.

In the third place, *Our finding joy that is deep and satisfying and lasting depends entirely upon what we do with Jesus*

Christ. We read in I Pet. 1:8: " Though now ye see Christ not, yet believing (in Him), ye rejoice greatly with joy unspeakable and full of glory." Every man and woman in this world is seeking the same thing. They are all seeking joy. But the great mass of men and women are seeking joy in ways in which joy was never found. Many are seeking joy in the pursuit of wealth and in the accumulation of wealth. Not one single man or woman in all this world's history ever found joy that was deep and satisfying and lasting in that way. Others are seeking joy in the pleasures of this world, in the dance, in the card table, in the theatre, in the movies, in any or all of the countless forms of pleasure of the present day. Not one single man or woman in all this world's history ever found joy that was deep and satisfying and lasting in any or all the pleasures this world has to offer. Others are seeking their joy in higher ways; for example, in music and in art. But not one single man or woman in all this world's history ever found joy that was deep and satisfying and lasting in music or in art. Others are seeking joy in study, the study of science and philosophy, or of history, or of literature. Not one single man or woman in all this world's history ever found joy that was deep and satisfying and lasting in that way. Others are seeking their joy in the acceptance of Jesus Christ as their Saviour, in whole-hearted surrender to Him as their Lord and Master, and in open confession of Him before the world, and by a life of daily conformity to His will as revealed in His Word. Every man or woman who has sought their joy in this way has found it, great joy, " joy unspeakable and full of glory."

One night when I was preaching in Christ Church in New Zealand, as I sat on the platform a note was handed to me. It read like this:

" DEAR DR. TORREY,—
    Can you tell me where I can find joy that is deep and lasting and satisfying? I have sought it everywhere but have not found it. I have sought it in the possession of wealth, but I have not found it there. I have sought it in dissipation and sin, but I have not found it there. I have sought it in music and in art, but I have not found it there. I have sought it in the study of philosophy and science, but have not found it there. I have sought it

in travel, I am just back now from a trip around the world, but
I have not found it there.   Can you tell me where to find it?"

As I preached that night I read this note, which was un-
signed, and I replied, " Yes, I can tell this person where she
can find joy that is deep and satisfying and lasting.   She can
find it in Jesus Christ."   A lady came up to me at the close
of the meeting and said, " I wrote that note.   I have sought
joy that was deep and satisfying and lasting.   I have sought
it everywhere.   I have sought it in the possession of wealth
for I have wealth, but I have not found it there.   I have
sought it in the pleasures of the world, but I did not find it
there.   I have sought it in dissipation and sin, but I have not
found it there.   I have sought it in music and art, but I have
not found it there.   I have sought it in the study of philosophy and science, but have not found it there.   I have
sought it in travel, I am just back now from a trip around
the world, but I have not found it there."   I sat down and
took my Bible and showed her Jesus Christ as the One Who
bore her sins in His Own Body on the cross, and as a risen
Saviour who could save her from the power of sin, and she
accepted Jesus Christ that night.   The next night she came
back to the meeting again and she arose and said, " I have
been seeking joy that was deep and satisfying and lasting
wherever I thought it might be found.   I sought it in the possession of wealth, but I did not find it there.   I sought it in
the pleasures of the world, but I did not find it there.
I sought it in dissipation and sin, but did not find it there.   I
sought it in music and in art, but I did not find it there.   I
sought it in the study of philosophy and science, but I did not
find it there.   I sought it in travel, as you all know I am
just back from a trip around the world, but I did not find it
there.   But," she continued, " last night I accepted Jesus
Christ and I have found joy that is deep and satisfying and
lasting."   No one can find it anywhere else than in Christ.
Anyone can find it in Him.   Your finding joy that is deep
and satisfying and lasting depends entirely on what you do
with Jesus Christ.

We had at one time in our Institute in Chicago as a student
a very distinguished noblewoman, one who, because of her

long line of titled ancestry was spoken of as the " daughter of a hundred earls," Lady Henry Somerset.   The day she left the Institute she made a few farewell remarks, and in these she said, " Once in the homeland I was summoned to see a woman in a very high position.   I hurried to the palace of my friend.   As I went up the marble stairway and noticed the costly paintings upon the wall and the beautiful statuary that adorned the hall I said to myself, I wonder if all this wealth and magnificence makes my friend happy.   I had not long to wait for an answer; for my friend hurried into the room, dropped into a seat by my side and burst into a flood of tears and poured out her heart-breaking sorrow.   A short time afterwards I had occasion to call upon a poor blind woman.   It was a dark, dismal, rainy day, and as I entered the cottage the rain was dripping through the poorly thatched roof and gathering in a puddle at the blind woman's feet.   As I saw her sitting there in her blindness and poverty, before I thought what I was saying I asked, Maggie, are you not miserable?   Fastening her blind eyes upon me she said, ' What, lady, I miserable, I, a child of a King, and hurrying on to the Mansion He has gone to prepare, I miserable?   No! No! Lady, I am happy.' "   A simple faith in Jesus Christ had brought to the blind woman in all her poverty a joy that all the wealth and exalted position had not brought to the other woman in all her exalted position.   Yes, there is just one way to find joy that is deep and satisfying and lasting, and that is by accepting Jesus Christ, and anyone here tonight, no matter how great your poverty or your sorrows or your misfortunes may be, can find joy that is deep and satisfying and lasting by a simple faith in the crucified and risen Son of God.

IV. OUR OBTAINING ETERNAL LIFE DEPENDS ENTIRELY UPON WHAT WE DO WITH JESUS CHRIST

In the fourth place, *Our obtaining eternal life depends entirely upon what we do with Jesus Christ.* We read in I John 5:11, 12, " And the witness is this, that God gave unto us eternal life, and this life is in His Son.   He that hath the Son hath the life; he that hath not the Son of God hath not the life."   When God sent His Son, Jesus Christ, down into this world He sent down eternal life in Him, and the moment anyone accepts Jesus Christ, that moment he gets what is in Jesus Christ, he gets eternal life, and there is no other way in which anyone can get eternal life.

What strange ideas people have as to the way in which eternal life is to be obtained. If I should go down from this platform tonight and put to some of you the question, " What must one do to get eternal life?" some of you, even some of you Christians, would reply something like this, " If one will fight hard against temptation and overcome it, and strive to live every day a life that pleases God and will read his Bible regularly every day and pray often and unite with the church and be baptized and go regularly to the Lord's Table and work hard to bring others to Christ, then perhaps at the end of a long life of struggle and of victory, and of Bible study and faithfulness in the performance of church duties, he may get everlasting life." Thank God that is not the teaching of this Book! The teaching of this Book is that one gets eternal life in an instant by the simple acceptance of Jesus Christ. He gets eternal life as a free gift (Rom. 6:23), and in the power of this eternal life he gets as a free gift through simple faith in Jesus Christ, he gets the victory over temptation, he leads a life pleasing to God, he studies his Bible and prays and works faithfully and successfully for the Master Who has given him eternal life as a free gift. Anyone in this building tonight, no matter what your past has been, no matter how many sins you may have committed, even though you have been a rank and outrageous infidel and blasphemer, even though you have spoken in terms of utmost contempt of God and of Jesus Christ and of the Bible, you may get eternal life in an instant right now, by simply believing on Jesus Christ. On the other hand, if you do not accept Jesus Christ there is nothing else that you can do that will bring you eternal life. You may try to live just as good a life as you know how, you may go regularly to church, you may fight hard against temptation, you may join the church, you may be baptized, you may go regularly to the Lord's Supper, you may give a tenth of your income to the church and you may try to bring others to Christ, but unless you have accepted Jesus Christ as your personal Saviour, and surrendered to Him as your Lord and Master, all of these things, good as they may be in their place, will not bring you everlasting life. Everlasting life is a free gift of God's grace, "The wages of sin is death; but *the free gift of God* is eternal life *in Christ Jesus* our Lord." (Rom. 6:23.)

Some years ago I was preaching in the city of Minneapolis. The hall in which I was preaching was on a main thoroughfare with the door opening directly on to the sidewalk. The hall was a blaze of light; for I always felt that a mission or a church should be the brightest place on the street. A man came down the street who had made an utter shipwreck of life. At one time he had been up in the world, he had been postmaster of the town where he lived. But he had gone down and down through drink. For a while he had been a waiter in the lowest saloon in Minneapolis at that time, the Jumbo; but he had gotten so low that they kicked him out of there, and this night he came down the street with a ten-cent piece in his pocket, all he had in the world. He had in his mouth the stub of a cigar, which I think he had picked out of the gutter. He came by our hall and mistook it for a free lunch joint or something of that kind. He entered with the stub of the cigar in his mouth and his hat on one side of his head. A lady at the door asked him to let her have the stub of the cigar, which she set aside, and to take his hat off, and then she led him up the aisle to the very front seat in the hall, as all the rest of the hall was crowded. He sat down right in front of me. Another man who had been saved from the deepest depths of degradation by the Lord Jesus Christ, was giving his testimony and it was a remarkable testimony. The man who had come in was quite drunk, and as the other man gave his testimony he leered up at me and said, "Do you believe that?" I replied, "Yes, I know this man's testimony is true, and the same Christ that saved him can save you to-night." Then as the other man finished his testimony I said to him, "Joe, take this man around to my office." The man stepped down from the platform and took him to my office back of the platform, and when the meeting was over I went in there and spoke with him. He was somewhat sobered and as I presented Jesus Christ to him, even into his befuddled mind there came enough light for him to understand the truth, and he put his trust in Jesus Christ then and there, and the

moment he did it he obtained eternal life.   The ten-cent piece
he had in his pocket when he entered the room was gone and
we had to pay for his night's lodging.   The next day we got
work for him, a very humble job, peeling potatoes in a cheap
restaurant.   In a few days he got a better job and then he
got a position with the Maple Leaf Railway, for he was a man
of ability.   They promoted him rapidly from one position to
another.   In the meantime I had moved to Chicago and he
was thinking of coming to Chicago to study for the ministry.
But his health gave way.   The railroad company thought so
much of him that at their own expense they sent him down to
Missouri to recover his health, but he died.   In the meantime his mother had rejoined him; and after his death she
sent me his picture, saying, " You were kind to my boy when
he was down.   He has now gone Home and I am sending you
this picture to remember him by."   I wrote his story on the
back of the picture and put it on the mantelpiece in my office
in Chicago, and whenever I was tempted to be discouraged I
would turn round in my revolving chair and look at the picture on my mantelpiece.   The face was that of a Christian
gentleman.   You would never have believed he was ever down
in sin.   Drunk as he was, he got eternal life that night by
simply believing in Jesus Christ; and any man or woman in
this audience can get eternal life the same way tonight, and
there is not a man or woman here who can get it in any
other way.

Your obtaining eternal life depends entirely upon what you
do with Jesus Christ.

V. OUR BECOMING THE CHILDREN OF GOD DEPENDS
ENTIRELY UPON WHAT WE DO WITH JESUS CHRIST

In the fifth place, *Our becoming children of God depends
entirely upon what we do with Jesus Christ.*   We read in John
1:12, "*As many as received Him, to them gave He the right
to become children of God, even to them that believe on His
name.*"   Here we are distinctly told that we become the children of God by the one act of receiving Jesus Christ.   If you
will receive Jesus Christ you will be a child of God the instant
you do it.   If you will not receive Jesus Christ there is nothing else you can do that will make you a child of God.   Here

again many Christians have strange notions, strange notions
as to how one becomes a child of God. If I should come to
many of you who profess to be Christians, in this audience tonight, and put to you the question, " How does one become a
child of God," many of you would answer me something like
this, " To become a child of God one must give up every
known sin, he must fight hard against temptation and overcome it, he must live a holy life, he must read his Bible regularly and say his prayers every day, he must go to church
regularly and join the church and be baptized and partake
regularly of the Lord's Supper and give a tenth of his income
to the church, and then perhaps at the end of a long life of
victory over sin and faithful attendance upon religious duties
and of active service for Christ and of generous giving, he
may become a child of God."   Again I thank God, thank God
that that is not the doctrine of this Book.   God in His own
Word tells us, as we have just seen, that one becomes a child
of God by the simple act of accepting Jesus Christ, and that
he overcomes temptation and leads a holy life and studies his
Bible and prays and works hard to bring others to Christ and
gives generously of his money, not in order to become a child
of God, but because he already is a child of God.   Anyone
here can become a child of God in a moment.

One night at the close of one of my meetings in Chicago
one of my elders was going around speaking to one and another in the church. He stepped up to a man, a stranger, and
said to him, " Are you saved?"   The man very positively replied, " I am."   Then the elder asked him, " When were you
saved?"   He replied, " About five minutes ago, while that man
was preaching."   Yes, one can be saved as quickly as that:
one can become a child of God as quickly as that.   You can
become a child of God right as you sit there, before I give
out the invitation, by simply receiving Jesus Christ.   The first
time that I ever visited London, in September, 1883, I stopped
in a lodging house on Cecil Street just off the Strand.   On
Sunday afternoon I went out to take a walk and started for
" The Seven Dials."   I had often read of " The Seven Dials "
in Dickens and other books, and I wished to see them.   As
I followed the map in my guide book and went through the
tangle of narrow streets and alleys that led at that time from

the Strand to " The Seven Dials," I passed by a brick wall
and I saw a little notice upon it about a foot wide and a few
inches high. On this sign it said that at three o'clock that
afternoon there would be an open air meeting on " The Seven
Dials." I thought to myself, I am in luck, I will not only
see " The Seven Dials," but I will see a London open air
meeting. When I reached " The Seven Dials " I found that
on six of the seven corners there were saloons. It was a very
hot September afternoon and the doors of the saloons all stood
open and I could see in. What surprised me as an American
was to see about as many women in the saloons as there were
men. Very soon a brawling company of drunken women
came out on the street, fighting and clawing one another. I
can see vividly tonight one woman as another woman tore her
nails down her face, ripping off streaks of skin. It was an
awful sight. But just then a little company of men and
women stepped out on " The Seven Dials " and began singing
hymns, and the mob quieted down and gathered around. Some
of the mob were still turbulent and tried to disturb the meeting, but soon all was quiet. As I stood looking at the company of people holding the meeting in the street, a gentleman
who stood beside me said, " I don't believe in this sort
of thing." I replied, " I do." As the mob quieted a little
temporary platform was put up and a gentle faced Christian
woman ascended the platform and began to preach the Gospel
to the crowd. As she finished her short and interesting address she said, " There is a little chapel around the corner, and
if any of you are interested, come in there and we will tell
you more." Well, I was interested and so were many others,
and we entered the chapel. It was the smokiest, dingiest
chapel I ever saw in my life. But this sweet faced Christian
woman went and stood behind the altar and explained in a
clear way the way of life, and said, " If any of you are Christians, won't you speak to those who are not?" I looked across
that dismal room and over on the other side I saw one of the
most disgusting looking women I had ever seen in my life,
up to that time. She was clad in filthy rags. She seemed
to be about fifty years of age. Her skin looked like leather
and her cheeks hung down in heavy flabs. I thought to myself, that woman certainly is not a Christian, and I went over

and sat down beside her and explained to her the best I knew
how, the way of life. Then I asked her if she would accept
Jesus Christ then and there, and she said she would. We knelt
together in prayer. I prayed and the woman prayed. The best
she knew how, she accepted Jesus Christ. What did we have
kneeling there side by side? a minister of God and a London
outcast woman? No, two children of God. The moment that
woman accepted Jesus Christ she was just as truly a child of
God as I was. And anyone here tonight, no matter what your
outward life may have been, no matter how conscious you may
be of the vileness of your heart, no matter how bad you may
have been in the sight of man or God, if you will here and
now accept Jesus Christ as your personal Saviour, the moment
you do it you will be as truly a child of God as any man or
woman on earth or in heaven.

Twenty-two years later I was back in London again, holding meetings in a tabernacle that had been put up for me on
the Strand, at the very spot where I had left the Strand to go
through that network of alleys and narrow streets to " The
Seven Dials." In the course of my sermon that night I referred to this incident of twenty-two years before. At the
close of the meeting an usher came up to me and said, " There
is a woman in the audience that wishes me to tell you that
she is the woman you heard preach that afternoon on ' The
Seven Dials ' twenty-two years ago and that she is still
at the same old work."

There are other things that depend entirely upon what we
do with Jesus Christ, but I have said already enough to prove
the statement with which I began, that if you do the right
thing with Jesus Christ, you will get everything that is worth
having for time and for eternity; but, if you do the wrong
thing with Jesus Christ, you will lose everything that is worth
having for time and for eternity. If you accept Jesus Christ
God will accept you, but if you reject Jesus Christ God will
reject you. If you accept Jesus Christ you will have peace
of conscience; but if you reject Jesus Christ there is nothing
else you can do that will bring you peace of conscience. If
you accept Jesus Christ you will have joy that is deep and
satisfying and lasting; but if you reject Jesus Christ there is
nothing else you can do that will bring you joy that is deep

and satisfying and lasting. If you accept Jesus Christ you will get eternal life at once, as the free gift of God's grace; but if you reject Jesus Christ there is nothing else you can do that will bring you eternal life. If you accept Jesus Christ, in an instant you will become a child of God; but if you reject Jesus Christ there is nothing else you can do that will make you a child of God.

Will you accept Jesus Christ right now?

One night I was preaching in Philadelphia in the South Armory on South Broad Street. I had been preaching for six weeks at the North Armory at the corner of North Broad and Susquehanna Streets, but we had transferred our meetings to the South Armory, and this was the last night of the first week. I was preaching on the same text upon which I am preaching tonight. There had come into the meeting that night two of the most notorious ward politicians in that part of the city, Magistrate James Briggs, or " Jimmy Briggs " as he was popularly called, and Ed. Cook. I don't think they had come from any desire to hear me or even out of mere curiosity. I think they wanted to see what was going on in their political bailiwick, but as I preached Magistrate Briggs became very much interested. One sentence that I uttered rivetted itself in his mind, " If you accept Jesus Christ God will accept you, but if you reject Jesus Christ God will reject you." He went out of the meeting without speaking to anyone and went to his home. Entering his home he went and stood over by the mantelpiece with his elbow on the mantel and said to himself, " Dr. Torrey said if I accept Jesus Christ God will accept me, but if I reject Jesus Christ God will reject me. I accept Jesus Christ right now," and instantly God accepted him. This was on Friday night. The following Sunday morning he went out to the Bethany Presbyterian Church, known as John Wanamaker's Church, because John Wanamaker was so active in the church. There was a men's meeting and an opportunity given to anyone who wished to speak. Magistrate Briggs arose to his feet and said, " Night before last I went to the South Armory to hear Dr. Torrey preach. Dr. Torrey said if I would accept Jesus Christ God would accept me, but if I rejected Jesus Christ God would reject me, and I accepted Jesus Christ and God has accepted me." Monday morning

Magistrate Briggs went down to court. The prisoners were brought in and the witnesses and the policemen stood in their places. Magistrate Briggs arose at the Bench and said, " Before I try any of these cases I want to tell you something. Last Friday night I went to the South Armory to hear Dr. Torrey preach. Dr. Torrey said if I would accept Jesus Christ God would accept me, but if I rejected Jesus Christ God would reject me, and I accepted Jesus Christ and God accepted me, and I advise all you prisoners to do the same." The next morning the Philadelphia papers came out with great headlines telling this incident, " Magistrate Jimmy Briggs preaches to his prisoners." It was the first I had heard of the incident or of Magistrate Briggs' conversion. But for years after, whenever I would go back to Philadelphia I was pretty sure to see Magistrate Briggs somewhere in the audience, and if I gave the people in the audience an opportunity to testify he would always rise to his feet and say, " When Dr. Torrey was here holding meetings in Philadelphia, I heard him in the South Armory and he said if I would accept Jesus Christ God would accept me, but if I rejected Jesus Christ God would reject me, and I accepted Jesus Christ and God accepted me."

Men and women, I have the same message for everyone of you here tonight. If you accept Jesus Christ God will accept you, no matter who you are, no matter what you have been, no matter what you have done. But if you reject Jesus Christ God will reject you, no matter who you are, no matter how many other good things you may do. Your acceptance before God depends entirely upon what you do with Jesus Christ. Will you accept Jesus Christ tonight as your personal Saviour and surrender to Him as your Lord and Master and confess Him as such before the world and strive to live from this time on to please Him in everything day by day? Every one of you who will, stand up.

X

WHO, THEN, IS JESUS?

"What shall I do then with Jesus which is called Christ?"

OUR subject tonight is, Who, then, is Jesus? We have the same text that we had last night, Matt. 27:22, "What shall I do then with Jesus which is called Christ?" I said last night that this was the most important question that any man ever asked or answered, for if we did the right thing with Jesus Christ we would get everything that was worth having for time and for eternity, but if we did the wrong thing with Jesus Christ we would lose everything that was worth having for time and for eternity. We saw last night that our acceptance before God depended entirely upon what we did with Jesus Christ, that if we accepted Jesus Christ God would accept us, but if we rejected Jesus Christ God would reject us. We saw that our finding peace of conscience depended entirely upon what we did with Jesus Christ, that if we accepted Jesus Christ we would find perfect peace of conscience, but if we did not accept Jesus Christ there was nothing else we could do to bring us peace of conscience. We saw also that our finding joy that was deep and satisfying and lasting depended entirely upon what we did with Jesus Christ, that if we accepted Jesus Christ as our Saviour and surrendered fully to Him as our Lord and Master, we would find joy that was deep and satisfying and lasting, but if we did not thus accept Him and surrender to Him there was nothing else we could do that would bring joy that was deep and satisfying and lasting. We saw in the fourth place, that our obtaining eternal life depended entirely upon what we did with Jesus Christ, that if we accepted Jesus Christ we would at once have eternal life, but that if we rejected Jesus Christ there was nothing else we could do that would bring us eternal life; and we saw last of all that our becoming the children of God depended entirely upon what we did with Jesus Christ, that, if we accepted Jesus Christ, we would become children of God the moment we accepted Him, but if we rejected Jesus Christ there was nothing else we could do by which we would become children of God.

At that point we stopped last night.

Tonight I wish to take your thoughts along a different line, and that is, what we must do with Jesus Christ.

First of all, let me say that everyone of us must do something with Jesus Christ tonight. We have Jesus Christ on our hands and we cannot get Jesus Christ off from our hands without doing something definite with Him. Pontius Pilate, who first asked the question of our text, had Jesus Christ on his hands and he tried to get Him off his hands without doing anything definite with Him. He did not wish to crucify Him, for He knew that He was an innocent Man and he did not wish to bring upon his own head the guilt of shedding innocent blood; but, on the other hand, he did not wish to release Him, for he knew that if he did he would bring upon his head the enmity of the Jews and that they would complain of his government to the Roman Emperor, and that his government would not bear examination. Therefore he tried to get Jesus Christ off from his hands without doing anything with Him. First of all he turned to the Jews and said, " Take *ye* Him and judge Him according to your law;" but they replied, " We have a law and by our law He ought to die, but we have not the power of death," and Pontius Pilate had Jesus Christ on his hands again. He then tried a second expedient: he heard someone mention the fact that Jesus was from Galilee; and the thought came to him at once, Galilee belongs to Herod's dominions, I will send Him to Herod to try Him. So he sent Him to Herod, and as he saw Jesus going up the road under the guard of the soldiers he had a great sense of relief: he thought to himself, I have escaped an exceedingly unpleasant predicament, I was not forced to condemn Him to be crucified and thereby bring upon my head the guilt of innocent blood, and I was not forced to release Him and thereby bring upon my head the enmity of the Jews. But his relief and satisfaction were very short-lived. He soon saw Jesus coming back again (for Herod sent Him back to Pilate), and he had Jesus Christ on his hands again. Then he tried a third expedient. It was the Jewish Passover week and at that time of the year

it was the custom for the Roman Governor to release to the
Jews one prisoner, whomsoever they chose; so he went out
and faced the crowd and said to them in his most urbane and
conciliatory way, " You have a custom at this time of year
that I should release unto you one prisoner whomsoever you
choose.   Do you choose Jesus Christ or ——" and then he
put over against Jesus Christ the most contemptible prisoner
he had in custody, Barabbas, a robber, a thief, a murderer,
thinking to himself, " they certainly will not choose Barabbas."   But to his dismay and horror the cry came up from
the frenzied mob, " Deliver unto us Barabbas."   And Pilate
had Jesus Christ on his hands again, and he asked the question of the text, " What shall I do then with Jesus which
is called Christ?"

We, too, have Jesus Christ on our hands tonight.   We must
do something definite with Him.   We cannot get Him off our
hands without doing something definite with Him.   Every
man and woman in this audience tonight cannot go out of this
place without having first done something definite with Jesus
Christ.   Let me tell you what you must do.

1.   First of all, *You must either accept Him or reject Him.*
There is no middle ground.   Jesus Christ offers Himself to
each one of us as our Saviour Who bore our sins in His Own
body on the cross, as our Lord and Master to Whom we
should surrender entire control of our life; and we must either
definitely accept Him as He offers Himself, to be our Saviour
and our Lord and Master, or else we must definitely reject
Him.   Not to accept Him is to reject Him.

There are many people who say, " I do not accept Him, but
neither do I reject Him."   Absolutely ridiculous!   Not to
definitely accept Him is to definitely reject Him.

Suppose some young man should offer himself in marriage
to some young woman.   She does not wish to accept him because she does not love him enough for that.   On the other
hand, she does not wish to reject him because she does not
wish to hurt his feelings, and so she says, " Charlie, I don't
accept you, but I want you to understand I don't reject you."
What absolute nonsense.   Not to accept is to reject, and not
to definitely accept Jesus Christ is to definitely reject Jesus
Christ, and every one of you will go out of this building to-

night either having definitely accepted Jesus Christ or having definitely rejected Jesus Christ.

2. In the second place, *We must either confess Jesus Christ or else we must deny Jesus Christ.* He Himself says so in Matt. 10:32, 33. These are His words, " *Whosoever* therefore *shall confess Me before men,* him will I confess also before My Father which is in heaven. *But whosoever shall deny Me before men,* him will I also deny before My Father which is in heaven." You see there is no middle ground: not to confess Jesus Christ is to deny Jesus Christ, and every one of you will go out of here tonight either having definitely confessed Jesus Christ or else you will go out of here tonight having definitely denied Jesus Christ. Which will it be?

One night I spoke to a friend who was going out of a meeting like this. I had often spoken to him before, and this night I said to him as he was leaving, " Will you confess Jesus Christ tonight?" " No, Mr. Torrey," he replied, " I have not gotten quite so far as that, but I want you to understand that I do not deny Him." I replied, " I do not understand anything of the kind. You have had the definite opportunity tonight to confess Jesus Christ. You have refused it. You are denying Him." And every one who goes out of this building tonight without having definitely confessed Jesus Christ will go out of here having definitely denied Jesus Christ.

3. In the third place, *You must either let Jesus Christ into your heart or you must shut Jesus Christ out of your heart.* The Lord Jesus Himself says so in Rev. 3:20. These are His Words, " Behold, I stand at the door, and knock: if any man hear My voice, and open the door, I will come in to him, and will sup with him, and he with Me." Jesus Christ is knocking tonight at the door of every heart here. Knocking, knocking, knocking—Who is it that is knocking? Jesus Christ, the Son of God, knocking at the door of your heart and knocking at the door of my heart tonight. Will you throw your heart's door wide open and say, " Come in, Lord Jesus," or will you bolt and bar the door of your heart and say, " Stay out, Lord Jesus "? Every one of you here tonight will do the one thing or the other. Every one of you will go out of this building tonight either having definitely let Jesus Christ into your heart

or having definitely shut Jesus Christ out of your heart.
Which will it be with you?

4.   In the fourth place, *We must either take our stand with
Jesus Christ or we must take our stand against Jesus Christ.*
He Himself says so.   You will find His words in Matt. 12:30,
" He that is not with Me is against Me."   According to Jesus
Christ's own statement there are just two classes of men and
women in this world; those who are for Him openly, confessedly, whole-heartedly, and those that are against Him.   And
if you do not take your stand openly, confessedly and whole-
heartedly with Jesus Christ then you take your stand definitely
against Jesus Christ.   Every one of you here tonight must
make your own choice.   You must either take your stand with
John, the beloved disciple, and Paul, the courageous disciple,
and Peter, the warm-hearted disciple, and with all the apostles and the martyrs and the heroes of our faith, and with all
that noble company of men and women who throughout the
centuries, have taken their stand for Jesus Christ, or else you
must take your stand with Pontius Pilate and Herod and
Annas and Caiaphas and Judas Iscariot and all that horrid
and despicable crew of the vicious and criminal and vile and
blaspheming, who, throughout the centuries, have taken their
stand against Jesus Christ.   Where will you line up?   Where
will you take your stand tonight?   Will you take your stand
with Jesus Christ or will you take your stand against Jesus
Christ?   Every man and woman in this building tonight will
go out of this building either having definitely taken your
stand for Jesus Christ or having definitely taken your stand
against Jesus Christ.   Where will you have taken your stand?
I could run a line through this building tonight and if I knew
you all tonight as well as God knows you, I could put every
man and woman in the building on one side of that line or
the other.   On the one side would be those who are for Christ
openly, confessedly, whole-heartedly for Christ.   On the other
side would be those who are against Jesus Christ.   Suppose
I did it.   Which side would you be on?

  How, then, will you take your stand tonight?   Will you
accept Jesus Christ or will you reject Jesus Christ?   Will you
confess Jesus Christ or will you deny Jesus Christ?   Will you
let Jesus Christ into your heart or shut Jesus Christ out of

your heart? Will you take your stand with Jesus Christ or will you take your stand against Jesus Christ?

II. WHO IS JESUS CHRIST WITH WHOM WE HAVE TO DO TONIGHT?

Before you decide this all-important question of what you shall do with Jesus Christ tonight, let me call your attention to another line of thought, and that is, Who this Jesus is Whom you must either accept or reject, Whom you must either confess or deny, Whom you must either let into your heart or keep out of your heart, Whom you must either take your stand for or take your stand against. Just Who is Jesus Christ?

1. In the first place, *Jesus Christ is your King, divinely appointed King.* This Peter declared on the day of Pentecost, in Acts 2:36, " Therefore let all the house of Israel know assuredly, that God hath made that same Jesus, whom ye have crucified, both Lord and Christ." "Christ" means "anointed King." Jesus Christ is your Divinely appointed and Divinely anointed King. They have a way of saying over in England that King George is their king by Divine appointment (and in a sense I believe it is true); but in a far higher sense Jesus Christ is your King by Divine appointment. If you reject Him you reject your Divinely appointed King, if you deny Him you deny your Divinely appointed King, if you shut Him out of your heart you shut your Divinely appointed King out of your heart, if you take your stand against Him you take your stand against your Divinely appointed King. In other words, YOU ARE GUILTY OF HIGH TREASON AGAINST YOUR DIVINELY APPOINTED KING.

Now high treason is the highest crime in the calendar, punishable by death, by the universal law of civilized nations. During the Boer War in South Africa certain subjects of Queen Victoria and the British Government took up arms against their queen and government. Some of these men were men of noble character. One of them was the nephew of the dearest friend I had in South Africa at that time, a nephew that he loved like a son. This nephew was arrested, tried for high treason. In the trial no question was asked about his character. Everyone admitted the nobility of his character.

The only question was, had he taken up arms against his queen and government? It was proved that he had, and they took him out and shot him. That is law. And I charge every man and woman in this building tonight who is out of Christ of high treason against your Divinely appointed King.

When I was in Maryborough, Australia, a man called upon me one day at the house where I was stopping. He was an unusually fine looking man. He had a high, dome-like forehead, overhanging eyebrows, a fine face, a fine head upon an unusually well built pair of shoulders. I showed him to a seat and he turned to me and said, " I want to ask you a question." I said, " What is your question?" He answered, " My question is this, what have you got against me?" I looked at the man in surprise and said, " What have I got against you? Why, sir, I have nothing against you. I do not even know who you are." He said, " Let me explain what I mean. I am not a Christian. I have never accepted Jesus Christ and I have no intention of accepting Jesus Christ. I have not confessed Him and I don't intend to. But I claim to be leading an upright life. As far as I know, I am doing my full duty toward everyone. I am doing my duty toward my wife and children. I am doing my duty toward my employers. I am doing my duty toward my neighbours. As far as I know, I am doing my duty in every relation in life, only I am not a Christian. What have you got against me?" I looked straight at him and answered, " I will tell you what I've got against you. Jesus Christ is your King by Divine appointment. You admit you have not accepted Him, that you have not taken your stand with Him. Therefore you have taken your stand against Him." Then I looked straight into the depths of those deep-set eyes and said, " Sir, I accuse you of high treason against Heaven's King." A dark cloud came over the man's face. He arose to his feet silently, hesitated a moment, and then without uttering a word he walked past me and out of the door. I followed him. Down the long hall he walked, never turning back, I following him. He opened the front door, pulled it to behind him without ever looking back and I followed him to the door. I looked out through the glass in the door and watched him as he walked down the long walk to the front gate. He never once looked back.

Coming to the gate he opened it in front of him, passed out of it without turning around, pulled it to behind him, I watching him from the door, and off he passed out of sight. Days, weeks, months, passed by. In the meantime I had gone to Tasmania and had returned to Australia and was speaking in the Alfred Hall in Ballarat, Australia. One afternoon as I came down from the platform a man was waiting for me at the foot of the platform steps. He said to me as I stepped up to him, " Do you recognize me?" " No," I replied, " I don't. I know I have seen you somewhere but I cannot place you." He said, " Do you recall accusing a man of high treason against Heaven's King?" I replied, " I have charged many a man with that." " Yes," he said, " But one particular man," and then described the circumstances that I have related above. Then it all came back to me. " Oh, yes," I said, " I remember you now." Then he looked steadily at me with those piercing eyes and said, " I have come way down from Maryborough to Ballarat to tell you, sir, that never again shall you accuse me of high treason against Heaven's King," and he reached out a strong hand and I put my hand in his. He clasped it and said, " Down!" and he sank down upon one knee and I sank upon mine and he handed in his allegiance to Heaven's King. Will you do it tonight? Again I repeat, I charge every one of you here tonight out of Christ of high treason against Heaven's King. Will you give up your awful treason and hand in your allegiance to Heaven's King tonight?

2. But Jesus Christ is more than your Divinely appointed King, *He is the Son of God*. If you reject Him, you reject the Son of God. If you deny Him, you deny the Son of God. If you shut Him out of your heart, you shut the Son of God out of your heart. If you take your stand against Him, you take your stand against the Son of God. But someone will say, " But, Dr. Torrey, don't you know that some of us don't believe that He is the Son of God." Yes, I know that very well; but did it ever occur to you that denying a fact does not alter the fact? A fact is a fact, whether you believe it or not. It is just as much a fact if you don't believe it as it is if you do believe it; and it is a fact that Jesus Christ is the Son of God, and your doubting the fact does not make it any less a fact, it only makes you guilty of trying to rob a Divine Person

of the honour, obedience and devotion which are His just due.
But we live in such a superficial age that many think all they
have to do to get rid of an unpleasant truth or fact is to simply
deny it.   But facts are stubborn things and cannot be gotten
rid of as easily as many think they can.   For example, there
are many in our day who do not wish to believe in the reality
of sickness and pain and sin and death.   I do not wonder that
they do not.   Sickness and pain and sin and death are very
disagreeable facts, and it is no wonder that people do not wish
to believe in the reality of them and welcome a philosophy that
denies them; but they are very real and they are solid facts,
just the same, and you cannot get rid of them by simply questioning their existence.   But these people think you can and
they say sickness and pain and sin and death do not really
exist, that they are simply " illusion " or " mortal thought."
" If you think you are sick, why then you are sick; but if you
deny sickness strongly enough you are not sick but perfectly
well.   If you think you have pain, you do have pain; but if
you deny pain you have no pain whatever.   If you think you
have sin, you have sin; but, if you deny sin, you are perfectly
righteous.   If you think you are going to die, you will die,
but if you deny death strongly enough and persistently enough
you will not die but live right on forever."   And they call this
" Christian Science."   It is nothing of the kind.   It is Buddhistic Nonsense.   In the first place it is not Christian.   It is
Buddhism pure and simple.   Some years ago there was a lady
in India, a very learned Hindu woman, versed in all the lore
of Buddhistic philosophy.   Her father was a pundit, a Hindu
philosopher; and she was a " pandita," an educated woman
teacher.   In the course of time she was led to see the folly
of Buddhism and accepted Jesus Christ and became a Christian.   She was perhaps the best known and most useful
woman in India, especially in her work among Hindu widows.
She was carrying on a great work in India which was largely
supported from America.   She visited America time and time
again, and always went to Boston where many of her sup-
porters lived.   On one of her later visits to Boston " Christian
Science " was very much to the front, and she was asked to
go to hear one of the leading teachers of " Christian Science."
She went and listened to this teacher as she spoke at great

length and fully expounded the teachings and philosophy of
" Christian Science." Pandita Ramabai listened to her in
silence until she had finished, and then she calmly said, " What
you are saying is nothing new to me. That is the philosophy
in which I was brought up. That is Buddhism pure and simple, and that is what I gave up when I became a Christian."
She was right. " Christian Science," " falsely so called," is
essentially Buddhistic.

But not only is it not Christian, it is not Science, it is nonsense. There is a large element of truth in it. It is true that
much of the sickness and pain in the world is imaginary, it
really is as the " Christian Scientists " say, " illusion " or
" mortal thought." There are many who think they are sick
but who really are not. They just imagine they are sick; and
they are the hardest kind of cases for the ordinary physician
to treat. They go to the Christian Science practitioner and
the practitioner tells them that their sickness is imaginary,
that it is " illusion "; and in telling them this they tell them
the exact truth. *Their* sickness is " illusion." He tells them
they are well and they believe it. They are well. They were
well all the time. Furthermore, the mind has a tremendous
influence over the body. A cheerful mind, a mind without
worry and anxiety, a mind full of hope, is the best medicine
in the world. It is better than all the physic and all the physi-
cians. A cheerful mind will even overcome such a chronic and
dangerous malady as Bright's disease, by sending more red
blood corpuscles through the kidneys. And, undoubtedly,
thousands upon thousands of people are far better physically
because of " Christian Science," and " Christian Science " is
true up to that point. I think it is more effective physically
than the constantly repeated formula of Coué or the mesmeric
shoutings, swayings, strokings and hallelujah incantations of a
certain type of self-styled " Divine Healers " or " Miracle
Men " or " Miracle Women." But while much of the supposed sickness in this world is " illusion," is imaginary,
there is sickness that is real and there is pain that is real and
there are thousands of people whose bodies are lying in premature graves who were really sick, but the Christian Science
practitioner persuaded them that they were not sick, that
they needed no medicine nor medical aid whatever. If they

had gone to a competent physician he would have given them
advice (or possibly medicine) that would have saved their
lives; but they were led to believe they were not sick when
they really were; and they are dead today.   I know a talented
woman who is totally blind today and has been totally blind
for years because she went, in the early stages of her trouble,
to a " Christian Science " practitioner instead of to a reputable
physician, who would have saved her from blindness.

When I was holding meetings in a city in North Carolina,
the leader of the " Christian Scientists " of that city took issue
with what I said, but she was herself a glaring example of the
very thing I said.   She had a little daughter.   This daughter
fell downstairs and seriously injured her head.   A little wise
help would have saved the child much suffering and would
have saved the child's life.   But the mother would not permit
a physician to be summoned, nor anything of any kind to be
done to alleviate the child's great sufferings.   The child
moaned and groaned and suffered for several days, but the
mother insisted on saying, " The child is not sick.   She is
not in pain.   She only thinks she is in pain," and by " Christian Science," by the denial of her suffering and her pain she
tried to relieve the child; but she failed utterly and the child
died.   They took the body of the unfortunate child out to the
cemetery and lowered it into the grave.   Her mother would
not even get out of the carriage and stand by the open grave
while the body was lowered, but sat in her carriage reading
" Science and Health."   She had another child who was taken
ill, but again she would not permit any treatment for the child,
simply denying the child's sickness and that child died too and
was buried.   Now this is cruelty, appalling cruelty, the sacrifice of a mother's love and a mother's duty to stubborn devotion to a false philosophy.   " Christian Science," falsely so
called, robs people of sympathy, of compassion, and it is the
most selfish system that was ever devised by the Devil.   It
centres one's thought entirely upon one's self; and " Christian
Science " has transformed many a tender-hearted, loving, sym-
pathetic mother into a self-satisfied, cruel monster with less
sympathy for her child than a mother lion has for her cub.

They had a Christian Science testimony meeting in Scran-
ton, Pa., one night.   One after another arose to tell what

Christian Science had done for them. Finally a man arose
and limped across the platform, toeing in, and said, " I thank
God Christian Science has cured me of being club-footed."
I do not wish to ridicule anyone's faith, but some things are
so essentially ridiculous that the only way to successfully com-
bat them is by exposure of how ridiculous they are. A little
boy whose mother was a Christian Scientist, ran in to his
mother and said, " Mother, Grandpa is sick." " No, no, my
child," she replied, " demonstrate your Science. Don't say,
' Grandpa is sick,' say, ' Grandpa thinks he is sick.' " The
little boy learned his lesson and ran out. A little while after
he came running in again and said, " Mother, Grandpa thinks
he's dead." The undertaker thought so too, and they buried
him. When Mrs. Mary Eddy died a few years ago Jacob
Fry, her most intimate friend, said that she was " in error,"
that is that she thought she was dead, but was not really
dead. But her error was so like reality and Mrs. Eddy was
apparently so much like other really dead people that they
thought it wise to bury her, and then the Christian Science
Church claimed her property which she had willed to them.
Now, either she was dead or she wasn't. If she wasn't dead
they committed a legal fraud by going into the court and testi-
fying she was dead and claiming her property, for a will is of
no effect until the testator dies. But if she was dead and they
had a legal right to the property as they claimed, then " Christian Science " is a fraud; for " Christian Science " says that
there is no such thing as death. Now you may take which-
ever horn of the dilemma you please, and in either instance
" Christian Science " is a fraud.

Then again, there are those who do not wish to believe in
an eternal hell. I do not wonder that they don't. It is an
awful thought. It is an appalling thought, to think there is
an eternal hell to which any man or woman shall ever go and
go forever. But we cannot get rid of the fact by simply denying the fact. There is a hell and those who do not accept
Jesus Christ will go there, and we cannot get rid of it by simply saying, " I do not believe there is any hell." Then again
there are those who do not wish to believe in the Deity of
Jesus Christ. If Jesus Christ is really Divine, God manifested
in the flesh, the Son of God in a sense that no other was ever

the Son of God, then it lays upon us a most solemn obligation
to accept Him, and it makes it the most dreadful, daring and
damning of all sins to reject Him.   And these people do not
wish to accept Him and so they look wise and say, " I do not
believe Jesus is the Son of God," and by denying His Deity
they think they have done away with it.   Oh, no!   Facts are
facts, and you cannot get rid of them by simply denying them.
And it is a fact that Jesus Christ is the Son of God.   He is
proven to be the Son of God by five unmistakably Divine
testimonies: first, By the testimony of the Divine life that
He lived, for He lived as never man lived; second, By the testimony of the Divine words that He spoke, for He spoke as
never man spoke; third, By the testimony of the Divine works
that He wrought, for He wrought as never man wrought;
fourth, By the testimony of His Divine influence upon all subsequent history; and fifth, By the testimony of the resurrection from the dead, the best proven fact of history, and the
Lord God almighty's stamp of endorsement on the claim of
Jesus Christ that He is the Son of God.   And you do not make
Him any less the Son of God by denying that He is the Son
of God.   No, you simply make yourself guilty of the appalling
sin of trying to rob a Divine Person of the faith which is His
due, the surrender which is His due, and the worship which is
His due.   Jesus Christ is the Son of God, and if you reject
Him you reject the Son of God; if you deny Him, you deny
the Son of God; if you shut Him out of your heart, you shut
the Son of God out of your heart; if you take your stand
against Him, you take your stand against the Son of God.
The most appalling and the most damning sin of which any
man or woman can be guilty is the sin of which you are guilty,
the sin of rejecting, denying, shutting out of your heart and
taking your stand against the infinite Son of God.

   3.   But *Jesus Christ is more than the Son of God, He is
your Saviour, He is the One Who was wounded for your transgressions and bruised for your iniquities, the One upon Whom
the chastisement of your peace was laid; He is the One Who
left Heaven with all its glory and came down to earth with all
its shame, to die upon the cross for you.   He is the One Who
was blindfolded, spit upon, scourged and crucified for you.*
If you reject Him, you reject the One Who was wounded for

your transgressions, bruised for your iniquities and upon Whom the chastisement of your peace was laid. If you deny Him you deny the One Who was wounded for your transgressions, bruised for your iniquities, the One upon Whom the chastisement of your peace was laid. If you shut Him out of your heart, you shut out of your heart the One Who was wounded for your transgressions, bruised for your iniquities, the One upon Whom the chastisement of your peace was laid. If you take your stand against Him, you take your stand against the One Who was wounded for your transgressions, bruised for your iniquities, the One upon Whom the chastisement of your peace was laid. The blackest, wickedest, most unpardonable, most monstrous and most infamous ingratitude of which any human being is capable of is the ingratitude of which you are guilty, the ingratitude of rejecting, denying, shutting out of your heart and taking your stand against the One Who was wounded for your transgressions, bruised for your iniquities and upon Whom the chastisement of your peace was laid.

One night as I walked down through the inquiry room in our church in Chicago a gentleman who was sitting there beckoned to me and asked me to come and sit beside him as he wished to talk to me. I sat down by his side and he said to me, " I want to ask you a question." " Very well," I said, " what is your question?" He said, " My question is this: I am not a Christian. I make no profession of being a Christian and I have no intention of becoming a Christian. But," he continued, " I do claim to be leading an upright life. As far as I know, I am doing my duty in every relation in life. I am doing my duty by my wife and children, I am doing my duty by my father and mother, I am doing my duty by my employers, I am doing my duty by my neighbours. In every way as far as I know I am doing my whole duty. Now," he said, " leading such a life as I claim to be leading, and, Mr. Torrey, I am leading that kind of a life, do you think if I do not accept Jesus Christ I will go to Hell just because I do not accept Jesus Christ?" I replied, " You most certainly will." " Well," he said, " all I have got to say is, it isn't fair." I said, " Wait a few moments and do some thinking. Suppose your mother was one of the best women that ever lived." He

said, " She is." I said, " Suppose your mother not only loved
you as mothers usually love their sons, but loved you far more
than mothers usually love their sons." He replied, " She
does." I said, " Suppose your mother so loved you she would
give her life for you if necessary." He said, " She would."
" All right, having such a mother as you claim to have, and
I really believe you have, suppose you do your duty by everyone else but by your mother; do your duty by your wife and
children, your duty by your father, your duty by your neighbours and friends, your duty by your business associates, your
duty by every man and woman you know except that one person, your mother, but this mother who so loves you, who has
done so much for you, who has made so many sacrifices for
you, when she is old and broken down, broken down largely
because of her many ministrations to you, you turn her out
on the street to starve and die, what would you say of yourself?" He instantly replied, " I would say I was a scoundrel."
I said, " What! a scoundrel, just because of your treatment
of one person when you have done your whole duty by everyone else, by your wife and children, your father and brothers
and sisters, your neighbours and friends, your business associates, everybody but that one person, a scoundrel just because
of your treatment of her?" " Yes," he replied, " I would say
I was a scoundrel." I said, " Please do some more thinking.
Jesus Christ is nobler than your mother or mine, nobler than
the noblest woman that ever lived. Jesus Christ loves you
more than any mother ever loved a son. Jesus Christ not only
would lay down His life for you if it were necessary; Jesus
Christ has already laid His life down for you. Now," I said,
" suppose you do your duty by everyone in the world but by
Jesus Christ. Suppose you should do your whole duty by your
father, mother, brothers and sisters, wife and children, neighbours and friends, business associates, by everybody but by
Jesus Christ, the Christ Who came down from Heaven to die
for you, this Christ Who was spit upon, blindfolded, buffeted,
scourged and crucified for you, this Christ Who was wounded
for your transgressions, bruised for your iniquities, upon
Whom the chastisement of your peace was laid, Him you reject and deny and shut out of your heart and take your stand
against. What have you got to say of yourself?" The man

was honest and he replied, " Mr. Torrey, I am a scoundrel."
I put it to you tonight. I do not say you are a scoundrel,
but what do you say of yourself? Even though you do your
whole duty by everyone else in the world but by Jesus Christ,
this Jesus Christ Who gave up Heaven and all its glory and
came down to earth with all its shame, for your sake, this
Christ Who gave up the praises of the angels, the archangel,
the cherubim and seraphim, and came down into this world
to be despised and rejected of men, to be scorned, to be
spurned, to be blindfolded, to be spit upon, to be scourged,
to be crucified, and to die that awful death of heart-breaking
agony in your place, this Christ Who was wounded for your
transgressions, bruised for your iniquities, upon Whom the
chastisement of your peace was laid, Him you reject, deny,
shut out of your heart and take your stand against. Now,
as you will have to answer before God in the Day of Judgment, what have you got to say of yourself? I put it to every
one of you tonight. What will you do with Jesus Christ tonight? Will you accept Him or will you reject Him; will
you confess Him or will you deny Him; will you take Him
into your heart or will you shut Him out of your heart; will
you take your stand with Him or will you take your stand
against Him? God help you to decide right.

It was an awful crisis in the life of Pontius Pilate when he
asked the question of the text. There sat Pontius Pilate on
the Roman judgment seat; and there stood Jesus of Nazareth;
there He stood in all the beauty of His perfect Manhood;
there He stood in all the glory of Incarnate Deity; there He
stood in all the wondrousness of His redeeming love; and there
sat Pontius Pilate deep in thought, trying to decide what to
do with Him. Two classes of opposing voices in Pilate's heart
were clamouring to be heard: The voice of conscience cried,
" Pontius Pilate, He is innocent; let Him go," the voice of
reason cried, " Pilate, He is innocent; let Him go," the voice
of common decency cried, " Pontius Pilate, He is innocent;
let Him go." Everything that was high and true and noble
in Pontius Pilate cried, " He is innocent; let Him go." But
listen! There are other voices in Pilate's heart that are also
clamouring to be heard, the voice of avarice lifts his strident
tones, " Pontius Pilate, He is innocent, yes, but, if you let

Him go, it will cost you money; crucify Him;" the voice of cowardice whispers hoarsely, " Pontius Pilate, He is innocent, yes, but, if you let Him go, think what it will cost you; crucify Him;" the voice of low, mean, political policy snivels, " Pontius Pilate, He is innocent, yes, but, if you let Him go, the Jews will complain of your government at Rome and your government will not bear inspection and you will lose your position; crucify Him."   All that was low and base and mean and vile and devilish in Pontius Pilate cries, " Crucify Him," and Pontius Pilate listened to the lower voices and decided wrong—and Pontius Pilate's name has come down to everlasting infamy.

It is a more awful crisis in the life of some of you here tonight than it was in the life of Pontius Pilate in that hour so long ago.   There you sit—there stands Jesus of Nazareth. There He stands again in all the beauty of His perfect Manhood.   There He stands in all the glory of Incarnate Deity. There He stands in all the glorious wondrousness of His self-sacrificing, dying and redeeming love.   And there you sit deep in thought.   In your heart, just as in the heart of Pontius Pilate of old, are the two kinds of voices clamouring to be heard, lower voices and higher voices, infernal voices and supernal voices, voices from hell and voices from heaven.   The lower voices are crying: The voice of avarice shrieks, " Yes, He is your Divinely appointed King.   Yes, He is the Son of God.   Yes, He is your Saviour.   Yes, He is the One Who was wounded for your transgressions and bruised for your iniquities, and upon Whom the chastisement of your peace was laid; but, if you accept Him, it will cost you money; it may cost you much money; reject Him, deny Him, shut Him out of your heart, take your stand against Him."   The voice of cowardice hisses, " Yes, He is your Divinely appointed King. Yes, He is the Son of God.   Yes, He is your Saviour.   Yes, He is the One Who was wounded for your transgressions and bruised for your iniquities and upon Whom the chastisement of your peace was laid.   *But,* if you accept Him, think of what others will say; reject Him, deny Him, shut Him out of your heart, take your stand against Him."   The voice of lust is thundering, " Yes, He is your Divinely appointed King. Yes, He is the Son of God.   Yes, He is your Saviour.   Yes,

He is the One Who was wounded for your transgressions and bruised for your iniquities, and upon Whom the chastisement of your peace was laid.   But, if you accept Him, you will have to give up your charming companion in sin.   Reject Him. Deny Him.   Shut Him out of your heart.   Take your stand against Him."   All things in you that are low and base and mean and vile and devilish are shouting in loud chorus, " Reject Him, deny Him, shut Him out of your heart, take your stand against Him."   But thank God higher voices also are crying in your heart tonight, voices from the fair heavenly world. The voice of conscience cries, " He is your Divinely appointed King, accept Him, confess Him, let Him into your heart, take your stand with Him."   The voice of reason cries, " Beyond a question, He is the Son of God, God manifest in the flesh; accept Him, confess Him, let Him into your heart, take your stand with Him."   The voice of gratitude cries with still more compelling tones, " He is your Saviour.   He is the One Who gave up all of Heaven's glory and came down to all this world's shame for you.   He is the One Who was spit upon, blindfolded, cruelly scourged until His back was all torn to shreds, crucified and died in awful agony of a breaking heart for you. He is the One Who was wounded for your transgressions, bruised for your iniquities, the One upon Whom the chastisement of your peace was laid.   Accept Him.   Confess Him. Let Him into your heart.   Take your stand with Him."   Everything that is high and everything that is holy, everything that is true and noble and decent in you cries, " Accept Him.   Confess Him.   Let Him into your heart.   Take your stand with Him."

How will you decide tonight?   God help you to decide right.

XI

A QUESTION TO WHICH GOD DEMANDS AN AN-
SWER FROM EVERYONE WHO IS HESITATING
TO PUBLICLY CONFESS CHRIST

*" And now why tarriest thou? arise, and be baptized, and
wash away thy sins, calling on the name of the Lord."*—ACTS
22 : 16.

MY subject tonight is, A Question to Which God Demands an Answer from Everyone Who Is Hesitating to Publicly Confess Christ. You will find that
question in Acts 22:16, " And now *why tarriest thou?* arise,
and be baptized, and wash away thy sins, calling on the name
of the Lord," especially the first part of the question, " Why
tarriest thou?" It was God Who asked the question. He
asked it of Saul of Tarsus. Saul of Tarsus was, as you know,
a bitter enemy of Jesus Christ. I doubt if Jesus Christ ever
had a more bitter, a more determined, a more relentless, a
more able or a more dangerous enemy than Saul of Tarsus.
Saul of Tarsus was a man of great sincerity, rare ability and
also of great determination. He had convinced himself that
Jesus of Nazareth was an impostor, that while He claimed to
be the Messiah and the Son of God, in reality He was nothing
of the kind; and with all the intensity of a strong, earnest,
intense and honest soul, Saul of Tarsus hated this One Whom
he believed to be such a colossal Impostor. He not only hated
Jesus Christ, but because of his hatred of Jesus Christ he
hated everyone who belonged to Him. His hatred was of a
most vehement and active character. He went up and down
the streets of Jerusalem, in and out of homes, sparing neither
age nor sect, arresting all men, women and children who professed to believe in Jesus Christ, upon whom he could lay his
hands and dragged them before the Jewish Sanhedrin to be
tried and to be punished. And whenever a vote was taken

he always voted for their death.   He fairly breathed an at-
mosphere of " threatening and of slaughter."   He gloated over
the shedding of Christian blood.   But at last he had exhausted all his opportunities of shedding Christian blood in
Jerusalem, but he had not exhausted his hatred of Jesus Christ
and of those who belonged to Him.   He heard that in far-
away Damascus, a hundred and fifty miles away, there were
other believers in Christ, and though they were entire stran-
gers to him, though he had never even seen them, he hated
them, hated them simply because they bore the name of Jesus
Christ.   He went to the Jewish authorities and requested of
them a commission to go to Damascus and do in Damascus
the same work he had done in Jerusalem, to arrest all believers in Jesus Christ and to bring them back to Jerusalem
to be punished.   He easily obtained the authority he sought
and started out on his journey.   It was a long and trying journey, one hundred and fifty miles on foot or on horseback,
across burning sands and desolate wastes; but Saul of Tarsus
pressed on day after day, urged on by his bitter hatred, not
even stopping to rest during the fierce heat of the noontime
sun.   At last he has almost reached his destination.   He is
on the last hilltop and Damascus lies in the valley at his feet.
Damascus was a city famed throughout the ancient world for
its beauty, a city of dashing rivers and flashing fountains, a
city of olive groves and of vineyards, a city of almost matchless beauty, a city of which an ancient Persian poet said,
" Damascus is a diamond in a setting of emerald."   But as
Saul of Tarsus stands upon the last hilltop and looks down
upon Damascus in its radiant beauty, he has no eye for its
beauty.   His only thought is, " In that city are some of these
accursed believers in Jesus as the Christ; but I will soon have
them in my power and be dragging them back to Jerusalem
to be punished."   He is about to press on, when suddenly
there shines around him a light above the light of the noontime sun and there in that light he sees standing the most
wonderful face and form he has ever beheld, the face and
form of the risen and glorified Jesus.   Overwhelmed with
terror and confusion he falls upon his face to the ground, and
out of the light there comes a voice and that voice calls, " Saul,
Saul, why persecutest thou Me?"   Back from the prostrate

man there comes the reply, " Who art Thou, Lord?"   Back
comes the crushing rejoinder, " I am Jesus Whom thou persecutest."   And from the thoroughly humbled man there comes
the eager cry, " What wilt Thou have me to do, Lord?"
" Arise, stand on thy feet, go into Damascus and there it shall
be told thee what thou shalt do."   Saul of Tarsus arises to
his feet, tries to look around; but finds he has been totally
blinded by the glory of the vision which he has beheld, and
he holds out his hand and is led as helpless as a child into
the city which he had expected to enter as a conqueror.

He goes to the house of a friend, locks himself in and for
three days and three nights sees no one, neither eats nor
drinks, but spends the time in fasting and in prayer.   But he
does not come out and openly confess Jesus as the Son of
God before the world in baptism; and at last God, weary with
waiting, sends to him a man " named Ananias," with the question of our text, " Why tarriest thou, Saul?   (What are you
waiting for?   You know now that I am the Son of God and
the Messiah for Whom you have been waiting, why do you
not come out and openly confess Me in baptism before the
world?)"

I believe that God is putting that same question to
every man and every woman, young and old, in this audience tonight who has not accepted Jesus Christ and publicly
confessed Him before the world: What are you waiting for
before you accept Jesus Christ and publicly confess Him before the world?

I wish it were possible for me to go down from this platform tonight and go from seat to seat to each one of you
individually and put to each of you the question of the text
and have you give me your honest answer as to what you
are waiting for before you accept Jesus Christ, and then I
would take up your answers and answer them.   I believe that
if I could do that I could lead almost every one of you who
is here tonight to accept and confess Jesus Christ.   But of
course that is impossible; for there are many of you and it
would take hours.   Furthermore, many of you would not give
me an honest answer.   So I am going to do the next best
thing.   We are going to have a time of perfect silence and
I am going to ask every Christian here in the audience tonight

to pray for those who are not Christians, and I am going to ask you who have not accepted Jesus Christ or have not publicly confessed Him before the world, to put to yourself the question, " What am I waiting for before I accept Jesus Christ and publicly confess Him before the world?"; and then I am going to take up your answers and answer them.   Now let us have a time of perfect silence; every Christian pray.   If you have some definite friend here tonight who has not publicly confessed Jesus Christ, pray for him.   And you who are not Christians, put to yourselves the question, " What am I waiting for before I accept Jesus Christ and publicly confess Him before the world?"   Have you asked yourself the question?   Have you honestly answered it?   Well, if you will give me your attention I will now take up your answers and answer them.

I.   I AM WAITING UNTIL I AM CONVINCED

Doubtless the answer that some of you gave to that question was, " I am waiting until I am convinced.   I am not convinced that Jesus Christ is the Son of God, nor that the Bible is the Word of God.   As soon as I am convinced that the Bible is God's Word and that Jesus Christ is God's Son I will accept Jesus Christ as my own Saviour and Lord and confess Him as such before the world."   Now if any of you made that answer I want to make you an offer, and that offer is, if you will come to me personally at the close of this meeting, I will show you a way to find out to an absolute certainty that the Bible is God's Word and that Jesus Christ is the Son of God.   Now, if you are an honest skeptic you will accept that offer.   If you do not accept it, never tell anyone again that you are a skeptic, you are a humbug.

Please notice exactly what I offer.   I do not offer to show you that Jesus Christ is the Son of God and that the Bible is the Word of God.   I offer to do something far better than that—I offer to show you a way to find out for yourself that the Bible is God's Word and that Jesus Christ is God's Son. Now, if you are a mere quibbler and simply wish to exhibit your skill at discussion and debate, I have no time to waste upon you; but if you are an honest seeker after truth and really wish to know the truth and are willing to obey it when you find it, I have unlimited time to give you. I would rather talk to an honest skeptic than to any other man I know. I was a skeptic once myself, and a thoroughly honest one. It has been one of the greatest joys of my life to lead countless skeptics and infidels and agnostics and atheists to an intelligent acceptance of Jesus Christ as the Son of God. But let me say, I have yet to find the first honest skeptic, infidel, atheist, agnostic, Unitarian or spiritualist, who really wished to know and obey the truth, whom I could not show a way to find out that Jesus Christ was the Son of God and the Bible the Word of God. I have made the offer which I have made here tonight literally around the world. The offer has been accepted by a great many men and women, men and women in all classes of society, from university professors and students down to the most illiterate of men and women, but so far as I know there is not one single person on earth tonight who has really accepted that offer who has not been brought to believe that the Bible was God's Word and that Jesus Christ was God's Son.

Let me give you an illustration, one of the first men that I ever led out of the fogs and miasma of doubt into the health-giving sunlight of an intelligent faith in God and in Jesus Christ and in the Bible. It was in my first pastorate. There was a man in my congregation who was a constant attendant but who had not publicly confessed Christ before the world. His wife and his daughter were members of our church but he was not. One Sunday night as I was going out of the building he stood between the two doors and I stepped up to him and said, " Mr. B., why are you not a Christian?" He instantly replied, " Because I don't believe anything." He went on to say, " I do not boast of it as so many men in this town do." (It was a notoriously infidel town. We had afterward a revival that changed the character of the town, but at that time it was notoriously infidel.) He said, " I do not boast of it as so many men in this town do, but I don't believe anything." I said to him, " Do you not believe there is a God?" Hesitatingly he replied, " Yes, I believe there is a God, I have not quite given up faith there is a God. I believe there is a Supreme Being." " Well," I said, " if there is a God, a Supreme Being, as you call Him, you ought to sur-

render your will to His.   You ought to take your stand upon
His will to follow it wherever it carries you.   Have you done
that?"   He replied, " I am trying to live just as near right as
I know how," and I believe he was, he was one of the most
universally respected business men in the town.   I replied,
" That is not what I asked you.   I asked you if you had taken
your stand upon the will of God to follow it wherever it carried you?"   He answered, " I have never put it just that
way."   I said, " Will you put it that way tonight?"   He said,
" I will."   " Now," I said, " do you believe God answers
prayer?"   " No," he said, " I do not.   I have lain awake
nights thinking about that, and I have about come to the conclusion that God does not answer prayer."   " Well," I said,
" I know He does, but that will not do you any good.   But
you can find out for yourself.   Will you pray this prayer,
' Oh, God, show me if Jesus Christ is Thy Son or not, and if
Thou shewest me that He is, I promise to accept Him as my
Saviour, and confess Him as such before the world '?"   He
said, " Yes, I will do that too."   This was Sunday night.
The following Thursday night, prayer meeting night in those
days in North-Eastern Ohio, I noticed that this man came into
the prayer meeting, which I think he had never done before.
As soon as I threw the meeting open this man arose and said,
" Friends, I was all in a mist, all in a fog.   I did not know
what I believed.   I did not know as I believed anything."
Then he told us what he had done.   Like an honest man he
had done exactly what he had promised.   Then he added,
" My doubts are all gone.   I do not know where they are
gone, but they are gone."   He came out and made a public
confession of Christ, united with our church, became one of
the most active men in the church and in the community.   He
was afterwards made superintendent of the Sunday School and
then a deacon of the church, and tonight he is with Christ
up in the glory.   Do you doubt that story?   Well try it yourself, then you will have one of your own to tell.   It has been
tried by a countless multitude.   It has never failed and it
never will, for Jesus Christ Himself says, " If any man willeth
to do His will, he shall know of the teaching, whether it is of
God, or whether I speak from Myself."   (John 7:17.)

II. I am Waiting Until I Have Enjoyed
the World Enough

But someone will say, " That is not my difficulty. That
is not what I am waiting for. I believe in the Bible. I believe that Jesus Christ is the Son of God just as much as you
do. But I am waiting *till I have enjoyed the world enough.*
When I have enjoyed the world enough then I will give up
the world and accept Jesus Christ." Let me say to you, you
are making a great mistake. You are making a great mistake
for three reasons.

1. In the first place, You are making a mistake because
you are proceeding upon the theory that one can live for this
world for a while and then tire of it and then can give it up
without a struggle. You never made a greater mistake in all
your life. The truth about the world is this, the longer one
lives for the world, the less he enjoys it; that is true, but the
tighter and tighter becomes its grip upon his soul. Take for
example, the love of drink. When a man first begins to drink
there is pleasure in it. Some will tell you there is not, but I
know that there is. The first glass of beer a man drinks, the
first glass of wine or champagne, there is pleasure in it, it makes
him feel like two men. But as a man goes on drinking there
is less and less pleasure in it until at last he hates the drink,
hates it as intensely as the most ardent prohibitionist. He
knows that the drink is robbing him of his brain power, he
knows it is robbing him of his physical strength, he knows
it is robbing him of his business capacity, he knows it has
robbed him of the love of his wife and the respect of his children, he knows it has robbed him of everything that makes
life worth living, and he hates it, oh, how he hates it! but
every time the appetite cracks its whip he goes up to the bar
and drinks that glass of liquid damnation to the very dregs.
Is that not true? You know it is true.

It is just the same way with the love of money. When a
man begins to accumulate money there is pleasure in it. The
first hundred dollars a man puts in the bank, the first thousand
dollars, oh, the joy of it, the glad sense that one is beginning
to be a capitalist. But as a man goes on accumulating wealth
there is less and less joy in it, until at last there is no joy at

all, but only an ever-increasing sense of anxiety and care and worry; but all the time that the joy of accumulating money decreases, the tighter and tighter becomes the grip of the almighty dollar upon that man's poor shrivelling soul. Is it not so? One night a good many years ago my wife and my two children and I were stopping at the home of a man in Northern Ohio. He was a man over seventy years of age. He had been successful in business. He had accumulated perhaps half a million dollars. He had more money than he knew what to do with, and he did not have a child in the world to whom to leave it. One foot was already in the grave and the other foot was so near in that just a short time before our visit they had to send post haste in the middle of the night for a doctor or both feet would have been in the grave. That night after my wife and his wife and our two children had retired, he and I sat up to talk together. What do you think he wanted to talk about? " Why," you say, " a man upwards of seventy years of age, with one foot in the grave and the other foot almost in, with more money than he knew what to do with and with not a child in the world to whom to leave it, certainly he wanted to talk about eternity." Did he? When my wife and children and his wife had gone and he knew that we were alone, he leaned that old white head over toward mine, and it was a fine looking head too—I was living at that time in Minneapolis, in the boom times, when men were making fortunes in a day—and he said with intense earnestness, " Archie, do you know any place in Minneapolis where I could invest a little money where it would bring big interest?" You laugh at that; but, when one stops to think of it, it was appalling. But so it is with the love of money, the longer one lives for money the less joy there is in it, but the tighter and tighter becomes its grip upon a man's poor, starving, shrivelling soul. The grip of the love of money upon the soul is tighter, far tighter than the grip of strong drink. It is easier far to save a whiskey fiend from the love of drink than it is to save a money fiend from the grip of the lust for the almighty dollar. I would rather undertake to save twelve whiskey drunkards than to save one money drunkard.

It is just the same way with the love of pleasure. When one begins the pursuit of pleasure, there is indeed pleasure in it. Oh, that first dance that a young girl goes to, it seems like fairyland. The first theatre she attends, it seems like Paradise. But as she goes on attending, there is less and less pleasure in it, until at last there is no pleasure whatever, nothing but a corroding sense of ennui, a sickening sense of weariness and disgust with yourself and everyone else. But as the joy of worldly pleasure diminishes, the power of the love of it increases. Come with me tonight to New York City and let us enter some of the theatres or operas there, whom will we see in the boxes? Only the young girls, the buds of society and their escorts? No indeed. We would see women old enough to be grandmothers, who ought to be at home putting their grandchildren to bed; but who sit there heavily rouged, with painted lips, with pencilled eyebrows, with low-cut dresses, diamond earrings sparkling in their ears, pearl necklaces lying on their shrivelled old necks, looking like skeletons tricked out with gewgaws and wondering why the young men in the orchestra chairs are not admiring their gorgeous display instead of ogling the ballet girls on the platform. You laugh at that too, but it is appalling. The same is true of the love of the world in all its forms, the longer one lives for the world the less pleasure there is in it, but the tighter and tighter becomes its grip upon the poor, withering soul. There will never come a time when it will be easier to give up the world than it is tonight, there will never come a time again when it will be quite so easy as it would be tonight. It would have been easier still a year ago, easier still longer ago than that, but never again will it be as easy as it is tonight. Oh, you who are waiting until you enjoy the world enough before you accept and confess Jesus Christ, you are making a fearful mistake.

2. But you who are saying, " I am waiting till I have enjoyed the world enough," are making a mistake for a second reason, and that is, because all the time that you are waiting until you have enjoyed the world enough you are losing every day the far greater joy that is to be found in Jesus Christ. It does not admit of a moment's question that an immeasurably greater joy is to be found through believing in Jesus Christ and absolutely surrendering to Him than is to be found in all that this world has to give; and all the time

that you are postponing accepting Jesus Christ in order that you may enjoy the world some more, you are losing every day the immeasurably greater joy that is to be found in Jesus Christ.   You are sacrificing real and satisfying joys to obtain emptiness and disappointment.

3.   But you are making a great mistake for a third reason, and that is, because *while you are waiting until you have enjoyed the world enough, you may be called out of it at any moment,* and " what shall it profit a man, if he shall gain the whole world, and lose his own soul?"   One night up in Dakota at the close of a meeting like this, as they were singing the last hymn, I walked down the aisle and spoke to one and another as I passed along.   Toward the rear of the building a young woman was standing, singing very heartily.   She was a gay-hearted girl with a roguish, laughing pair of eyes.   I think I never saw but one other pair of eyes so full of gentle but irrepressible laughter as hers.   I stepped up to this young woman and said, " Why are you not a Christian?"   She turned those laughing eyes upon me and said with a toss of her head, " Because I enjoy the world too much."   I looked into those laughing eyes and said nothing more than to quote the words of our Lord Jesus, " What shall it profit a man, if he shall gain the whole world, and lose his own soul?" (Mark 8:36), and passed on.   After some days the meetings came to a close. I had preached my last sermon, the last song had been sung. I had gone home to the house where I was stopping, intending to take an early train to Minneapolis the next morning. While I was talking with the family the maid came in and said, " There are two persons who wish to see you in the other room."   I went to the other room and one of them was this girl with the laughing eyes, but her eyes were laughing no longer, no, there was a very solemn look in those eyes.   I asked her what she wished.   She replied, " I don't enjoy the world any longer.   Ever since you spoke to me that night in the church, your words, ' What shall it profit a man, if he shall gain the whole world, and lose his own soul?' have been ringing in my ears, and I have had no peace and I have brought my friend around with me for you to tell us what to do to be saved."   Oh, I would to God that I could burn that same question into the heart of everyone in this audience tonight who

is giving up Christ that they may gain the world. "What shall it profit a man if he shall gain the whole world, and lose his own soul?" Ah, suppose while you are waiting until you have enjoyed the world enough you are called out of this world, as you may be any day or any hour? What shall it profit a man to gain the whole world, and lose his own soul?

III.   I am Waiting for My Friends

But some of you will say, " That is not my difficulty at all. It is not that I love the world and am waiting until I have enjoyed the world enough; *I am waiting for my friends.* There is some friend or friends whom you dearly love, and if they would come to Christ you would come too, and you are waiting for them, you don't wish to come alone. That is true of many of you here tonight. Lovers are waiting for their sweethearts, sweethearts are waiting for their lovers, husbands are waiting for their wives and wives are waiting for their husbands, friends are waiting for friends. There are many of you here tonight who would come to Jesus Christ tonight and confess Him tonight if only your loved ones would come too. What shall I say to you?

1. Just this, *You come to Jesus Christ first and bring your friends with you.* If your friends love you as much as you love them, if you come to Christ they will come too. Which is better, for you to come to Christ and bring your friends with you or to let your friends drag you down to hell with them? I was at dinner one night with a friend who was in the ministry, a Congregational minister. After dinner he said to me, " Would you like to hear the story of my life?" I replied, " I would very much like to hear it." " Well," he said, " my wife and I had been married for fourteen years and a half. We were happy together, as things go. We had similar tastes. I had a good position, I was superintendent of the schools in the city where I lived. One Saturday night as my wife and I sat talking together my wife said to me, ' Husband, I have been thinking the matter over and have decided that I ought to become a Christian and unite with the church, and I am intending to unite with the church tomorrow.' ' Oh,' I replied, ' don't do that. That will separate us from one another. We have lived happily together for fourteen and a half years, we

have had similar tastes; but I have no intention of uniting
with the church, and, if you should unite with the church,
don't you see that that would separate us from one another?'
She replied, 'Husband, I love you. You know I do. I would
do anything I could conscientiously to please you, but I have
made up my mind I ought to accept Christ and unite with the
church.' Then I answered, 'Well, you can accept Christ. I
won't object to that, only don't unite with the church,' " and
he continued, " We agreed on that compromise, that she could
accept Christ but not unite with the church. This went on
for about six months. Then one Saturday night we were talking together again and she said, 'Husband, I have been trying
to be a Christian outside of the church for six months and
I have failed.' " (Everyone who attempts that fails. No one
ever succeeded in being a successful Christian without Christian fellowship.) Then she continued, " ' I have made up my
mind to unite with the church tomorrow.' I was very angry.
I said, 'Wife, we have been married fifteen years, we have
lived happily together; but if you unite with the church you
are no more to me, you can go your way and I will go mine.' "
That was a severe test to put a loyal wife to; but that
wife was loyal, loyal not only to him but loyal to God. And
men, listen, any loyalty to you on the part of your wife that
is not founded upon loyalty to God, is not a very safe thing
to trust. This wife was loyal to her husband and loyal to
God, and she replied, " Husband, you know I love you, you
know I would do anything I could conscientiously to please
you; but I must please God first, and I know it is my duty
to unite with the church and publicly confess my faith in
Christ and I am going to do it tomorrow morning." Then
he said, " I was very angry and I said to my wife, ' Very well,
you can unite with the church. I have no intention of doing
so. From henceforth you are nothing more to me. You can
go your way and I will go mine.' We separated. We retired
to our rooms for the night. She went to her room and I went
to mine. I went to bed but not to sleep. Eleven o'clock came
and I was still awake, very angry, getting angrier all the time.
The clock struck twelve. I was still awake, very angry, getting
more and more angry all the time. The clock struck one and I
was still awake, getting angrier and angrier every minute. Two

o'clock came, and I cried from my room, 'Wife, I'm converted.' We went into the church together." When he told me, he was a successful Congregational minister. He is now in heaven. If that wife had waited for him he would never have come, but she came first and he loved her and he came too. Oh, you men and women who are waiting for your friends, you come first and if your friends love you as you do them, they will come too. It is far better for you to take them to heaven with you than to let them drag you down to hell with them. If you wait for them to come, neither you nor they will ever come, you will be lost together.

2. But some one will say, "Suppose they won't come?" Then you would better come without them; for it is far better to go to heaven alone than to go to hell in company. If there were not another person in this building tonight that started for heaven, if I were not a Christian, I would start tonight even though I had to start alone; for it is far better to go to heaven alone than it is to go to hell in the best company on earth. There is no good society in hell. Heaven is the place where all the best society is; Hell is the place where all the bad society is; and it is infinitely better to go to heaven alone than to go to hell in the very best society on earth. Men and women sometimes say to me, " I had a friend that I loved dearly and who is now dead, if that friend has gone to hell I want to go there too." You are making a great mistake. Suppose when you get to hell you find that your friend is not there. That is not at all impossible. But even suppose when you get to hell you find them there, do you suppose you will love them and enjoy them in hell? There is no love in hell. Hell is the place where everybody hates everybody else; and one of the darkest experiences of that eternal midnight world of woe will be the way in which the intensest love of earth is turned into the intensest hatred down there, and the way you hate the people whom you now love.

I shall never forget a startling experience that I had in my first pastorate. It was four miles away from Hiram, Ohio, where Hiram College of the Disciple denomination is located. Before my going to this town there had been a great revival in Hiram and many people had been converted. One night when the evangelist gave the invitation for all who would

accept Christ to come to the front, a lady arose from her place
to do so; but her husband, sitting back of her, laid his hand
on her shoulder and forced her back into the seat. He would
not permit her to go forward. She never made another attempt. Then she began to drift and drift and drift, until she
drifted into utter infidelity. That is the way most people
become infidels. There is a time when they see their duty
and see it clearly, but they will not take the step; and the
Spirit of God leaves them and they become " darkened in
their understanding " and they drift into sheer infidelity.
You ask any infidel you know if there was not a time when
he was under conviction, when he felt he ought to be a Christian and when he refused to yield, and many of them, if they
tell you the truth, will admit that there was a time when they
felt they ought to become a Christian, but they refused to
yield and drifted into infidelity. It was so with this woman.
She drifted into utter infidelity. They moved to the town
where I began my ministry. A revival came to that town.
The whole town was moved. All classes of people were being
converted. The ranks of the infidels were being broken and
the infidels became greatly alarmed. In order to interfere
with the work they sent off for an infidel lecturer to come to
the town and lecture. His coming to the town was a blessing;
for many went to hear him that did not dare to come out to
the meetings; and when they heard the inane nonsense that
he talked they were so utterly disgusted that they gave up
their infidelity and came to Christ. I remember one woman
in particular. On the first night that the infidel lecturer
spoke, she said to her husband, " Let us go and hear Professor
Jamieson." He said, " Why do you want to go and hear him?
You don't believe as he does." She replied, " I don't know
what I believe, I don't know as I believe anything." So they
went. As they were going down the stairs out of the hall
that night this woman turned to her husband and said, " Husband, I have learned one thing tonight anyway." He replied,
" I would like to know what you have learned from that mass
of nonsense." She replied, " I have learned that I believe
in the Bible. I never knew before that I did; but when I
heard that man's absurd arguments and his ridiculous abuse
of the Bible I found out that I really believe the Bible."

She came to me a few days afterward and said she wished
to accept Christ and unite with the church and she did accept
Christ, united with the church and became one of the most
faithful and most useful members in my church. I met this
man again some time later and I said to him, " Professor
Jamieson, I am glad you came to this town, you have done a lot
of good." " Well," he said, " I am very glad if I have done
any good." " Yes, you converted a lot of people I couldn't.
When they heard the nonsense you spoke, they made up their
minds to believe in the Bible and accept Jesus Christ." But
to come back to my story—while they were waiting for this
infidel lecturer to come, this lady of whom I was speaking,
who had become an infidel because she had yielded to her husband instead of to the Spirit of God, said to a friend of hers,
" I can hardly wait until Professor Jamieson gets here." She
did not wait. One Saturday night there was a neighbourhood
card party. She was present at the party. It was a very
respectable card party. I don't think they were playing for
money, I am very sure they were not. They were just playing for pleasure. Ten o'clock came and they were still playing cards. Eleven o'clock came and they were still playing
cards. Twelve o'clock Saturday night came and they were
still playing cards. The first day of the week had come—the
Lord's Day—and they were still playing cards.—Sabbath
breaking and card playing go constantly hand in hand.—At
one o'clock on the Lord's Day morning, as this woman sat
playing cards, she suddenly sprang from the table, clapped
her hand on the side of her head, cried, " Oh!" and dropped
dead beside the card table. I would rather die somewhere
else. I shall never forget my first meeting with that woman's
husband after that awful tragedy. One morning a few days
later I entered the Post Office by one door and he came in
by another. I don't think he had ever spoken to me before,
but now, as he saw me, he hurried across the Post Office with
his hand extended and I held out my hand and he took it.
Oh, he gave it such a pressure. How I pitied that man! He
knew that his wife had gone to hell and that he was to blame.
Oh, you men who are standing between your wives and Jesus
Christ, there is a dark hour coming for you, that hour when
you look down upon the face of your wife as she lies there

silent in the coffin, and know she has gone out into a Christless eternity and that you are to blame.

I said this once in Birkenhead, England, just across the Mersey from Liverpool. A few days afterward a man met me on the streets of Liverpool and stepped up to me and said, " I heard you the other night in Birkenhead and you told the story of the man who had stood between his wife and Jesus Christ, and who was responsible for her going out into a Christless eternity. You said also, ' Men, you men who are standing between your wives and Christ, there is an awful day coming for you, a day when you will look down upon the face of your wife as she lies there silent in the coffin and know she has gone out into a Christless eternity and that you are to blame.' " He continued, " Dr. Torrey, you say that wherever you go. You described my case exactly. I was standing between my wife and Jesus Christ. I went home from that meeting and I went to my wife and together we accepted Jesus Christ." But to come back to this man of whom I was speaking, he became a very warm friend of mine; he would do almost anything I asked him to do. People were amazed at the things he would do at my request, but there was one thing I could not get him to do. I could never get him to accept Jesus Christ. Now he also has gone into eternity. Do you suppose that when that wife saw him entering that dark world where she was that she welcomed him with open arms and said, " Oh, Egbert, I am so glad you have come here, I so love you and we will be so happy together here "? No, not for one moment, rather would she say, " Egbert, I loved you on earth, I hate you now. If it had not been for you I would have been in the world of eternal joy, but here I am in this dark world of everlasting woe and you are to blame. I loved you then; I hate you now."

Oh, men and women out of Christ, who have loved ones out of Christ and who are waiting for them to come, you come first and bring them with you. If they will not come with you, come without them.

There are others of you who gave other answers to the question. I will not take them up tonight. I will take them up tomorrow night. Let me say as I close, anyone here who is waiting for anything before accepting Jesus Christ as your

Saviour and surrendering to Him as your Lord and Master, and publicly confessing Him as such before the world, is making a great mistake.   You are running a fearful risk.

A mighty preacher in America of days long gone by, the Rev. Daniel Baker, illustrates this in a striking way.   He pictured a man on the deck of a steamer crossing the ocean. It is a bright, sunshiny day.   There is scarcely a breath of wind and the vessel glides smoothly along.   The surface of the deep is almost like a mirror, except where here and there it is kissed into light, dancing ripples by the gentle zephyrs that now and then fall upon it.   The man is leaning over the rail of the vessel with something in his hand that shines with wondrous glory as it lies in the palm of his hand in the sunlight.   Now and then he casts it into the air and watches it as it falls sparkling, glittering, glowing in the sunlight, and he catches it.   Again and again he casts it into the air watching eagerly as it falls through the sunlight and catches it. After he has done this many times, another man who is watching him steps up to him, lays his hand upon his shoulder and says, " What is that you have in your hand?"   He replies, " A diamond."   " Is it of any value?"   " Of great value?   Look at it, see the size of it, see the glory of it, it is of almost priceless value.   All I have in the world I have put into that gem and I am going to a new country and will sell it and realize upon it."   " But don't you think you are taking a great risk in tossing it so carelessly in the air?"   " Oh, no," he replies, " I have been doing this for the last half hour and I have never missed it yet."   " Yes, but the boat might give a sudden lurch, you might cast it too far in the air or too far out." "Oh," he replies, " there is no danger, watch me."   And again he tosses it in the air and it flashes and sparkles and glows as it falls through the sunlight.   He watches it eagerly and catches it as it falls.   Again he casts it in the air; again it shines with wondrous light and he watches it eagerly and catches it.   Again he casts it in the air.   Oh, how it flashes and glows as it falls through the sunlight.   How eagerly he watches it.   But it is a little farther out now.   He reaches as far as he can over the rail of the vessel; but it is too far out.   It is beyond the utmost reach of his fingertips, it falls into the ocean.   There is a little splash and that priceless gem sinks, sinks, sinks to the bottom of the sea and the frightened man grasps the rail of the vessel, leans far over, strives to penetrate the depths of the ocean and cries, " Lost! lost! lost! My all is lost forever!"

But some of you will say, " That is not a true story, that is too absurd to be true. No man would be such a fool as that." Yes, that is a true story. The man is in this audience tonight. Thou art the man! That ocean is eternity, that vessel is life. As you sail this ocean of eternity you hold in your hand a priceless gem, worth more than any diamond that human eye ever gazed upon in wondering admiration, your soul, worth more than this whole round earth; for " What shall it profit a man, if he shall gain the whole world, and lose his own soul?" And you are tossing it up day after day, risking its eternal loss; and I step up to you tonight and lay my hand on your shoulder and say, " Friend, what is that you have in your hand?" and you reply, " My soul," and I ask, " Is it worth anything?" " Worth anything?" you say, " Worth anything? Worth more than the whole round earth, for ' What shall it profit a man, if he shall gain the whole world, and lose his own soul?' " and then I say, " You are taking an awful risk." " No, no," you say, " there is no danger whatever. I have been doing this for the last five years, the last ten years, the last fifteen years, and my soul is not lost yet." " Yes, but there will come a last time." " No, no," you say, " there is no danger. Watch me," and again you whirl your soul in your carelessness in the air, and you watch it as it falls and you catch it, and again you whirl it into the air and watch it as it falls and catch it. Again tonight you whirl it into the air. Ah! too late, once too often. Far out it falls. You reach after it, you cannot reach it and it goes sinking, sinking, sinking, not into the depths of the ocean but into the depths of a hopeless eternity, and you grasp the rail of the vessel and look after your soul and cry, " Lost! lost! lost! My soul is lost forever." Oh, men and women, don't risk that precious, priceless soul another night. Put it tonight where it will be forever safe. Put it in the keeping of Jesus Christ tonight. Accept Christ as your Saviour tonight, confess Him tonight.

XII

WHAT ARE YOU WAITING FOR?

" And now why tarriest thou? arise, and be baptized, and wash away thy sins, calling on the name of the Lord."—Acts 22:16.

MY subject tonight is, What Are You Waiting For? We have the same text we had last night, Acts 22:16, " And now why tarriest thou? arise, and be baptized, and wash away thy sins, calling on the name of the Lord," especially the first part of the verse, " Why tarriest thou?"

We saw last night it was God Who asked the question, He asked it of Saul of Tarsus, the most bitter and most determined and most relentless, the ablest and the most dangerous enemy of Jesus Christ the world has ever known. We saw that God was putting that same question today to everyone who had not accepted Jesus Christ as his Saviour and surrendered to Him as his Lord and Master and confessed Him as such before the world.

Last night we had a few moments of absolute silence in which I asked every Christian to pray for those who were not Christians; and everyone who was not a Christian to put to himself the question, " What am I waiting for before I accept Jesus Christ as my Saviour and publicly confess Him as such before the world?" and then I offered to take up the answers each one made and to answer them. We had time last night to take up three answers. The first answer that we took up, was the answer of those who say, " I am waiting until I am convinced; I am not yet convinced that the Bible is the Word of God and that Jesus Christ is the Son of God, and I am waiting until I am convinced. As soon as I am convinced that the Bible is God's Word and that Jesus Christ is God's Son I will accept Jesus Christ as my Saviour and will confess Him as such before the world;" and I made an offer to those who made that answer that if anyone of them would come to me at the close of the meeting I would show them a way to find out for themselves that beyond a question the Bible is the Word of God and that Jesus Christ is the Son of God. And if there are any here tonight who were not here last night I repeat that offer to you.

We next took up the answer of those who say "I am waiting until I have enjoyed the world enough." We saw that all these were making a great mistake, that they were making a great mistake for three reasons. First of all, because they were proceeding upon the theory that one could live for the world for a while and then tire of it and give it up without a struggle, whereas the truth was that the longer one lived for the world, the less joy there was in it that was true, but while the joy grew less the bondage to the world became greater all the time, and that there would never be another time in which it would be quite so easy to give up the world as it is now. We saw they were making a mistake for a second reason, because every day that they were waiting until they enjoyed the world some more they were losing the far greater joy that was to be found in Jesus Christ. And we saw that they were making a mistake for a third reason, because while they are waiting until they enjoyed the world enough they might be called out of it, and "What shall it profit a man, if he shall gain the whole world, and lose his own soul?"

We took up one more answer last night, the answer of those who say, "I am waiting for my friends;" and we saw that the only wise thing to do was to come to Christ first ourselves and then to bring our friends with us, for it was infinitely better that we should come to Christ and take our friends to heaven with us, than that we should allow our friends to drag us down to hell with them. And we saw, furthermore, that if our friends would not come to Christ with us, then we would better come alone, for it was far better to go to heaven alone than to go to hell in company. But that did not cover all the answers that were made, and I am going to take up the remaining answers tonight.

I. I am Waiting for Feeling

The answer that some of you will give to the question is, "*I am waiting for feeling.*" I believe that that is true of a great many of you here tonight. There are many people in this world who would like to become Christians, that would like to become Christians at once, but they have an idea there is some peculiar sort of feeling one must have before they can come to Christ, and they have not that feeling yet, and they are waiting till they get it. That is doubtless the case with some of you here tonight.

First of all, let me ask you a question. What kind of feeling are you waiting for? What kind of feeling do you think it is necessary to have before one becomes a Christian? I will get two entirely different answers to that question.

1. Some of you will say, "*I am waiting for the joy and peace that Christians talk about. When I get that joy and peace I will confess Christ before the world.*" But " the joy and peace that Christians talk about " is the result of having come to Christ, of having accepted Him as our Saviour and surrendered to Him as our Lord and Master and of having confessed Him before the world. You do not expect, do you, the joy of having come to Christ and of having confessed Christ before you actually come? Suppose I should call upon some friend who was very sick. I go to the bedside of my friend and I say, " What is the trouble?" He replies, " I have the influenza. It seems as if I ached in every bone in my body and I am burning up with fever." Then I say, " I had the influenza a year ago (I did not, but we will suppose I had for the sake of the illustration), and I took a certain remedy and the first dose made me a great deal better, and in two or three days I was perfectly well." My friend replies, " Is that true, what was the remedy you took?" and I tell him the name of the remedy. He calls his son and sends him at once to the drug store to obtain the remedy. The son soon returns with the bottle in his hand. The sick man hands it to me and says, " Is that the remedy you took?" " Yes." " And you say the first dose made you better and that in two or three days you were perfectly well?" " Yes." " Oh," he says, " I am so glad you came." I go away and in three or four days I go back to see my friend again. I expect to find him well, but to my amazement I find him still in bed and sicker than before. I go to his bedside and say, " Are you no better?" " Better? No, I am a great deal

worse. Oh, how I ache; I am almost burning up with fever."
Then I say, " Did you get the remedy that I told you about?"
" Why, yes. Don't you remember I got it while you were
here?" "Oh, yes. Did you take the remedy?" "No, I
didn't take it. You said the first dose made you a great deal
better and I did not feel any better, and therefore I did not
take the remedy." What would you think of a man who
talked like that? What would you say? " Why, man, take
the remedy. You don't expect to get the results of taking the
remedy, do you, before you take it?" No one talks that way
about the ordinary affairs of life. It is only about **religion**
they talk in that irrational way. Do you expect the result
of having come to Christ and of having confessed Christ before you come to Him and before you confess Him? Why
man, take the remedy, take Christ tonight and confess Him
tonight, and then you will get the joy and peace that Christians talk about.

When Mr. Alexander and I were holding meetings in Melbourne, Australia, there came into the inquiry meeting one
night a bright, intelligent young woman and I spoke with her
personally. She said to me, " I want to become a Christian."
I replied, " Why then don't you become one right now?" She
replied, " Because I have no feeling." I said, " What kind
of feeling do you want?" She said, " The peace and joy that
Christians talk about. A great many of my friends have been
converted in your meetings, and they are all talking about the
joy and peace they have found." I replied, " The joy and
peace your friends have found are the result of having come
to Christ and having confessed Christ. You don't expect the
results of having come to Christ and having confessed Christ,
do you, before you actually come?" Then I continued,
" Don't you know that you are a sinner?" " Yes," she replied, " I certainly know I am a sinner." But to make sure
of it I took her to the Word of God and showed her by the
Word of God that she was a sinner, a lost sinner. Then I
said, " Don't you know that Jesus Christ died for your sins?"
" Yes," she replied, " I know that Jesus Christ died for my
sins." But to make sure of that I took her to the Word of
God again and showed her that Jesus Christ had died for our
sins. " Now," I said, " will you accept Him as your

Saviour?" She said, " I will." We knelt down and I prayed
and she prayed. We got up and she said, " I don't feel any
different yet." I replied, " I did not suppose that you would,
you have not gone far enough yet. You have not yet publicly confessed Christ. Now, you cannot do it here tonight
for everyone has gone, but whomever you go home with tonight you tell them what you have done." The next noon
when I went to the Town Hall, to the meeting for business
men, a note was handed to me. It was from this young lady.
She said, " Dear Dr. Torrey, within fifteen minutes after the
time I left the Exposition Hall last night I had all the feeling
I could stand. I went home with my brother. My brother
is not a Christian. I told him what I had done and my heart
was filled with peace and joy."

2. But others will say, " That is not the feeling I am waiting for. Of course no one will get the joy and peace of a
Christian until they have accepted Christ and confessed Him,
but *I am waiting for conviction of sin.*" There are a great
many in this world who think it is necessary to have a certain amount of conviction of sin before they can accept Christ.
God forbid that I should even seem to say anything against
conviction of sin. I believe in conviction of sin. I like to
see people under deep conviction of sin, just as they were on
the day of Pentecost, but I do not read in my Bible that any
person must have a certain amount of sorrow for sin before
they can accept Jesus Christ. What my Bible tells me is
that, What we must do to gain pardon, is to *forsake* sin, not
shed tears over it. I read in Isa. 55:7: " Let the wicked *forsake his way* (forsake it, mind you, not shed tears over it),
and the unrighteous man his thoughts: and let him return
unto the LORD, and He will have mercy upon him; and to our
God, for He will abundantly pardon." You will notice that
it does not say we are to feel sorry for our sins, but to quit
our sins. I have seen people apparently very sorry for sin.
I have seen them shed tears and groan and sob and yet not
forsake their sins; and they were not saved. I have seen a
man fall prostrate on the floor and lie there rigid and then
sob and shake over his sins, but he would not accept Christ
and he was not saved. I have seen others who never shed
a single tear, but who turned from their sins and accepted

Jesus Christ as their Saviour and who surrendered to Him as
their Lord, and they were saved. We read in the Bible that
on the day of Pentecost people were *" pricked in their heart "*
and cried unto Peter and the rest of the apostles, " Men and
brethren, what shall we do?" and there were three thousand
converted and born again that day; but we read in the six-
teenth chapter of the Acts of the Apostles regarding Lydia
that the Lord " opened her heart " so that " she attended
unto the things that were spoken of Paul." There seems to
have been no excitement, no great feeling, no tears. Then
we read, " She was baptized, and her household;" and she
became one of the most satisfactory of Christians. Getting
saved is not a matter of shedding tears, it is not a matter of
mere emotion, *it is a matter of simply accepting Jesus Christ.*
The Bible nowhere says that we are saved by conviction of
sin, but that we are saved by receiving Jesus Christ. No matter how great one's conviction of sin may be, if he does not
receive Jesus Christ he will not be saved. And on the other
hand, even if anyone has no perceptible sorrow for sin at all,
if they receive Jesus Christ they will be saved. God's Word
makes that plain as day in John 1:12, where we read, " As
many as *received Him* (not as many as shed tears, or were
under deep conviction of sin, but, " as many as *received
Him* "), to them gave He the right to become children of God,
even to them *that believe on His name."* It is not feeling
sorry for sins that saves, but simple faith in Jesus Christ.

I knew a man in Chicago who came to me time and time
again, he was a drinking man and I would talk with him and
pray with him and he would shed tears. They would fairly
run down his cheeks. But he did not give up his drinking,
and did not accept Christ. That went on, I think, for as long
as two years. Then one day he came to me, and, as far as
I can recall, he did not shed a single tear. But he accepted
Jesus Christ and gave up his drink, and became a transformed
man. All his tears did not save him: his accepting of Christ
did save him. Let me drive it home: IT IS NOT FEELING
SORRY FOR SIN, BUT FORSAKING SIN AND ACCEPTING JESUS
CHRIST THAT SAVES.

I was holding a meeting one night in one of the Baptist
churches in Chicago. In the after meeting I went down and

talked with a gentleman of perhaps thirty-five years of age
and his wife. I said to this man, " Why are you not a Christian?" He replied, " I would like to be a Christian, I hope
to be a Christian some day. My father was a Baptist minister and my mother was one of the best women that ever
lived; and I, too, hope to be a Christian some day." I said,
" Why do you not accept Jesus Christ tonight?" He replied,
" I have no conviction of sin." Then turning to me he said,
" You believe in conviction of sin, do you not?" I said,
" Yes, indeed, I do; and I think that anyone who has sinned
as much as you or I ought to have conviction of sin. But,"
I added, " I do not read anywhere in my Bible that it is neces-
sary to have a certain amount of conviction of sin to be saved.
What my Bible tells me is that the thing we must do to be
saved is to forsake sin and accept Jesus Christ as our personal Saviour and confess Him as such before the world."
Then I said, " Do you not know that you are a sinner?"
" Yes," he said, " I know I am a sinner." " Do you not know
that Jesus Christ died for your sins?" " Yes, I know that
Jesus Christ died for my sins." " Don't you know that, if
you will accept Jesus Christ tonight, He will save you tonight?" He replied, " Yes, I know if I accept Jesus Christ
tonight, He will save me tonight." " Then, why don't you
accept Him right now?" He replied, " I have no feeling."
" Oh," I said, " bother the feeling. What business are you
in?" He replied, " I am in the real estate business."
" Well," I said, " suppose I should call at your office tomorrow morning and offer to sell you a fine corner lot here in
Chicago for Five Thousand Dollars and you knew that you
could turn within twenty-four hours and sell that lot for ten
thousand dollars, but for some reason or other you did not
feel like buying it, what would you do?" " I would buy it
quick, feeling or no feeling," he replied. " Well," I said,
" why do you not have as much sense in religion as you have
in business? Don't you know you are a sinner?" " Yes, I
know I am a sinner." " Don't you know Jesus Christ died
to save you?" " Yes, I know that Jesus Christ died to save
me." " Don't you know that if you accepted Him tonight
He would save you tonight?" " Yes, I know that if I accepted Him tonight He would save me tonight." " Don't you

know that that would be the best paying investment in all the world?" "Yes," he said, "I know that would be the best investment I could make in all the world." "Well," I said, "will you do it?" He said, "I will." "All right," I said, "let us kneel down and tell God so." All three of us knelt. I prayed, he prayed and his wife prayed. They came out into a bright Christian experience. I went back to that church a few months later and he had made such rapid progress in the Christian life they had already made him a trustee in the church.

There are only two things that anyone needs to know and only one thing anyone needs to do in order to be saved: the first thing we need to know in order to be saved is that we are sinners. You all know that, do you not? You know that you are a sinner. The second thing we need to know is that Jesus Christ is an all-sufficient Saviour. You know that, do you not? The one thing and the only thing we have to do is simply to accept Him as our own Saviour; and the moment we do that one thing, accept Jesus, and show that we have done it by confessing Him before the world, that moment we are saved, feeling or no feeling.

Men and women, listen, Jesus Christ is an all-sufficient Saviour from the power of sin by His resurrection power. The moment you accept Him as your own Saviour and trust God to forgive you because Jesus Christ died in your place, and look to Him to deliver you from the power of sin, and surrender to Him as your Lord and Master and confess Him as such before the world, that moment you are a saved man or woman, feeling or no feeling. Will you thus accept Him tonight?

II. I am Waiting Until I am Better

But someone will say, "That is not my difficulty at all, *I am waiting until I am better. I am not good enough to come to Christ and I am waiting until I am better."* I believe that is true of a great many thoroughly sincere and very earnest people. They would like to become Christians; they see the beauty of Christian life; they see the wisest thing anyone can do for time and for eternity is to accept Jesus Christ as Saviour and surrender to Him as their Lord and Master;

but they do not think they are good enough yet to come to Christ and they are waiting until they are good enough before they come. What shall I say to you? Listen to what Jesus Christ Himself says, in Matt. 9:12, 13, " They that are whole need not a physician, but they that are sick. . . . *I am not come to call the righteous, but sinners."* Jesus Christ is a Physician, a Physician of the soul. Who needs a physician? The man who is sick; and the sicker a man is the more he needs the physician. Suppose I should call on some friend who was very sick. I find this man tossing upon his bed in great pain and see that he is dangerously ill. I turn to my friend and say, " You are very sick." He replies, " Yes. I know I am very sick." I continue, " You are dangerously sick." " Yes, I know I am dangerously sick." I add, " You need a physician and you need him at once." " Yes," he says, " I know I need a physician, and I need him badly, and I need him at once. But I am too sick to send for a physician. I am waiting until I am better before I send for the doctor." What would you think of a man who answered you in that way? Would you not say, " Why man, the fact that you are very sick is the reason why you should send for the doctor at once." No sensible man talks in that way about anything but religion. Listen! the fact that you are so sinful is the very reason why you should come to Christ immediately. There is not one man or woman here tonight who is good enough to come to Christ on their merits, but thank God, there is not one of us so sinful that Jesus Christ will not accept us if we come. He Himself says, " Him that cometh to Me (no matter who he is or how bad he is) I will in no wise cast out." (John 6:37.) There is not a man or woman on earth so sinful but Jesus Christ will receive them and save them if they will only come to Him. If you wait until you are good enough to come to Christ on your merits you will never come and you will be lost forever, but if you will come to Christ and accept Him as your Saviour and surrender to Him as your Lord and Master, and confess Him as such before the world, no matter how bad you are Jesus Christ will accept you and save you tonight.

I was preaching one Sunday morning in our church in Minneapolis. At the close of the service, one of my deacons walked down the aisle speaking to different people that he met. He stepped up to a well dressed and prosperous looking man and said to him, " Are you a Christian?" "No," he replied, " I am not a Christian." Then the deacon asked him, " Why are you not a Christian?" He replied, " Because I am too great a sinner to be saved." The deacon instantly exclaimed, " Praise God!" The man looked very much mystified that a deacon should be praising God that he was so great a sinner. I had not yet left the platform, and the deacon turned to me and said, " Come down here, Brother Torrey. Here is a man who says he is too great a sinner to be saved, praise the Lord!" I understood what the deacon meant, and went at once to the man with whom he was talking. I asked him, " Is what the deacon says true?" " Yes," he replied, " I am too great a sinner to be saved." I immediately opened my Bible to I Tim. 1:15 and put it in his hands and asked him to read it. He read, " This is a faithful saying, and worthy of all acceptation, that Christ Jesus came into the world to save sinners; of whom I am chief." " Well," he said, " I am ' chief,' " and it turned out that he was a great sinner. He had deserted his wife in Toronto and was up in Minneapolis squandering his time and manhood in gambling and in sin. And if there is any contemptible man on earth, it is the man who runs away and leaves his wife to take care of herself, and then spends his time, his money and his manhood in sin. Furthermore, this man had lost thirty-five thousand dollars the week before at the gaming table. He said, " I am ' chief.' " I said, " Well, then, it means you." " It is a precious promise," he exclaimed. I said, " Will you accept it right now?" He said, " I will." Then I said, " Let us kneel down and tell God so." We knelt down. I prayed. He prayed. He arose a saved man. I do not think the conversation was any longer than I have related it to you tonight. He attended our meetings for several days and then had to leave the city for the far Northwest. I expected to hear from him, but did not. Some months passed by,—about a year. In the meantime, the deacon who had introduced me to this man had been away for several months in St. Paul. After his return, he said to me one day, " Do you remember that man that I introduced you to one morning in the church, who said he was too great a sinner to be saved?" I said, "Yes, indeed I do." He said, "Have you ever heard from him?" I said, "No, I have often wondered why I have not heard from him." He said, "Let me tell you about him." Then he said, "You know I have been away all winter in St. Paul. Well, that man was there too. I have seen him pretty much every night for months at the meeting to which I went, earnestly working to lead others to Christ. He sent to Toronto for the wife whom he had deserted, and she came to him, and they are so happy in their reunited life that they have adopted a little child out of the orphan asylum to make the home complete." The same Christ Jesus, Who on that Sunday morning saved this man who thought he was too great a sinner to be saved, can save anybody in this audience tonight, no matter how great your sins may be.

III. I am Waiting Until I am Sure I Can Hold Out

But someone else will say, "That is not my difficulty, I know that Jesus Christ saves sinners and that the more sinful I am the more quickly I need to come to Him, but *I am waiting until I am sure I can hold out*." I believe that is true of a great many people in this world. They sincerely desire to be Christians, but they know that they are very weak and they are afraid that if they start out in the Christian life they will fail and they do not wish to bring reproach on Jesus Christ; so they are waiting until they are sure they can hold out. What shall I say to you? Listen to what God Himself says in Jude 24, 25, "God our Saviour is able to keep you from falling, and to present you faultless before the presence of His glory with exceeding joy." It is not at all a question of your ability to hold out, but only of God's ability to keep you; and there is no question at all about that. There is not a man or woman in this building tonight who can hold out in the Christian life twenty-four hours in their own strength; but thank God, there is not a man or woman in this building tonight so weak but that God can hold them to the end, if they will just give up their own efforts to keep themselves and let God " keep " them " through Jesus Christ our Lord."

Sometimes a man will stand up in a meeting and full of self-confidence will say, " Friends, I have accepted Jesus Christ tonight. You know me. You know how strong my will is, and I want you to know that I don't propose to backslide as so many do. I am in for the whole war. I propose to hold out to the end." Now, when I hear a man talk like that, full of self-confidence, I know he is going to backslide inside of six weeks every time. But another man will stand up and say, " Friends, I have accepted Jesus Christ tonight. You all know me. You know how weak I am. You know how unable I am to keep my good resolutions. You know how often I have signed the pledge and failed to keep it. You all know that I haven't strength to continue in the Christian life a single day. But tonight I have accepted Jesus Christ as my personal Saviour and I am trusting Him to keep me." When I hear a man talk that way, I know that he is going to continue to the end. The time will never come when you can hold out in the Christian life in your own strength; but tonight the time has already come when, if you put your trust in Jesus Christ for Him to do the keeping, you can hold out to the end.

How many men I have known who started out in the Christian life utterly weak. They had no strength at all; but they put their trust in Jesus Christ to keep them. For many years I had a very dear friend. He is in heaven now. That man had become an utter wreck through drink. He had committed a hundred and thirty-nine forgeries and the police were hunting for him. He had spent the night before in the lock-up. He had gone to the police sergeant and asked him to lock him up for the night; for he knew he was on the verge of delirium tremens. It was a night of awful horror. The next night he went to the Cremorne Mission in New York City. He heard Jerry McAuley tell how the Lord Jesus Christ had saved him, and when Jerry said, " If there is anyone who wants to be saved tonight let him come to the front," he went up the aisle and said to Jerry McAuley, " Pray for me." Jerry replied, " Pray for yourself." But he did not know how to pray. He had forgotten how. But he knelt down and cried out, " God be merciful to me, a sinner," and before he got up he was a transformed man. He became one of the most beautiful Christian characters I ever knew. One time I was in Washington at a Conference. Mr. Wanamaker, who was then Postmaster-General of the United States, attended the Conference, and said to me, " I want you to come around to my house for dinner." I went. When I was ushered into the drawing room, whom should I see sitting there but this man, Sam Hadley and his wife, honoured guests in the home of the Postmaster-General of the United States; the former forger, the man who had no will power left, the hopeless and helpless drunkard, but now saved by simple faith in Jesus Christ.

There is not a man or woman in this audience tonight so weak, so helpless and so hopeless that Jesus Christ can not hold you to the end, if you will only put your trust in Him. Listen to what God says in another place in the Bible, Isa. 41:13, " Fear thou not; for I am with thee: be not dismayed; for I am thy God: I will strengthen thee; yea, I will help thee; yea, I will uphold thee with the right hand of my righteousness." That is God's promise: and how many a man with will power all gone, no strength left to continue in anything that is good, has put his trust in this promise and trusted the almighty God to hold him up; and God has done it. One night in Chicago I was speaking in a mission. At the close of the meeting I went and sat down beside a man who burst into tears as soon as I began to talk with him. I said, " What is the trouble?" " Oh," he said, " I would like to be a Christian. My mother was a fine Christian woman and she has died and gone to heaven. And I had a fine Christian wife and she has died and gone to heaven. And I had a little daughter, and she was a Christian. She died last week and has gone to heaven; and I would like to go too." I said, " Why don't you accept Christ tonight?" " Oh," he said, " I can't. I am a drunkard. I have no will power left." Then I read him this passage from the Word of God, " Fear thou not; for I am with thee: be not dismayed; for I am thy God: I will strengthen thee; yea, I will help thee; yea, I will uphold thee with the right hand of my righteousness." And that poor, helpless man put his trust in Jesus Christ then and there. How many a man has stood at the bottom of the shining path that leads up to heaven and to eternal glory; and as he looks up that shining pathway it seems to him as

if he could almost look within the gates at the top. Within
those gates a mother had passed and is now in the glory;
through those gates a wife had passed and is now in the
glory; through those gates some beloved child had passed and
is now in the glory. And oh, how he longs to go there too;
but the way seems so steep and he so weak that he dares not
start,—and then a hand is let down from heaven; it is the
hand of God; and he hears a voice saying, " Fear thou not;
for I am with thee: be not dismayed; for I am thy God: I
will strengthen thee; yea, I will help thee; yea, I will uphold
thee with the right hand of My righteousness." And he has
put his poor, weak hand in that mighty hand of God and God
has led him on and on and on, and up and up and up, and
many such a one has already entered into the glory. Will
you trust God and His promise and start tonight?

IV. I am Waiting Until I Have Done Something That I Could Not Do if I Were a Christian

But someone will say, " Oh, that is not my difficulty at all:
that is not what I am waiting for. *There is something I wish
to do that I could not do if I were a Christian, and I am
waiting until I have done that and then I will accept Jesus
Christ and confess Him before the world.*" That is the way
with a great many, probably the way with many of you here
tonight. There is something you wish to do in business that
is not exactly straight and honourable and you know you could
not do it if you were a Christian, and you are waiting until
you have done that before you become a Christian. Others
of you have something that you wish to do in a political way
that you could not do if you were a Christian and you are
waiting until you have gained your political end before you
accept Christ. Others of you have some plan for the pursuit
of pleasure that you could not carry out if you were a Christian, and you are waiting until you have done that before you
become a Christian. There are many like that; many, I presume, in this audience tonight. What shall I say to you?
Listen to what God says, " Seek ye *first* the kingdom of God,
and His righteousness." (Matt. 6:33.) The first thing to
attend to is " the kingdom of God " and your eternal welfare.
The wise man puts first things first, and your eternal welfare

is the first thing. IF YOU PUT ANYTHING ELSE BEFORE THE ACCEPTANCE OF JESUS CHRIST YOU WILL LOSE YOUR SOUL. Let those words of Christ sink into your heart, " Seek ye first the kingdom of God. Seek ye *first* the kingdom of God. Seek ye FIRST the kingdom of God." How many there are who have lost their souls for all eternity by putting something else before the acceptance of Jesus Christ.

Mr. Finney tells of a man in New York State who was under deep conviction of sin. He had a personal interview with Mr. Finney and Mr. Finney urged upon him an immediate acceptance of Jesus Christ and an immediate confession of him before the world. But the man replied, " Mr. Finney, I am running for the Legislature. Some of my friends have put me up for this office and I must see them before I take a step like this. They may think it will prejudice my chances of election." Mr. Finney urged upon him that it was not a question between him and the friends who put him up for office, but a question between him and God. But he said, " No, they have put me up for this office and I think I owe it to them to consult them first." He went away to consult with them, and came back and said, " Mr. Finney, my friends say I must not think of taking the step at this time: that if I do it will prejudice my chances of election, and I believe I owe it to them not to do anything that will prejudice my chances of election." Mr. Finney urged upon him the grave peril of the foolish course he was pursuing; but the man would not yield. He was successful in the election, he was elected to the New York Legislature. He went there to take his place. Shortly after taking his seat in the Legislature he was suddenly taken very ill and died in awful agony of mind. He had sold his soul for a position in the Legislature. Oh, listen! listen! If you put anything else before the salvation of your soul through the acceptance of Jesus Christ you will lose your soul.

A Methodist minister in a certain place where I was holding meetings, told me this story from his own experience. He said that in a former pastorate a young lady in his congregation was brought under deep conviction of sin. He urged upon her an immediate acceptance and confession of Jesus Christ; but the young woman said, " No, Mr. Sawyer, there

is to be a dance next week and I have made up my mind to
attend that dance.   Now if I accept Jesus Christ I could not
go to that dance.   I will go to that dance and I will promise
you I will never go to another, and I will accept Jesus Christ
and confess Him before the world."   Mr. Sawyer urged upon
her the danger of the course she was pursuing; but she was
obstinate and said, " No, I will not accept Christ this week.
I will go to that dance, and after that is over I promise you I
will accept Christ and confess Him and never go to another."
All of the minister's pleadings made no impression upon her.
She went to the dance, caught cold, had lung fever, went down
to the gates of death.   Her pastor called upon her and urged
upon her an immediate acceptance of Christ.   He said, " You
are very ill; they think you are dying; they think there is
no hope of your recovery.   Accept Jesus Christ now.   You
promised me you would accept Him when the dance was over.
The dance is over, accept Christ."   She shook her head and
said, " No, no, I know I am very sick, I know I am near to
death, I do not expect to live; but I cannot accept Christ now.
I refused to take Him last week when I was well and strong
and now I am sick and dying I cannot accept Him," and she
died without Christ and without hope.   Ah, you men and
women who are putting off the acceptance of Christ until you
have done something you think you could not do if you were
Christians, unless you give that up and accept Jesus Christ
now, right here tonight, the overwhelming probability is that
you will lose your soul and spend eternity in hell.

V.   I am Waiting Until I Die

But someone else will say, " That is not my difficulty, *I am
waiting until I die.   I am going to enjoy this world just as
long as I can, and when I find out I am going to die and can
enjoy it no longer I will give it up and accept Christ and be
saved.*"   Now that is true of a great many.   As a rule they
do not put it in that blunt way, but that is their real thought.
They are going to enjoy the world just as long as they can,
and then, when they see they are near death and see the world
slipping out of their hands anyway, they propose to give it
up and accept Christ.   A young lady in Sherman, Texas, said
to me one night bluntly and frankly in so many words when

I urged upon her an immediate acceptance of Christ, " Dr. Torrey, I love the world, and I am going to have it just as long as I can, and when I see I am going to die I will accept Jesus Christ and get salvation too." You don't put it in that straightforward way, but that is true of many of you tonight. What shall I say to you?

1. First of all, let me ask you a question, *Have you any guarantee that you will not die tonight?* Is there a man or woman in this audience tonight who would be so foolish as to dare to stand up and say, " I am absolutely sure I will not die tonight?" I think not. Not one of us can tell how soon the summons may come. Time and time again in my experience as a minister of the Gospel I have spoken to people who were apparently in perfect health and strength, who were in eternity before another day had passed.

2. Let me ask you a second question, *Have you any guarantee that, when you do die, you will not die suddenly?* People take it for granted that they are going to have a long, lingering illness and plenty of time to think and to repent and accept Christ and attend to the affairs of eternity. But is that the way most people die in these days? Most people that I know, especially out here in California, who have died, died suddenly. And it is largely so everywhere. My father was walking around the room, dressed. He had not been in bed a day. He lay down on the sofa and was gone almost immediately. My oldest brother was sitting up talking to friends, he lay back on a pillow and was gone instantly. I expect to go that way, if I die at all. Thank God, I am ready and would rather die suddenly than with a long, lingering illness. Have you any guarantee that you will not die suddenly and with no opportunity for repentance?

3. Let me ask you a third question, *Have you any guarantee that when you do die, even if you have a long, lingering illness, that you will have any disposition to repent?* Many people take it for granted that one of the best places in the world to repent is on the deathbed. My experience is, and it has been a wide experience and a long and large experience, that *a deathbed is the poorest place in the world for repentance.* I have been at many deathbeds. I have gone miles in the darkness of the night and in the storm, sometimes on foot,

sometimes in a carriage and sometimes on horseback to stand beside a dying man and to try to lead him to Christ; and I am ready to go again,—but I would rather speak to one man in good health and in full possession of his faculties, than to a dozen men on their deathbeds; I would have more confidence that something of real value was to be accomplished. Of all the professed deathbed repentances that I have ever seen I have never known but one, of the genuineness of which I was at all confident. I have known one, but only one. The men and women who wait until they die before they repent are in the overwhelming majority of cases lost forever. Once speaking in Rogers Park, a suburb of Chicago, I made the remark I made a few moments ago, that of all the death-bed repentances of which I had known, I had never known but one, of the genuineness of which I was at all confident. A physician over seventy years of age came to me at the close of the meeting and said, " Did you say that of all the death-bed repentances of which you had known you had never known but one, of the genuineness of which you were at all confident?" I replied, " Yes, that is exactly what I have said." He said, " Let me tell you of my experience. I have been a physician for upwards of fifty years. I am a Christian. I always make it a point to talk to my patients about their soul's welfare. I have been at many a deathbed, but I have never seen in all my life one deathbed repentance that I thought was genuine." IF YOU WAIT UNTIL YOUR DEATH-BED BEFORE YOU ACCEPT JESUS CHRIST, THE OVERWHELMING PROBABILITY IS THAT YOU WILL BE LOST FOREVER.

My first winter in Chicago I got home late one night after a very busy day. In the morning I had been lecturing to my students, answering letters and doing other things. In the afternoon I had been studying. At night I had been out preaching. It was after eleven o'clock at night when I reached home. My wife had already retired. I went into the sitting room and turned up the droplight; and, as I did so, I noticed that my wife had pinned a note to the tube of the droplight. I opened it and read, " Dear Archie, There is a man dying down at 228 North Clark Street. They think he cannot live through the night. They want you to call. Now whatever hour you get home tonight, don't go to bed until you have seen that man." It was late, it was cold out, and I was tired, I wanted to postpone it until the next day; but I thought, No, the man may die tonight. So I turned down the light again, put on my overcoat and cap, drew on my gloves and started for 228 North Clark Street. It was only four or five blocks from my house. I had no difficulty in finding the building, but I had great difficulty in finding the flat in the building. At last I pushed a door open, and within I saw a number of people standing around a bed upon which a man was lying. I knew none of them, but they all seemed to know me and passed out of the room as soon as I entered, and left me alone with the dying man. I saw he was near his end and whatever was done must be done quickly. I stepped at once to his bedside and put my right hand on the outside rail of the bed and the other hand beyond him, and then bent over him so as to be sure he would hear every word I said. It was over thirty-four years ago, but I remember it as vividly as if it were last night. Oh, how eagerly that dying man looked up into my eyes. I began to explain to him as simply and as briefly as I could just what he must do to be saved. He drank in every word as I was explaining to him the way of life, and, oh, how eagerly he was looking up into my eyes. Suddenly there was a little gurgle in his throat; and I was looking down into the eyes of a dead man and a dead man was looking up into my eyes, and I was trying to tell a dead man what to do to be saved. Too late!

Oh, men and women, whatever you are waiting for, put away your delay and accept Jesus Christ right now.

XIII

MR. MOODY'S LAST TEXT

"And they all with one consent began to make excuse."
LUKE 14:18.

MR. MOODY preached his last sermon in the old Convention Hall in Kansas City, Mo., late in the year 1899. The building was crowded, about fifteen thousand people, if I remember the capacity of the building correctly, being present. Before he finished his sermon it was noticed by some that he staggered and leaned upon a piano, but he finished the sermon and God blessed it and many found Christ that night. But he knew that his condition was serious, and he telegraphed me in Chicago, " Torrey, I am feeling poorly. Come to Kansas City and take my Saturday meetings and help me on Sunday." I immediately boarded a train for Kansas City, but when I arrived there found they had already taken him away on a private car to his Northfield home, where a few days before Christmas, 1899, he passed triumphantly into the glory.

When I was in Kansas City holding meetings last April, a man who heard that last sermon of Mr. Moody's came to me and said, " Won't you preach on Mr. Moody's last text?" I replied, " I don't know what Mr. Moody's last text was." Then he told me what the text was and something about the meeting and I preached on that text and God blessed the preaching of His Word.

You will find the text in Luke 14:18, " And they all with one consent began to make excuse." In these words our Lord Jesus Christ describes how the great majority of men in His own generation would receive the Gospel invitation. Instead of receiving it with glad alacrity and appreciative gratitude that one would naturally expect that they all would, the vast majority of men begin to trump up excuses for not accepting it at all. The Gospel invitation has been received in

exactly the same way throughout the centuries and is received
in exactly the same way by the average man today. Instead
of accepting it with the responsive gratitude and appreciative
eagerness that one would naturally expect of intelligent men,
they begin to search for some excuse for not accepting it at
all. The Gospel invitation is an invitation to a feast, to the
most bountiful and joyous feast that was ever spread on earth,
but the average man and average woman treat the invitation
to it as if it were an invitation to a funeral. Nothing more
clearly reveals the blindness and desperate wickedness of the
unregenerate heart than the way in which men and women
treat God's wondrous invitation of infinite grace and mercy.
That invitation, as we have said, is an invitation to a Royal
Banquet, but men treat it as if it were an invitation to
a funeral. If the king of England should make a feast next
week and invite to it some of the leading men and women of
the realm, everyone that received an invitation to that feast
would move heaven and earth if necessary, to be present;
but when the great King of kings and Lord of lords, the eternal and almighty God, spreads His Royal Banquet and in-
vites to it men and women like you and me, instead of mov-
ing heaven and earth to get there at any cost, we search
through heaven and earth for some excuse for not coming at
all. God's inviting us to His Son, Jesus Christ, and to heaven
and eternal life in Him, is the culmination of all His wondrous dealings with us in Christ, and it is amazing that men
and women treat that invitation as they did in Jesus Christ's
day and as they do till this day. It is well-nigh incompre-
hensible that they do so treat it. I can understand men's
trampling under foot the law of God; what I cannot understand is men's trampling under foot the grace of God and
the love of God manifested in His giving His Son to die for
us on the cross of Calvary, and their treating with the contempt that they do, the invitation of His grace to come to the
Royal Banquet that He has spread for us in the Gospel of
His Son. The only possible reasonable explanation of it is
the one given in the Bible, that " the (natural) heart is deceitful above all things, and desperately wicked." (Jer. 17:9.)

Our Lord Jesus, in the parable of which our text is a part,
gives us three specimen excuses that men made for not ac-

cepting the invitation to the Royal Feast. The excuses are all alike in this, that each one of them appears reasonable at the first glance, but on careful examination is found to be absolutely unreasonable and utterly absurd. That is the point of it, our Lord Jesus wishes us to see how utterly irrational and ridiculously absurd are all the excuses that men make for not coming to Christ. The excuse the first man made was, " I have bought a piece of ground, and I must needs go and see it: I pray thee have me excused." Now at the first glance that appears like a good reason. Buying a piece of land is an important transaction and no sensible man wishes to buy land without first seeing it. But notice exactly what this man said, " I *have* bought a piece of land." The land was already purchased. The transaction was finished. There was therefore no hurry about seeing it at once. By the way, what sensible man ever buys land first and goes to see it afterwards? I remember some men that did that very thing when I was living in Minneapolis in the boom times. A real estate agent went down into Wisconsin to sell some land near Lake Harriet, one of the most beautiful parts of the coming great city. He represented this land as being well located, right near the lake, indeed touching the lake, and having good soil, and on this representation a number of men down there bought lots. Afterward one of these men came to Minneapolis to see his lot. He found that it was indeed near the lake, very near, it did touch the lake, but alas! it was at the bottom of the lake and touched it on the under side. It was good soil, but there were six feet of water on top of it. The fact is this man in the parable had no reason and so he trumped up an excuse. That is just what an excuse is, a substitute for a reason. There is no man on earth that has a good reason for not coming to Christ and therefore men trump up " *excuses.*"

The second man's excuse was equally absurd. He said, " I have bought five yoke of oxen, and I go to prove them: I pray thee have me excused." Now, that, too, at the first glance looks like a good excuse. Nobody wants to buy oxen until he has tested them and found out that they are well broken, but remember what this man was invited to, " a supper," a night meal; what intelligent man ever goes to try oxen at night?   This man also had no reason and simply trumped up an excuse.

The third man's excuse was the most absurd of all, " I have married a wife, and therefore I cannot come."   Now if the invitation had been an invitation to a funeral that might have been a perfectly legitimate excuse, no man wants to take a bride to a funeral; but he was not invited to a funeral but to a feast, who ever knew a bride who was not glad to go to a reception?   Why did he not go and take his wife with him? Women were welcome at feasts in that land.   The fact is, this man had no *reason* and therefore he also just trumped up an excuse.

That is just the way it is today.   As I have said, no man on earth has a good reason for not coming to Christ; so men who in the wickedness of their hearts do not wish to come trump up excuses to cover up their wickedness and to justify their foolishness.

Now you laugh at these men's excuses, but is there a man here tonight or woman here tonight who has a better excuse than any one of these three men had?   Every excuse that men make today for not coming to Christ, while it may appear at the first glance to be reasonable, when you come to examine it, is found to be just as absurd and unreasonable as those of which our Lord tells us in the parable.

We are going to take up tonight some of the excuses that men make in our day for not coming to Christ, and carefully examine them.

I.   There is Too Much to Give Up

One of the most common excuses that men and women make in our day for not coming to Christ is, *There is too much to give up*.   Now that is as unreasonable as any excuse our Lord mentions in the parable.   " What," someone will say, " do you mean to say, Dr. Torrey, there is nothing to give up when one comes to Christ?"   No, I do not mean to say that at all.   I know there is something to give up when men come to Christ; oftentimes there is much to give up.   I doubt if anyone ever came to Christ without having been obliged to give up something that they thought very dear in order to do it.   " If that is so," you will say, " how can you say the excuse is absurd?" It is absurd for three reasons.

1. First of all, the excuse is absurd because, *The only things that God asks you to give up are the things that are doing you harm.* God never asked any man to give up any really good thing. We have God's Own Word for that in Ps. 84:11, " The LORD God is a sun and shield: The LORD God will give grace and glory: *no good thing* will He withhold from them that walk uprightly." God never asked anyone to give up anything that it was really for their highest good to keep. The only things that God asks us to give up are the things that are doing us harm and that we are far better off without. He has given us a wonderful guarantee of that. What that guarantee is you will find in Rom. 8:32, " He that *spared not His Own Son,* but *delivered Him up for us all,* how shall He not *with Him also freely give us all things?"* When God gave His Son to die upon the cross of Calvary for you and me, He gave the very best that He had to give, that which was dearest to Him and that it cost Him so much to give, and do you suppose that after God has given His Own Son up to die for you that He will withhold from you anything that it is really good for you to have?

I was talking with a young lady in an inquiry meeting in New Haven many years ago, when Mr. Moody was holding evangelistic services in that city. I had known this young woman before I was converted, and seeing her in the inquiry meeting went over to speak to her and to urge her to accept Jesus Christ. As I talked to her she said, " Mr. Torrey, I would like to be a Christian, but there is too much to give up. You know how I love the world and I am not willing to give it up for Christ. I can't come to Christ, there is too much to give up." I replied, " Do you think God loves you?" " Yes," she answered quickly, " I know that God loves me." I said, " How much do you think God loves you?" She answered, " He loved me enough to give His Son to die for me." " Very well," I said, " if God loved you enough to give His Son to die for you, do you think He will ask you to give up anything that is for your good to keep?" " No," she said, " He certainly will not." " Do you wish to keep anything it is not for your good to keep?" She hesitated a moment and said, " No, I don't." Then I said, " Do you not think you

had better take Jesus Christ right now." She said, "Yes, I
will," and she did. Was that not good sense? I put the
same question to you tonight, Do you think God loves you?
You know He does. How much do you think He loves you?
You know He loved you enough to give His Son to die for
you. Well, if God loved you enough to give His Son to die
for you, do you think He will ask you to give up anything
that is for your good to keep? He certainly will not. Do
you wish to keep anything that is not for your good to keep?
If you have any sense you certainly do not. Well, then, do
you not think you would better come to Jesus Christ right
now? Be as wise as that young woman in New Haven and
say right now, before I finish my sermon, "I will come: I
will take Jesus Christ tonight."

2. The excuse is foolish for a second reason, and that is
because, *What you have to give up when you take Christ is
nothing to what you get.* It is very easy to give up pennies,
is it not, if one gets dollars in exchange for them? It is easy
to give up tin, is it not, when you get gold in exchange for it?
It is very easy, is it not, to give up the prettiest pieces of col-
oured glass one ever saw, if one gets real diamonds and pearls
and pigeon blood rubies in exchange for them? And it is very
easy to give up the baubles of this world's pleasures and this
world's gain, when one gets the real diamonds and pearls and
emeralds and pigeon blood rubies of the Kingdom in exchange
for them.

Suppose there were in this city a young girl with a very
pretty face, but without much money and with still less sense.
This girl could not afford real diamonds so she purchased
Brazilian pebbles and wore them. She could not afford to
wear real pearls so she bought some "am I pearls" made out
of oyster shells and wore them. She would like to have had
a real gold ring with a real emerald set between two diamonds,
but she could not afford them so she wore a rolled gold ring
with a piece of green glass set between two paste diamonds.
A sensible young fellow belonging to a richer class of society
comes along and falls in love with this girl. You say "no
sensible fellow would fall in love with a girl like that." You
cannot tell what a man will do when he falls in love. This
young fellow takes his girl out to many social functions, but

he is always ashamed of this sham jewelry that she wears, and every time he takes her out he hears his friends laughing at her and at him. So one night he musters up courage and he calls upon his best girl and he says to her, " Mary, there is something I want to talk to you about. I don't want to hurt your feelings, but I feel I must speak about this." " Oh, John," she says, " say anything you like." " Mary, I wish you would throw away that sham jewelry you wear. All our friends are laughing at us because you wear it." " Oh," she replies hesitatingly, " I don't believe people know it is sham." " Yes, Mary, everybody knows it is sham. Won't you give it up?" She hesitates and says, " I would be willing to do almost anything for you, John, but this is all I have." " Mary, won't you give it up for my sake?" Still she hesi- tates to promise to throw it away, and John goes home that night with a very heavy heart; for it is a dark day for any young fellow when he finds out that his best girl hasn't real good sense. But a few nights later he comes back again hopefully, yes, radiantly happy. He has in his hand a beau- tiful Russia leather box. He says, " Mary, I have something I want to show you," and he holds out this Russia leather box. She gazes eagerly at it. He presses a spring in the front and the cover flies back and there, lying upon fine white satin lies a beautiful pair of two karat diamond earrings, diamonds of the very first water, and a beautiful pearl necklace of large and perfectly matched pearls, and a beautiful platinum ring set with three large diamonds, gems of the very first quality. " Look there, Mary," he says. How Mary's eyes glisten. She sees lying upon the white satin the beautiful diamond ear- rings large and wonderful, the costly pearl necklace and the platinum ring with the three wonderful stones set in the plati- num. " Oh, John," she exclaims, " how beautiful they are! Whom are they for?" " For you, Mary, if you will only throw away that sham jewelry that you are wearing." How long would it take Mary to take those Brazilian pebble ear- rings from her ears, those bogus pearls from her neck and that sham ring from her finger and cast them all into the fire? Oh, men and women, throw away these sham jewels of the world upon which you have set your heart, and get in place

of them the real diamonds and pearls and pigeon blood rubies
of the Kingdom.

I suppose that no one ever gave up more for Jesus Christ
than the apostle Paul, and yet Paul says, in speaking of the
things he had given up for Christ, " What things were gain
to me, those I counted loss for Christ. Yea, doubtless, and
I count all things but loss for the excellency of the knowledge
of Christ Jesus my Lord: for Whom I have suffered the loss
of all things, and do count them but vilest refuse, that I may
win Christ."

3. The excuse is foolish for a third reason and that is,
because, *What you have to give up for Christ is nothing to
what Jesus Christ gave up for you.* Oh, when you and I stop
to think of what Christ gave up for us, how He gave up all
the glory of heaven and came down to all the shame of earth
for us, how He gave up the praises of the angels and the archangel, of the cherubim and the seraphim, and came down to
this world to be despised and rejected of men, to be spit upon,
to be blindfolded, to be buffeted, to be crowned with thorns,
to be scourged until His back was torn to shreds, for us, to
be nailed to the cross of Calvary for us and to die of a broken
heart on that cross for us, oh, when you and I stop to think
of what Christ sacrificed, gave up and suffered and endured
for us, how mean and pitiable it is for us to talk about the
paltry things that we have to give up to come to Him.

II. THERE ARE SO MANY HYPOCRITES IN THE CHURCH

Someone will say, " Well, that excuse is absurd, but I have
a good one." What is your excuse? *" There are so many
hypocrites in the church."* Now that excuse is more absurd,
if possible, than the first excuse. " What," some of you will
say, " do you mean to say there are no hypocrites in the
church?" No, I do not mean to say anything of the kind.
I know that there are hypocrites in the church. I suppose
nobody has had a better opportunity to find that out than I
have. " Well," you say, " if you admit that there are hypocrites in the church then it seems to me the excuse is a good
one." No, it is not a good one, it is a perfectly absurd excuse. It is absurd for three reasons.

1. First of all, *The excuse is absurd, because the fact that*

someone else professes to be loyal to Jesus Christ when he is not is no reason to any intelligent man for refusing to be loyal to Christ at all. In point of fact the very fact that somebody else professes to be a Christian when he is not, is all the more reason for your, if you have any sense and any decency, professing to be loyal and really being loyal. What would you think of a man whose mother was one of the finest women who ever lived, but who had a brother who professed to be loyal to that mother but was not, and therefore he would not even profess to be loyal to her? You would go to him some day and say, " Your mother is one of the finest women that ever lived." He replies, " Yes, I know she is." " And yet you are not loyal to her." " No, I am not loyal to her and I am not at all ashamed of myself for not being loyal to her. I have a good reason for not being loyal to her." " What is your reason for not being loyal to such a mother as you have?" " I have a brother who professes to be loyal to her but who really is not, and that is why I do not even profess to be loyal and am not." What would you think of a man who made a remark like that? Would you not say, " Man, if you were any sort of a man, the very fact that you have a brother who professes to be loyal to such a noble woman as your mother is, but who really is not loyal to her, would be all the more reason for your professing to be loyal to that mother and really being loyal to her?" And to a man who has any sort of decency and self-respect, the very fact that there are so many who profess to be loyal to our glorious Lord and Master Jesus Christ, but who are not loyal and who bring dishonour on Him by their hypocrisy, would be all the more reason for professing to be loyal to Him and really being loyal to Him.

2. But the excuse is absurd for a second reason, and that is, *Because while there are hypocrites in the Church almost all the good people are in the Church also.* If there were a church of a hundred members and ninety-nine of them were good, earnest, consistent Christians, and one of them was a poor, crooked stick of a hypocrite, you would overlook the entire ninety-nine good, earnest, consistent Christians and fix your entire attention upon that one wretched hypocrite. You know you would. Why is that? I will tell you why it is.

It is because you are a hypocrite outside the Church and you are looking for some hypocrite inside the Church to hide behind. I never knew an exception to that. Whenever I find a man who is talking about the hypocrites in the Church I know I have found a man with a guilty conscience every time. He knows he is a hypocrite outside the Church and he is looking for a hypocrite inside the Church to hide behind.

Some years ago there was a British colonel who returned to England from long service in India. This colonel had not a good word to say of missions or missionaries. That is the way with some returned army officers and some returned civil service servants in England, they have not a single good word to say about the missions or missionaries. Their own lives in India have been corrupt, and the work of the missionaries has interfered with their evil plans, and they try to get even with the missionaries by talking against missions and missionaries. Thank God, that is not true of all returned army officers and civil service servants. Some of the finest Christians I met in India were army officers and civil service servants, but unfortunately it is true of some. Well, this colonel was of that sort. One night he was out at a dinner at which a returned missionary was also present. Some of the other guests thought they would have some sport at the expense of the missionary; so they set the old colonel going. One of them said to him, " Colonel, did you meet any Hindu converts while you were in India?" The colonel replied with scorn, " Hindu converts, I should say not. I was in India twenty years and I never saw one single convert." Then the man turned to the returned missionary and said, " Dr. ———, what have you got to say to that?" The doctor was very quiet and turned to the colonel and said, " Colonel, did you see any tigers while you were in India?" " Tigers?" said the colonel, " Did I see any tigers in India? I should say I did; I shot lots of them." The missionary quietly replied, " Well, I was in India thirty years and never saw a tiger." Do you see the point? The missionary was not looking for tigers: the colonel was not looking for converted Hindus. The unconverted kind suited his purpose best. And you are not looking for consistent Christians, you know you are not. You are looking for " hypocrites." Why? Because you have a guilty conscience and you are looking for hypocritical Church members to hide behind. Did it never occur to you that you cannot hide behind anything that is not bigger than you are yourself? What a small, mean, measly specimen of humanity you must be that you can hide behind one of these little, contemptible hypocritical Church members.

3. The excuse is absurd for a third reason and that is, *Because all these hypocrites in the Church, unless they repent, are going to hell to spend eternity there, and unless you accept Jesus Christ pretty soon you are going to hell too, to spend eternity there. Now which is better, to spend a few years here on earth with a few hypocrites and all the good people, or to spend all eternity in hell with all the hypocrites and all the bad people?* Come now like a reasonable man and give that excuse up and accept Jesus Christ right now. Will you?

III. I am Not a Great Sinner and Do Not Need an Atoning Saviour

But someone else will say, " I see that excuse is perfectly absurd, but I have a good one." Well, let us hear your excuse? " I am not a great sinner and do not need an atoning Saviour." That is the excuse a great many are making in this city tonight and they fancy it is a good one; but in reality it is the most absurd of all. You say, " Why is that excuse absurd?" I will tell you why it is absurd: Because every last one of you that is saying you are not a great sinner and do not need an atoning Saviour, is a very wicked man or a very wicked woman. "No," you reply, "I am not wicked, I am moral, I am upright, I am leading an honourable life, I am doing my duty as far as I know it in all the relations in life." Let me repeat it (and I will prove it to you directly) that every man and every woman here tonight who is refusing to come to Christ because you think you are not a great sinner and do not need an atoning Saviour, is a very wicked man or a very wicked woman. You say, " How do you make that out?" Because everyone of you, while you are doing a great many excellent things, are at the same time breaking the very first and greatest of all God's commandments. What is the first and greatest of God's commandments? Let me read it

to you from God's Own Word, Matt. 22:37, 38, " Jesus said
unto him, Thou shalt love the Lord thy God with all thy
heart, and with all thy soul, and with all thy mind. *This* is
the first and great commandment." Now if this is the first
and great commandment, what must be the first and great
sin? Of course, not to keep this commandment. Well, are
you keeping it? Do you love God with all your heart, and
with all your soul, and with all your mind? Have you put
God first in everything, God first in business, God first in
politics, God first in social life, God first in home life, God
first in study, God first in pleasure, God first in everything?
You know that you have not. Then you have broken this
first and greatest of all God's commandments, and *is not the
man or woman who breaks the first and greatest of God's commandments a very wicked man or a very wicked woman?*
You are a great deal better than many other men on some
of the minor moralities of life, those that concern man's relation to man. Many men have stolen: you never have.
Thank God for that. Many men are dishonest in business:
you have never been dishonest in business. Thank God for
that. Many men have been impure in their lives: you never
have. Thank God for that. Many men tell obscene stories:
you never tell one. Thank God for that. Some men have
killed other men: you never have killed another man. Thank
God for that. Now, on these minor moralities of man's duty
to man you have been a great deal better than some other
men; but on the first and great morality, the morality that
concerns man's duty to God, you have failed utterly; and
therefore where you have succeeded is nothing in comparison
to where you have failed. Man is finite and God is infinite,
and it is one of the simplest and most indisputable principles
of mathematics that no number of finites ever equals infinity,
and if you should do your whole duty by every member of
the human race, all of whom are finite, and fail in your duty
to the one infinite God, where you did your duty would be
as nothing to where you failed. Are you not a very wicked
man or a very wicked woman? Some years ago I was preaching in the town hall in Sydney, Australia. There were five
thousand people present that night, and I was preaching on
the same subject I am preaching on tonight, and I made the

same point that I have just made.   There was a lady present,
a woman of exemplary character and large culture and high
position.   The next day I received a letter from this lady.
She said, " Dear Dr. Torrey, I wish that you would pray for
me.   I am a woman whom you convinced last night that she
was a very wicked woman.   I came to the meeting supposing
I was a very good woman.   I have been trusting in my
morality, I thought I was far better than most women, but
you showed me last night that I was a very wicked woman
and I want you to pray for me."   Oh, I pray God tonight
that He will show many of you who think you are so good in
yourselves that you do not need an atoning Saviour; I say,
I pray God that He will show you tonight and make you feel
tonight you are a very wicked man or a very wicked woman;
for that is what you really are, and unless your eyes are
opened to that fact and you see your need of just such a
Saviour as your Lord Jesus is, and unless you take Him as
your own Saviour pretty soon, you are going to be lost
forever.

IV. There is so Much in the Bible That I Cannot
Understand and Cannot Believe

But someone will say, " I have a good excuse and you will
have to admit it is good."   All right, what is your excuse?
You reply, " *There is so much in the Bible that I cannot understand and so much that I cannot believe.*"

Your excuse is as absurd as any I have mentioned.   " No,"
you say, " it is not absurd.   It is a fact that there is much
in the Bible that I cannot understand and cannot believe.   I
can't see how to reconcile the Bible with the established teachings of modern science and modern philosophy."   Let me
show you that the excuse is absurd.   Let me ask you a question, Is there not much in the Bible that you can understand
and that you can believe?   You will certainly have to admit
that there is.   Now let me ask you another question, Are you
living up to that part of the Bible that you do understand
and that you do believe?   You know that you are not.   Well,
it will be time enough to talk about those parts of the Bible
that you cannot understand and that you cannot believe when

you are living up to those parts of the Bible you can understand and that you do believe.

What would you think of a man who was half starving and who was brought in and given a seat at a table that was loaded with all the substantials and all the luxuries of the season; as he looks over that table he sees many dishes that he thoroughly understands and he greatly needs and that he would greatly enjoy and that he knows are perfectly wholesome; but he sees two or three little dishes that he has never seen before and he does not understand them and he does not know whether they are wholesome or not, and so, though he is half starved, he refuses to eat of the dishes that he does understand and that he knows are good and wholesome, until someone explains to him the mysteries of the dishes that are new and strange to him? What would you think of a man like that? To be perfectly frank, would you not think he was a fool? Now here in the Bible is spread a rich spiritual feast. You know that much of it is valuable, the very highest truth in the world, such truth as is found in no other book in all the world, and you know you need that truth; but there is some obscure passage in the Bible, or some doubtful passage in the Bible, that you cannot accept and you refuse to eat any of this wholesome food until everything is explained to you about these other parts that you do not understand and that you cannot believe. Is that good sense? I tell you the trouble with some of you men and women is that you need a little ordinary " horse sense."

One night there was brought to me in the inquiry room a fine looking, intelligent, thoughtful young man. I sat down to talk with him. I said to him, " Why are you not a Christian?" He replied at once, " Because there is so much in the Bible I cannot understand and cannot believe." I said, " What, for example?" " Well," he said, " the first chapter of Genesis. I cannot believe that. I cannot see how to reconcile it with the teachings of modern science." " Well," I said, " let us leave the first chapter of Genesis alone for the present. Can you believe in Jesus Christ?" " Oh, yes," he said, " I can believe in Jesus Christ all right. I have no trouble about Him." " Well then," I said, " believe on Him, accept Him." " What," he said, " accept Christ before I understand the first chapter of Genesis and can reconcile it with the teachings of modern science?" "Certainly, you are in no position to understand the first chapter of Genesis until you have first of all accepted Jesus Christ. Now," I said, "will you accept Him?" He at once replied, "I will," and he did. Was that not good sense on his part? And I put it up to you tonight. Let us set aside for the time these difficult passages in the Bible which seem to you unbelievable. Can you not believe in Jesus Christ? Is it not proved by incontrovertible evidence that beyond a question He is the Son of God? And is it not clear that He died on the cross of Calvary and bore your sins in His Own Body on the cross? And do you not know that you need a Saviour just such as Jesus is? Will you accept Him as your Saviour tonight and surrender to Him as your Lord and Master tonight and confess Him as your Saviour before the world tonight? Is it not as clear as day that the fact that there are some things of very minor importance in the Bible which you cannot believe is no reasonable excuse for your not acting upon those tremendously important parts of the Bible you can and do believe? I was saved while I was still an evolutionist, and I stayed saved after I learned better and gave up the evolutionary hypothesis.

V. I WANT TO WAIT

Let us look at one more excuse. It is a very common one, "*I want to wait.*" Oh, how often that excuse has been made to me when I have urged upon people the necessity of immediate acceptance of Jesus Christ. They have brought up one excuse after another and they have all been answered, and their final resort is, "I want to wait." That is the Devil's last ditch; and he gets a multitude of people mired and destroyed in that last ditch. When you have answered all the excuses that men can make, then the Devil whispers to them, "Tell him you want to wait." One of the most dangerous things about that excuse is that it is so indefinite. People do not set a time for their waiting. If they would only set a definite time as to how long they wanted to wait, the excuse would not be so perilous. Let me ask you definitely, How long do you want to wait? Do you want to wait a year or a month or a week or just a day? HOW LONG DO

YOU WANT TO WAIT?   A young woman in Scotland came one day to the great Dr. Chalmers.   As Dr. Chalmers talked to her and urged upon her the necessity of an immediate acceptance of Christ she finally said, " Dr. Chalmers, I want to wait. I don't wish to accept Christ just now." The great Dr. Chalmers replied, " How long do you wish to wait?   Do you wish to wait a year and not have an opportunity under any circumstances, no matter what comes up, to accept Jesus Christ for a whole year?"   She thought a moment and said, " No, Dr. Chalmers, I would not like to say that; for I might die within a year."   " All right," said Dr. Chalmers, " do you want to wait a month and not have another opportunity for one whole month, no matter what occurs, to accept Jesus Christ?"   She hesitated again and then said, " No, Dr. Chalmers.   I would not like to wait a month and not have *an opportunity under any circumstances* to accept Jesus Christ, for I might die within a month."   " All right, then," said Dr. Chalmers, " do you want to wait a week and not have another opportunity, no matter what occurs, to accept Jesus Christ for a whole week?"   Again she hesitated and then she said, " No, I would not like to say that.   I would not like to say I wanted to wait a whole week and not have an opportunity under any circumstances, no matter what might come up, to accept Jesus Christ for a week; for I might die within a week."   " All right," said Dr. Chalmers, " would you like to wait a day, twenty-four hours, and not have another opportunity, no matter what might occur in the next twenty-four hours, to accept Jesus Christ?"   Again she said, " No, Dr. Chalmers, I would not like to say even that; for I might die within twenty-four hours."   " All right," said Dr. Chalmers, " don't you think you had better accept Jesus Christ right now?" and she broke down and said, " I will."   I put the same question to you tonight, Do you want to wait a whole year, twelve months, and not have another opportunity under any circumstances, no matter what comes up, to accept Jesus Christ for a whole year?   I am sure that every sensible man or woman here would say, " No, I would not like to wait a whole year and not have another opportunity under any circumstances, no matter what comes up, to accept Jesus Christ for one whole year."   Well, would you like to wait a month and not have another opportunity after this, under any circumstances, no matter what might come up, to accept Jesus Christ for a whole month? Every sensible man and woman among you will say, "No, I would not like to say that I would like to wait a whole month and not have another opportunity no matter what might occur, to accept Jesus Christ for one whole month." Would you like to wait one week, until one week from tonight and not have another opportunity for one whole week, not until one week from tonight, no matter what may occur, to accept Jesus Christ? Certainly there is no really intelligent and sensible person here tonight would say, "I want to take my chances and not have another opportunity, no matter what may occur, to accept Jesus Christ for one whole week." Do you want to wait another day and not have another opportunity for twenty-four hours, no matter what may occur, to accept Jesus Christ? Every really intelligent man and woman in this audience who is out of Christ will say, "No, I don't want to wait twenty-four hours even and not have another opportunity, no matter what may occur, to accept Jesus Christ for another twenty-four hours." Well then, do you not think you had better accept Him right now? Will you do it?

Dr. Talmage told once of a woman of the world who retired one night but could not sleep. She got to thinking about eternity and the affairs of her soul. After tossing around for some time she arose, lighted the gas, went to her writing desk, took a sheet of paper and wrote down this resolution, "One year from tonight I will attend to the affairs of my soul." Signed it, turned out the light and got into bed again. But still she could not sleep through thinking of eternity and of her lost condition. After a while she arose again, again she lighted the gas and sat down at her writing table and wrote a better resolution, "Six months from tonight I will attend to the affairs of my soul." She turned out the gas again and got into bed, but still she could not sleep. After tossing about for a while she got up, lighted the gas again, sat down at her writing table and wrote a still better resolution, "One month from tonight I will attend to the affairs of my soul." Again she turned out the light and retired, but still she could not sleep: so many things might occur in a month.

Again she arose, lighted the gas, sat down at the writing table and wrote a still better resolution, " Two weeks from tonight I will attend to the affairs of my soul." The time seemed short. She turned out the light, got into bed again but still she could not sleep: there were many possibilities in even two weeks and she might lose her soul by waiting two weeks; so she arose again, lighted the gas, sat down at the table and wrote a still better resolution, " One week from tonight I will attend to the affairs of my soul." Again she turned out the light and got into bed and that resolution satisfied her. One week seemed a short time. She went to sleep, awakened in the morning and that night went to a ball, caught a cold which settled on her lungs. She went into delirium and then just one week later she regained consciousness long enough to say, " I am one week too late," and passed unsaved into eternity.

Men and women, there is not one of you here tonight out of Christ that has a good reason for not accepting Jesus Christ tonight. There is awful peril in delay. Throw all your false excuses to the wind and come to Jesus Christ right now and accept Him as your personal Saviour, surrender to Him as your Lord and Master and confess Him as such before the world.